The
DOG

The

DOG

The most complete, illustrated, practical guide to dogs and their world

David Alderton

CHARTWELL
BOOKS, INC.

A *Quill* BOOK

©Quill Publishing Limited 1984
First published in the United States in 1984 by
Chartwell Books Inc
A division of Booksales Inc
110 Enterprise Avenue, Secaucus, New Jersey 07904

ISBN 0-89009-786-0

This book was designed and produced by
Quill Publishing Limited
32 Kingly Court
London W1

Art director Nigel Osborne
Editorial director Christopher Fagg
Senior editor Liz Wilhide
Art editor Alex Arthur
Editor Sabina Goodchild
Editorial assistant Michelle Newton
Illustrators Elaine Keenan, Charlotte Kennedy,
Richard Phipps, John Woodcock
Paste-up Jimmy Brewster, Bob Burns, Nigel Daniels

Filmset by QV Typesetting Limited, Kingly Court, London W1
and Leaper & Gard Limited, Redfield, Bristol
Origination by Hong Kong Graphic Arts Services Centre Limited, Hong Kong
Printed by Leefung Asco Printers Limited, Hong Kong

Quill would like to extend special thanks to David Gunn at
the Royal Veterinary College.

CONTENTS

CHARACTERISTICS OF THE DOG

Man and dog have been closely associated for many centuries — in fact, while its precise origins are unknown, the dog is thought to have been the first domesticated species. Throughout history, the dog has fulfilled a variety of roles — as a guard dog, herder, hunting companion and guide — although today it is probably best loved for the affection and friendship it offers as a pet.

Different breeds vary tremendously in appearance and physical characteristics, but all dogs share certain fundamental behavioral traits of obedience, loyalty and adaptability. They can also be distinguished from other mammals by their sensitive natures.

THE ORIGINS OF THE DOMESTIC DOG

The earliest remains of domestic dogs, discovered in Denmark, may date back as far as 10,000 BC, preceding the Neolithic period. Domestication also occurred early in the East; evidence indicates that dogs were kept in Jericho by 6500 BC. In ancient Egypt, dogs were portrayed on various artefacts, and dog mummies have been found alongside those of pharaohs in the Pyramids. Most early European dog remains, found in localities from Ireland south to Spain, date from the Bronze Age (3000 BC) on. Dogs had been introduced to North America by early settlers from Asia in about 5000 BC, long before Europeans set foot on the continent.

Early domestic dogs were relatively uniform in appearance, medium-sized and rather reminiscent of the dingo overall. Bigger forms were gradually developed to act as draft animals; as settlements became more stable, demands arose for more specialized types of dog, for example, to herd stock or catch vermin. By Roman times, breeds of a sort had developed. Although they were not distinguished, as breeds are today, on grounds of color, size and other specific features, they had certain characteristics, such as good scenting ability, in common.

Deliberate modification of breeds is a relatively recent phenomenon, which began in earnest in Europe and North America about 150 years ago and

The Egyptians revered the jackal-headed god, Anubis, the caretaker of the dead. This god either took the form of a dog (left), or, as in this Roman statue (above left), a dog with a man's body. The Romans believed Anubis conducted the souls of the dead to the Underworld. Dogs were also kept as pets in the ancient world, however, as this fourth-century BC Greek relief illustrates (top). The Roman funeral urn (above) also shows the dog as part of a family group.

is linked to the rise of showing. The domestic dogs of today are bred in a very wide range of shapes, colors and sizes. It has been calculated that perhaps as few as 20 mutations account for the wide diversity which exists in contemporary breeds, and there may have been as many as 4,000 generations of domestic dogs in which these mutations have become evident. Some popular traits, such as the flattened face of the Bulldog and the Basset's shortened legs, have been reported in wild dogs. Through human interference, by selectively preserving such mutants as they occurred, various breeds have been nurtured, whereas in the wild, it is highly unlikely that dogs displaying these characteristics would have survived for any length of time.

Some breeds have been developed to carry out particular functions, and so are more specialized than their wild counterparts. Wild dogs hunt by a combination of sight and scent, are fast on their feet, yet can be stealthy when necessary. Refinement and emphasis of particular features has given rise to dogs with outstanding pace, such as the Greyhound, and hounds able to hunt effectively by sight alone, such as the Afghan. This process of evolution is still continuing. Some domestic breeds have become extinct during recent times, such as the Ban Dog, once used for guarding purposes in Britain. Others, such as the Molossus of Rome, have contributed to the development of such contemporary breeds as the Great Dane, but no longer exist themselves.

The hunter *The aggressive nature of dogs has been exploited by man throughout the ages. As long ago as 2000BC the Assyrians trained dogs to fight in battle and used them as hunting companions. This detail taken from the bas-relief of Asshurbanipal (c.2000BC) shows mastiff-type dogs pursuing wild asses (below left). Here the Assyrian hunters have already shot their arrows and have set the dogs on the beasts. The Greeks also used dogs for hunting. This Greek vase* (above left) *illustrates a scene taken from a mythological tale, where Actaeon the hunter is turned into a stag by Artemis and then eaten by his own dogs. The Romans, too, found many uses for the dog, particularly for hunting as this aggressive portrayal reveals* (below right).

ANCESTORS OF THE DOMESTIC DOG

It is now thought that only one wild species was involved in the domestication of the dog, although opinions differ as to which it was. The golden jackal *(Canis aureus)*, which occurs in northern Africa, southern Europe and Asia, would seem an obvious choice — it is medium-sized and is found close to human settlements. Significant anatomical and behavioral differences between the dog and the golden jackal, however, lend strength to the theory that a form of the grey wolf *(Canis lupus)* was the true ancestor of the dog. Wolves will mate freely with domestic dogs, and the offspring of these unions are fertile. Both dogs and wolves are pack animals, unlike jackals, which live chiefly in pairs. The dentition of the wolf more closely resembles that of the dog; wolves also bark distinctly, whereas the golden jackal is more given to wailing and yelping.

The main problem with this theory is the discrepancy in size between wolves and dogs. Wolves, however, formerly occurred over a very much wider range than they do today and, although populations in the north of Europe and Asia consisted of big animals, the wolves on the southern limits of the range were smaller, with reduced carnassial teeth, like dogs. Researchers have also found that dogs and grey wolves share a large number of behavioral patterns.

The wolf Nearly 40 races of wolf are recognized around the world; Canis lycaon, Canis lupus, Canis pallipes *and* Canis lupus chanco *are thought to be the most likely ancestors of the domestic dog* (below). *Wolves are highly social animals, like dogs,* (far right) *and have a similar pattern of dentition* (right).

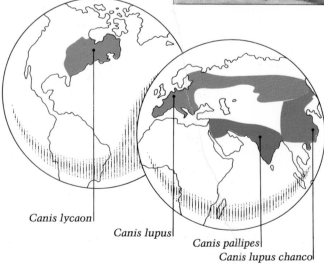

Canis lycaon

Canis lupus

Canis pallipes

Canis lupus chanco

Below *Jackals are usually solitary animals by nature, unlike wolves and dogs, but they may well have been involved in the ancestry of the dog. They often occur close to human settlements.*
Left *There are a number of semi-domesticated dogs found in various parts of the world. The dingo is probably the best-known member of the Pariah group, introduced to Australia by the aborigines. Other Pariah dogs have been fully domesticated in the Middle East.*

Several types of dog are still semi-domesticated today, but whether they are domestic stock that has reverted to the wild, or have never been fully domesticated, is not known. They are found across a wide area extending from Europe and Asia to Africa, and are known collectively as 'Pariahs'. Pariah dogs were used to found the Canaan Dog breed. Although these dogs vary in certain respects, such as coat length, they are all about the same size and of similar coloration, usually reddish-brown. Most have raised ears, flattened at their tips instead of completely erect.

The dingo *(Canis dingo)* is classed as a member of the Pariah group, and was introduced by man to Australia certainly by the late Pleistocene era, about a million years ago. Dingoes are still kept as pets and hunting dogs by Aborigines, who were the original inhabitants of the country; other dingoes are wild and have been persecuted since white settlement began, because of the threat they pose to sheep farming. Dingoes bear certain similarities to early domestic dogs but also have some wolf-like features, such as relatively large carnassial teeth. They will hybridize successfully with domestic dogs, and the resulting offspring are both fertile and often extremely cunning hunters, wreaking havoc among sheep flocks.

WILD DOGS

There are about 36 recognized species of wild dog, naturally distributed over all the major continents, apart from Antarctica and Australia. Wolves, jackals and dingoes, the domestic dog and the coyote are all grouped together in the genus *Canis*, whereas foxes are classified separately in the genus *Vulpes*. Members of the genus *Vulpes* occur throughout the northern hemisphere, extending into parts of Africa, and have also been introduced successfully in recent times to Australia. The red fox *(Vulpes vulpes)* has a huge range, which closely corresponds to the old distribution of the grey wolf. Its introduction to Australia, in order that fox-hunting could take place, was an ecological disaster, since it had virtually no competition from indigenous predators and rapidly established itself throughout much of the country. South American species are generally included in a separate genus, *Dusicyon*, and remain the least studied of all the wild dogs.

Some islands, including the Philippines, Formosa, Malagasy, New Zealand and New Guinea, do not have wild populations, although a dog closely related to the dingo was introduced to New Guinea by primitive man. Populations of wild dogs occur in a wide range of environments, from the frozen far north, where the arctic fox *(Alopex lagopus)* lives, to the steamy heat of the Amazon basin, which is a home for various species. The arid conditions of the Sahara do not deter Rüppell's sand fox *(V. ruppelli)*, while similar species are found in identical terrain in Asia. Wild dogs are highly adaptable, as demonstrated by the increasing penetration of suburban areas of Britain by the red fox.

Above right The hyena is classified in its own family, Hyaenidae, but is related to cats (Felidae), dogs (Canidae), and bears (Ursidae); it resembles the dog superficially. Highly territorial, hyenas live in 'clans' of up to 80 animals. They are excellent hunters, able to catch and swallow a hare in 55 seconds. They make a noise like laughter when they feed.
Right One of the world's most efficient predators is the African hunting dog (Lycaon pictus), also known as the Cape hunting dog. This species is unique among dogs in that it does not possess dew claws on the front feet; it is also the only spotted wild dog. Living in packs of between 10 and 40 members, the hunting dog's habitat is grassland and bush.

Wild relatives of the domestic dog *The domestic dog has 36 wild relatives. These include the oddly proportioned maned wolf from South America* (Chrysocyon brachyurus) *(1); the North American coyote* (Canis latrans) *(2); the side-striped jackal of central Africa* (Canis adustus) *(3); the South American forest fox* (Cerdocyon thous) *(4); the South American bush dog* (Speothos venaticus) *(5); the South American small-eared dog* (Atelocynus microtis) *(6); and the African fennec* (Fennecus zerda) *(7).*

The red fox (Vulpes vulpes) (left) *has an immense range, thriving near man. It is solitary, except during the breeding season and is small and alert. Farmed for its fur, hunted and trapped, it is one of the most well-known wild dogs. The Arctic fox* (Alopex lagopus) (above) *ranges the furthest north of all land mammals except the polar bear. It is the only wild dog to have a seasonal change in color.*

Working dogs *The Greyhound is renowned for its great speed and is raced professionally on tracks (right). In contrast is the more amateur sport of terrier racing, which may be organized outside in a field (below). Both sports use a dummy prey.*

Right *Coursing dogs chase live hares, which are set up by beaters. Two dogs race against each other at a time.*
Above right *A working sheepdog must be carefully trained. The intelligent Border Collie is one of the most popular breeds for herding work.*
Far right *Pointers are exceptionally useful dogs for the hunter. This German Short-haired Pointer has caught the scent of the prey and stands quietly, pointing its nose and whole body toward the spot, quivering. The hunter can then flush out the bird or animal.*

PHYSICAL CHARACTERISTICS

In spite of their range in size, all dog breeds have a basically similar skeletal structure. Differences are possibly most conspicuous in the skull. At one extreme, breeds such as the Greyhound possess a long, narrow head, described as dolichocephalic, while at the other end, the compressed skull of the brachycephalic breeds such as the Bulldog, creates a square impression. In the middle are those such as spaniel-types, with a skull of intermediate length known as mesoticephalic.

The overall conformation of a dog is a reflection both of the skeleton and the overlying musculature. Show standards specify the 'type' or appearance that would represent the ideal dog of the particular breed in question. In the case of the Clumber Spaniel, for example, the offical KC standard demands 'very powerful and well-developed hind-quarters', so the muscle masses are prominent.

There are cases where the bones of limbs are drastically stunted, giving rise to achondroplasia. This is exemplified by the short-legged Dachshund, where the abnormality has become normal. In other cases developmental problems arise if the skeletal structure is not fully formed when the puppy is

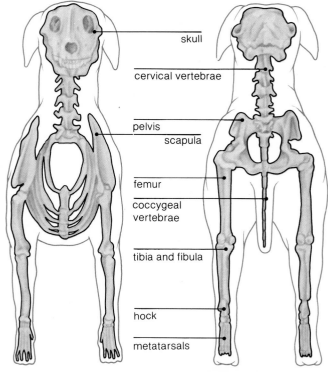

skull
cervical vertebrae
pelvis
scapula
femur
coccygeal vertebrae
tibia and fibula
hock
metatarsals

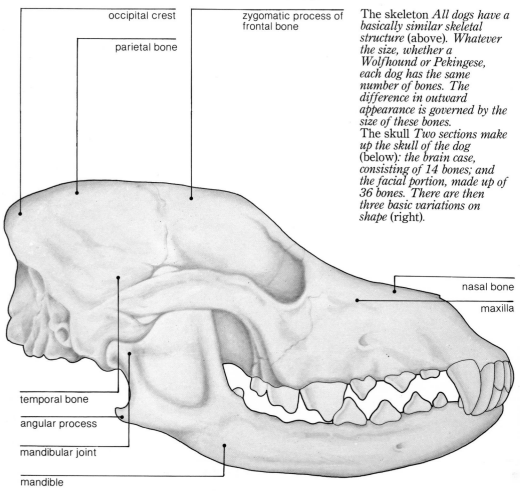

occipital crest
zygomatic process of frontal bone
parietal bone
nasal bone
maxilla
temporal bone
angular process
mandibular joint
mandible

The skeleton *All dogs have a basically similar skeletal structure* (above). *Whatever the size, whether a Wolfhound or Pekingese, each dog has the same number of bones. The difference in outward appearance is governed by the size of these bones.*
The skull *Two sections make up the skull of the dog (below): the brain case, consisting of 14 bones; and the facial portion, made up of 36 bones. There are then three basic variations on shape (right).*

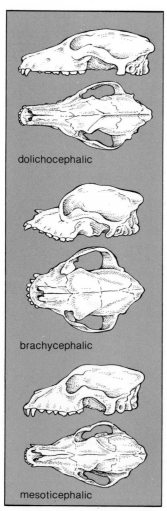

dolichocephalic

brachycephalic

mesoticephalic

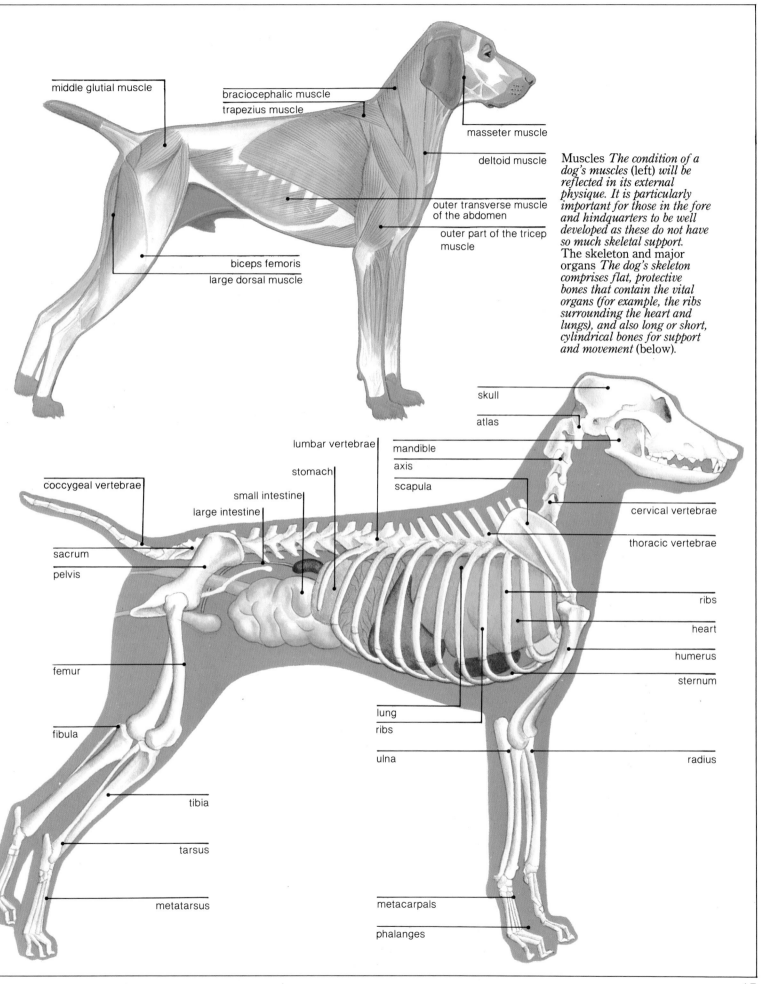

middle glutial muscle

braciocephalic muscle

trapezius muscle

masseter muscle

deltoid muscle

outer transverse muscle
of the abdomen

outer part of the tricep
muscle

biceps femoris

large dorsal muscle

Muscles *The condition of a dog's muscles* (left) *will be reflected in its external physique. It is particularly important for those in the fore and hindquarters to be well developed as these do not have so much skeletal support.*
The skeleton and major organs *The dog's skeleton comprises flat, protective bones that contain the vital organs (for example, the ribs surrounding the heart and lungs), and also long or short, cylindrical bones for support and movement* (below).

skull

atlas

lumbar vertebrae

mandible

stomach

axis

coccygeal vertebrae

small intestine

scapula

large intestine

cervical vertebrae

sacrum

thoracic vertebrae

pelvis

ribs

heart

femur

humerus

sternum

fibula

lung

ribs

ulna

radius

tibia

tarsus

metatarsus

metacarpals

phalanges

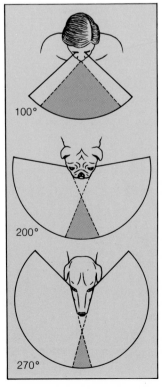

Sight Dogs have a greater field of view than humans because their eyes are located on the side of their heads. Whereas a human has a range of 100°, a dog with wide-set eyes can have as much as 270° (above). A dog whose eyes are more foward-pointing, however, will not have such a coverage, as the diagram illustrates (right). Dogs also have better sight in bad lighting than humans. This is partly because of the reflective layer (tapetum lucidum) at the back of the eye, but also because they have relatively more rod receptors on their retina, which respond to poor light.

100°

200°

270°

born. This means that the humerus does not fuse with the shaft of the bone in the forelimbs, which should occur within the first year. An x-ray examination will confirm this condition and it may be corrected by surgery.

Sight

The dog's vision is not good in bright light, although moving objects can be detected. At dusk, however, or in semi-darkness, the dog retains this sense, whereas humans perceive little at low levels of light intensity. The reason for this concerns the ratio of the two types of light-sensitive cells, cones and rods, on the retina. Cones are most effective in good light, whereas rods respond to dull light. The dog's retina is comprised of a relatively high proportion of rods compared to cones. Cones are also responsible for color vision, so dogs are not able to appreciate colors as clearly as humans, although some color recognition is possible.

Another feature that assists vision in poor light is the tapetum lucidum. This structure is located behind the retina and acts like a mirror, reflecting light rays back through the retina and increasing their stimulatory effect on the rods and cones. For this reason, the eyes of dogs (and cats) glow

greenish-yellow in the dark when a light is shone upon them.

As a hunter, the dog needs a wide field of vision to locate prey; binocular vision is also necessary to pinpoint the exact position of prey. The two different images received from both eyes naturally overlap to a certain extent, and are superimposed by the brain to create this facility.

Hearing

While dogs are able to hear sounds of a much higher pitch than humans, both can only appreciate low frequencies down to about 20 hertz. The dog's ability to hear high-frequency sounds helps it to locate and catch rodents, which may remain undetected by its owner. Dog whistles with frequencies of about 30 hertz are virtually inaudible to the human ear, but can be detected by a dog a long distance away. Their earflaps are able to locate the source of the sound much more precisely than human ears can. Dogs are now being trained to help deaf people, both in the United States and Britain, by warning them, for example, that a telephone is ringing or a baby is crying. They are equipped with orange leads, to distinguish them from the guide dogs, which wear white harnesses.

Hearing *A dog has much more acute hearing than its owner* (below). *Although both have a similar lower limit, dogs can hear sound frequencies up to 100,000Hz, whereas the upper limit for* humans is about 20,000Hz. *In practical terms this means that dogs can detect sounds of a higher pitch, such as those given out by a special dog whistle, which are inaudible to the human ear.*

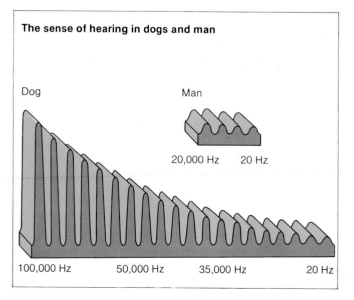

The sense of hearing in dogs and man

Dog   Man

20,000 Hz   20 Hz

100,000 Hz   50,000 Hz   35,000 Hz   20 Hz

Smell

The sense of smell is very highly developed in the dog, and it possesses large numbers of specialized olfactory cells to detect scents. By breathing with its nostrils flared, a dog can increase the volume of air passing to these cells, and Jacobsen's Organ, a structure not present in humans, located above the roof of the mouth, can also detect particles of scent in the air. In order to accommodate the increased input from the olfactory regions, the area of the brain responsible for processing such information, known as the rhinecephalon, is correspondingly large.

Puppies are, however, born with a very limited sense of smell. It is also possible to affect the scenting ability of a dog. Feeding a dog animal fat will cause this sense to diminish, while a lack of food promotes increased receptivity. Aniseed oil obtained from the plant *Pimpinella anisum* is used to lay trails for drag hunting. Tests have shown that hounds have no preference for the strong smell of the oil, as is sometimes supposed, but it is easy for them to follow.

Teeth

The dog has two sets of teeth during its lifetime. The first, deciduous set is comprised of 28 teeth, and is followed by a permanent dentition of 42 teeth. The incisors at the front of the mouth are small; the adjoining canines are large and pointed, and are us-

Sense of smell At least 100 times better than man's, the dog's sense of smell has been refined by selective breeding. Certain breeds have more highly developed senses of smell than others. This ability has been put to use in various ways. 'Sniffer dogs' help to locate explosives or narcotics (below). Tracking, hunting and retrieving are activities that rely on the dog's ability to detect odors at low concentrations (above).

ed for killing prey and ripping flesh. The first molar of the bottom jaw and the fourth premolar of the upper jaw, which are enlarged and known as carnassial teeth, are also used in this way. The other premolars are responsible for crushing food, and the molars for chewing, although dogs generally bolt their meals, rather than masticating food for any great length of time.

Temperature control

Unlike the cat, the dog is unable to retract its claws and dog prints always show the impression of claws in front of the pads. Between the toes are eccrine sweat glands, the only sweat glands used for heat loss on the dog's body. In hot weather, the dog may leave wet footprints because of these glands. The other type of glands, the apocrine glands, occur over the body itself, but are essentially scent glands, and are responsible for the dog's odor.

The major means of temperature control is by panting, evaporating moisture to cause heat loss. Although most water would appear to be lost from the tongue and oral cavity, in reality, the nasal cavities are more significant. There are lateral nasal glands just inside the nostrils that supply moisture both for heat loss, and to moisten the surface of the nose and improve the sense of smell. As its body temperature rises, the dog will first breathe exclusively through its nose, but if the temperature continues to increase, then it will breathe through the nose and exhale, or pant, through its mouth.

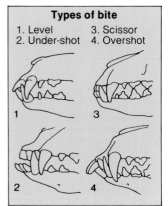

Types of bite
1. Level
2. Under-shot
3. Scissor
4. Overshot

Teeth The pattern of dentition does not differ significantly between types of domestic dog, but selective breeding has influenced the distribution of teeth in the jaws (left). Certain breeds, such as the Borzoi, have long mouths, whereas the reduced facial area of the Pekingese means that the teeth are relatively compressed in the mouth. In some breeds, notably the Chihuahua, the 'milk' or first teeth may not fall out of their own accord.

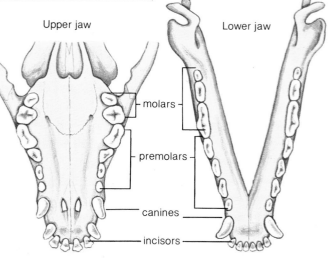

Upper jaw — Lower jaw

— molars
— premolars
— canines
— incisors

Panting Unlike humans, dogs do not sweat over their whole body, since their eccrine sweat glands only occur between their toes. Panting is therefore an important method of temperature control (left). Evaporation of water from the nasal and oral cavities cools the body. Water must always be available to make up this fluid loss.

BEHAVIOR

Most dogs are pack animals by nature, often hunting in groups in the wild. Within these social groups, there is always an order of dominance, based on strength, gender and age. The domestic dog, although most often kept singly, retains its social instincts; for this reason, it is both easy to train and dependent on its human companions for affection and attention.

Pets and working dogs respond to their owners as they would to the dominant member of the pack, provided the owner maintains control and consistency of approach. Dogs are popularly regarded as intelligent animals and, while they can certainly be taught to perform a variety of tasks and tricks, this reputation may rest more on their innate sense of dominance within a social order.

Social groupings can be noticed at an early stage, with puppies in a litter falling into a recognizable pattern. Later in life, such natural instincts may well surface in the form of fighting with other dogs. Unlike cats, which fight for the right to a territory, dogs more often fight to establish some form of local hierarchy.

Communication

Communication is carried out by altering the body posture and by vocalization. The ears and tail are especially important in communication. When suspicious, the dog will keep its ears raised and its tail erect. When strange dogs approach each other, the first contact will be nose-to-nose, with tails partially lowered. The dogs will then circle cautiously and sniff each other's genital regions. A familiar dog or person will be greeted with tail-wagging. When playing, the dog will drop repeatedly onto its forelimbs, wagging its tail, and then bound off and resume the posture nearby. A dog with a tail between its legs is adopting a submissive stance, and may even roll over onto its back. Raised fur, 'hackles', along the back, with curling lips revealing the teeth indicates an aggressive or nervous individual ready to bite or attack.

Some breeds bark more than others; the Basenji is incapable of barking effectively because of the structure of its larynx. Barking may indicate excitement or the presence of an intruder. Dogs start to bark when they are around three weeks old; prior to this time, they may whine, but such noises in later life are an expression of pleading, usually made to their owners, rather than to other dogs. Sudden injury will cause a dog to yelp. Baying or howling is most common in hound breeds, and this call is invariably uttered when the dog is standing still. It might be a means of keeping in touch with other members of the pack, since other dogs often respond in a similar way after a dog has howled.

Fighting *Play is often a method of emphasizing an order of dominance between individuals; where this has not been established, shows of aggression leading to actual fighting may take place* (right). *Serious injuries are rare, however, since a vanquished individual will make a quick retreat out of harm's way. Aggression is expressed not only by vocalization — snarling, growling and barking — but also by certain types of posture.*

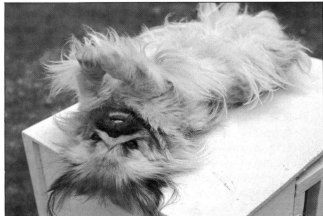

Top left *When two strange dogs meet, they first make direct nose-to-nose contact, before moving around to sniff each other's genital regions.*
Center left *Rolling over, to expose the underparts, is a characteristic gesture of submission.*
Above *The tricks that a dog learns are often just refinements of innate behavioral traits. The natural inclination of a dog to sit is the basis for teaching a trick such as 'begging'.*
Left *Dogs will instinctively dig both to retrieve and bury. Their keen sense of smell and natural inquisitiveness reinforce this behavior.*

BREEDS OF THE WORLD

There are over 350 different breeds of dog recognized around the world. Some of these are localized varieties; others well-known and well-established favorites. The major governing canine authorities — the Kennel Club (KC) of Britain, the American Kennel Club (AKC) and the Fédération Cynologique (FCI) of Europe — each classify breeds into different groupings, according to common characteristics. For easy reference, breeds are arranged here alphabetically, by their official names.

CLASSIFICATION OF BREEDS

The grouping of breeds varies according to the rules laid down by the various governing canine authorities. The European authority, the Fédération Cynologique Internationale (FCI), recognizes 10 distinct groups, whereas, in the United States, under American Kennel Club (AKC) rules, dog breeds are divided into six groups. The AKC also has a Miscellaneous Class for breeds that are not recognized but are attracting increasing interest. When a breed is recognized and officially admitted to the AKC Studbook, it is regrouped in the appropriate section to compete for championship points. The Kennel Club (KC) in Britain also has six basic groupings, but does not grant championship status to some of the breeds that are recognized by the AKC, and vice-versa.

Each recognized breed has a breed standard, controlled by the governing authority. Standards specify optimum size, weight, physical type, colour, markings and other features on which dogs can be judged at shows.

KEY

International groupings by KC, AKC and FCI

- CD Companion dog
- CO Coursing dog
- D Dachshund
- G Gundog
- GD Guard dog
- HD Herding dog
- H Hound
- SH Small hound
- LH Large hound
- NS Non-sporting dog
- SD Sporting dog
- T Terrier
- TO Toy
- U Utility
- W Working

FCI groupings

1 Herding dogs, guard dogs, sheepdogs
2 Guard dogs and hauling dogs
3 Working terriers
4 Dachshunds
5 Hounds for hunting large game
6 Hounds for hunting small game
7 Gundogs, except British and American breeds
8 British and American gundogs
9 Companion dogs, including toy breeds
10 Coursing dogs

Small Dogs (up to 12in/30cm high)

BREED	CLASSIFICATION			HEIGHT	WEIGHT	PAGE
	KC	AKC	FCI			
Affenpinscher	TO	TO	CD	9½-11in	6½-9lb	30
American Toy Terrier				6-9in	4-6lb	33
Australian Silky Terrier	TO	TO	T	9in	8-10lb	34
Australian Terrier	T	T	T	10in	10-11lb	35
Bichon Frise	TO	NS	CD	Up to 12in	7-12lb	40
Bolognese			9	11-12in 10-11in	5½-9lb	42
Border Terrier	T	T	T	10in	13-15½lb 11½-14lb	42
Cairn Terrier	T	T	T	12in	14lb	46
Chihuahua	TO	TO	CD	6-9in	2-6lb	49
Chinese Crested Dog				12in	7-12lb	49
Dandie Dinmont Terrier	T	T	T	8-11in	18lb	53
English Toy Terrier	TO	TO	CD	10-12in	6-8lb	56
French Bulldog	U	NS	CD	12in	28lb 24lb	60
Griffon Bruxellois	TO	TO	CD	7in max	5-11lb	66
Havanese				12in	7-12lb	68
Happa Dog				9in	12lb	72
Japanese Chin	TO	TO	CD	9in max	7lb	72
King Charles Spaniel	TO	TO	CD	10in	8-14lb	75
Long-haired Dachshund	H	H	D	5-9in	18lb 17lb	78
Lundehund			6	9-10in	13lb	79
Maltese	TO	TO	CD	10in max	6½-9lb	79
Mexican Hairless Dog			9	11in	9-18lb	80
Miniature Pinscher	T	T	CD	10-12in	10lb	81
Norfolk Terrier	T	T	T	10in	10-12lb	82
Norwich Terrier	T	T	T	10in	10-12lb	82
Papillon	TO	TO	CD	8-11in	9-10lb	84
Pekingese	TO	TO	CD	6-9in	11lb 12lb	84
Podengo (small form)			5	8-12in	9-11lb	86
Pomeranian	TO	TO	CD	12in	4-4½lb 4½-5½lb	86
Poodle (Toy)	U	TO	CD	under 11in	15lb	87
Pug	TO	TO	CD	10-11in	14-18lb	89
Scottish Terrier	T	T	T	10-11in	19-23lb	96
Sealyham Terrier	T	T	T	12in max	20lb max 18lb max	97
Shih Tzu	U	TO	CD	10½in max	10-18lb	98
Skye Terrier	T	T	T	10in	25lb	99
Smooth-haired Dachshund	H	H	D	5-9in	25lb max 23lb max	100
Tenerife				12in	7-12lb	105
Tibetan Spaniel	U		CD	10in	9-15lb	105
Volpino			9	11-12in 10-11in	9lb max	107
Welsh Corgi — Cardigan — Pembroke	W	WD	HD	12in 10-12in	29lb 20-24lb 18-22lb	107 107
West Highland White Terrier	T	T	T	11in	15-22lb	109
Wirehaired Dachshund	H	H	D	5-9in	20-22lb 18-20lb	111
(Miniature)					10-11lb max	112
Yorkshire Terrier	TO	TO	CD	9in	7lb max	113

Table of breeds
While official classifications are important for those intending to breed and exhibit dogs, size is an important consideration for the pet-owner. This chart arranges the 350 breeds of the world in five groups, according to size. Although many breed standards specify a specific height and weight, other figures are more approximate. The females of some breeds are slightly smaller and lighter than the males; in these cases, the second set of measurements refer to bitches. A page number is given for each breed, for easy reference to the A-Z section. The chart also includes the official classification of each breed in KC, AKC and FCI groupings.

Cairn Terrier Chihuahua Bruxellois

Small Dogs (12-18in/30-45cm high)

BREED	CLASSIFICATION			HEIGHT	WEIGHT	PAGE
	KC	AKC	FCI			
American Cocker Spaniel	G	SD	G	15in 14in	24-28lb	32
American Staffordshire Terrier		T	T	17-18in 15-17in	38-44lb	32
American Water Spaniel		SD		15-18in	28-45lb 25-40lb	33
Basenji	H	H	SH	17in 16in	24lb 21lb	36
Basset Artésian Normand			6	10-14in	33lb	36
Basset Bleu de Gascogne			6	12-15in	35-40lb	36
Basset d'Artois				14in	35lb	36
Basset Fauve de Bretagne			6	14-16in	40-44lb	36
Basset Griffon Vendéen — small version			6	14-16in 13-15in	40-44lb 37-42lb	37
Basset Hound	H	H	SH	13-15in	40-51lb	37
Beagle	H	H	SH	13-16in	18-30lb	38
Bedlington Terrier	T	T	T	16in	18-23lb	38
Berner Laufhund			6	16in	33-40lb	40
Boston Terrier	U	NS	CD	15-17in	Lightweight 15lb Middleweight 15-20lb Heavyweight 20-25lb	43
Bulldog	U	NS	GD	12-14in	55lb 50lb	45
Cavalier King Charles Spaniel	T		CD	12-13in	12-18lb	47
Cesky Terrier			3	11-14in	13-20lb	47
Chow Chow	U	NS	CD	18in min	55-60lb	50
Clumber Spaniel	G	SD	G	16-18in	55-70lb 45-60lb	50
Cocker Spaniel	G	SD	G	15½-16in 15-15½in	28-32lb	50
Coton de Tulear			9	12¼in 11in	8¾lb 7¾lb	52
Drever			6	12½-16in	33lb	54
Dutch Hound				18in max	40lb	55
Egyptian Sheepdog				18in	35-40lb	55
Erz Mountains Dachsbracke			6	13-17in	22lb	57
Eurasier			2	14in	25lb	58
Field Spaniel	G	SD	G	18in	35-50½lb	58
Finnish Spitz	H		SH	17-20in 15½-18in	31-36lb 23-29lb	58
German Hunting Terrier			3	13-16in	20-22lb 17-19lb	60
German Spitz			9	16in	40lb	62
Glen of Imaal Terrier				14in	30-35lb 30lb	63
Harlequin Pinscher			9	12-14in	22-26lb	68
Hungarian Puli	W	W	HD	16-17½in 14-16in	28½-33lb 22-28½lb	68
Iceland Dog			I	12-16in	25-30lb 20-25lb	70
Irish Terrier	T	T	T	18in	27lb 25lb	70
Italian Greyhound	TO	TO	CO	13-15in	6-10lb	72
Jack Russell Terrier				10-15in	10lb +	72
Japanese Small-sized Dog			9	16in 14in	30lb	73

BREED	CLASSIFICATION			HEIGHT	WEIGHT	PAGE
	KC	AKC	FCI			
Japanese Spitz			9	12-16in 10-14in	22lb	73
Japanese Terrier			3	15in max	15lb	73
Jura Laufhund			6	16-18in	40-44lb	73
Keeshond	U	NS	CD	18in 17in	55-66lb	74
Kramjohrländer			9	15-18in	26lb	75
Lakeland Terrier	T	T	T	14½in max	17lb 15lb	76
Lhasa Apso	U	NS	CD	10in	13-15lb	78
Lowchen (Miniature)	TO		CD	10-14in	4-9lb 10-11lb max	79
Luzerner Laufhund			6	16in	40-44lb	79
Manchester Terrier	T	T	T	16in 15in	18lb 17lb	80
Mudi			I	14-19in	18-29lb	81
Norbottenspets			2	16in	26-33lb	82
Norwegian Buhund	W		HD	17¾in +	44-55lb	82
Poodle — Miniature — Standard	U	NS	CD	11-15in 15in +	26lb 49lb	87 87
Schapendoes			I	16in	30lb	95
Schipperke	U	NS	CD	10-13in	12-16lb	95
Schnauzer	U	W	GD	19in 18in	33lb	95
(Miniature)	U	T	CD	14in 13in	13-15lb	95
Shar-Pei				18-20in 16-18in	44-55lb 35-45lb	97
Shetland Sheepdog	W	W	HD	14½in 14in ± 1''	14-16lb	97
Smooth Fox Terrier	T	T	T	16in	16-18lb 15-17lb	100
Smoushond				16in	15-18lb	101
Staffordshire Bull Terrier	T	T	T	14-16in	28-38lb 24-34lb	102
Steinbracke			6	16-18in	40-49lb	103
Sussex Spaniel	G	SD	G	15-16in	45lb 40lb	104
Swedish Vallhund			I	13in 12¼in	20-31lb	104
Tahl-Tan Bear Dog				16in	30lb	105
Tibetan Terrier	U	NS	CD	14-16in	18-30lb	106
Welsh Terrier	T	T	T	15½in max	20-21lb	109
Westphalian Dachsbracke			6	12-14in	33-40lb	110
Whippet	H	H	CO	18½in 17½in	18-28lb 12-20lb	110
Wire Fox Terrier	T	T	T	15½in	18lb ± lb 16lb	111

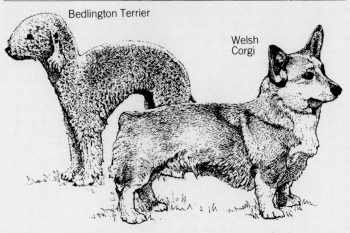

Bedlington Terrier

Welsh Corgi

Medium-sized Dogs (18-24in/45-60cm high)

BREED	CLASSIFICATION			HEIGHT	WEIGHT	PAGE
	KC	AKC	FCI			
Aidi			2	20-24in 18-20in	66lb	30
Ainu			2	19-20in 18in	50-55lb	30
Airedale Terrier	T	T	T	23-24in 22-23in	44lb	31
Appenzell Mountain Dog			2	22in 20in	49-55lb	34
Ariègeois			6	22-24in	66lb	34
Australian Cattle Dog			I	18-20in 17-19in	40-50lb 35-45lb	34
Australian Kelpie			I	18-20in 17-19in	25-30lb 20-25lb	34
Austrian Hound			6	18-20in	33-49lb	35
Austrian Pinscher			2	14-20in	26-40lb	35
Balkan Hound			6	18-21in 17-20in	44lb	35
Barb				18-20in 17-19in	40-50lb 35-45lb	36
Barbet			6	22-24in	33lb	36
Bavarian Schweisshund			6	20in	55-77lb	37
Beagle Harrier			6	17-19in	44lb	38
Bearded Collie	W		HD	21-22in 20-21in	66lb	38
Berger de Languedoc				16-20in	50-60lb	39
Berger Polonais de Vallée			I	17-20in	60lb	40

BREED	KC	AKC	FCI	HEIGHT	WEIGHT	PAGE
Black Elkhound			5	18-20in	44lb	41
Border Collie				21in	40-50lb / 34-40lb	42
Bourbonnais Pointer			7	22in	40-57in	44
Bouvier des Ardennes				24in	55lb	44
Boxer	W	W	GD	22-24in / 21-23in	66lb / 62lb	44
Brittany Spaniel	G	SD	G	17½-20½in	30-40lb	45
Bull Terrier	T	T	T	21-22in	52-62lb	46
Canaan Dog			2	19½-23½in	39½-55lb	46
Cane de Pastore Bergamasco			I	24in / 22-23in	71-84lb / 66lb	46
Catalan Sheepdog			I	18-20in / 17-19in	40lb / 35lb	47
Chien Courant de Bosnie à Poil Dur			6	22in	55lb	48
Chien Courant de la Vallée de la Save			6	23in	55lb	48
Chien d'Artois			6	20-23in	40-53lb	48
Chien Francais Tricolore			5	20in	49-55lb	49
Chinese Hound				22in	60lb	50
Croatian Sheepdog			I	22-24in	66-88lb	52
Dalmatian	U	NS	CD	23-24in / 22-23in	55lb	53
Dunker			6	19-22in	35-49lb	55
Dutch Partridge Dog			7	22-24in	44lb	55
Elkhound	H	H	LH	20½in / 19½in	50lb / 43lb	55
English Springer Spaniel	G	SD	G	20in	50lb	56
Entlebuck Mountain Dog			2	20in	55-60lb	57
Epagneul Francais			7	22-24in / 21-23in	44-55lb	57
Epagneul Pont-Audèmer			7	20-23in	40-53lb	57
Estonian Hound				20in	40-45lb	57
Finnish Hound			6	21½-24in	55lb	58
Flat-coated Retriever	G	SD	G	22-23in	60-70lb	58
German Hound				19in	45-50lb	60
German Sheep Pudel				24in	75lb	62
Golden Retriever	G	SD	G	22-24in / 20-22in	70-80lb / 60-70lb	63
Grahund			5	19-20in	66lb	64
Grand Griffon Nivernais			6	20-24in	49-55lb	65
Greek Greyhound			6	19-22in / 18-21in	38-44lb	66
Greenland Dog			2	24 in + / 22in +	66lb	66
Griffon à Poil Laineux			7	22-24in / 20-22in	44-55lb	66
Griffon Bleu de Gascogne de Petite Taille			6	17-20in	30lb	66
Griffon Fauve de Bretagne			6	20-22in / 19-20in	44lb	67
Haldenstövare			6	19½-23½in / 18-22½in	55lb	67
Hanoverian Schweisshund			5	22in / 20in	84-99lb	67
Harrier		H	SH	19-21in	45-55lb	68
Hungarian Vizsla	G	SD	G	22½-25in / 21-23½in	48½-66lb	69
Hygenhound			6	19-24in	44-55lb	69
Irish Setter	G	SD	G	21-24in / 20-23½in	40-55lb / 33-49lb	70
Irish Water Spaniel	G	SD	G	21-23in / 20-22in	55-60lb	70
Istrian Hound			6	18-23in	40-44lb	71
Italian Hound			6	20-23in / 19-22in	40-62lb	72
Japanese Middle-sized Dog			2	20-22in / 18-20in	44-55lb	73
Karelian Bear Dog			5	20-23½in	44-49lb	74
Kerry Beagle				18-20in	45lb	74
Kerry Blue Terrier	T	T	T	18-19in	33-37lb	74
Kuvasz		WD	HD	23 in + / 20in +	110lb	75
Labrador Retriever	G	SD	G	22-22½in / 21½-22in	55-75lb	76
Laika				20in	50-60lb	76
Lapinporokoira		.	I	19-22in / 17-19in	66lb	77
Lapphund				20in	44lb	77
Large Munsterlander	G	.	G	24in / 23in	55-65lb / 55lb	77
Macellaio Herding Dog				20in	70-80lb	79

BREED	KC	AKC	FCI	HEIGHT	WEIGHT	PAGE
Northeastern Sleigh Dog				23in	60-65lb	82
Nova Scotia Duck Tolling Retriever				20in	65lb	82
Old Danish Pointer			7	20-23in / 19-21in	40-53lb	83
Old English Sheepdog	W	W	HD	22in +	66lb	83
Perdigeiro Português			7	22in / 20in	44-60lb	84
Perro de Presa			2	23in	150lb	85
Pinscher			2	18-19in	13-18lb	86
Podengo (medium form)			5	16-22in	35-44lb	86
Poodle Pointer			7	22in	60lb	88
Porcelaine			6	22-23in / 21-22in	55-62lb	89
Portuguese Cattle Dog			2	22-24in / 20-22in	66-88lb / 44-66lb	89
Portuguese Sheepdog			I	17-19in	26-40lb	89
Portuguese Water Dog			2	17-19in	26-40lb	89
Pumi			I	20in / 16in	18-39lb	90
Rough Collie	W	W	HD	22-24in / 20-22in	45-65lb / 40-55lb	91
Sabueso			6	20-22in / 19-20in	55lb	92
St Germain Pointer				20-24in / 21-23in	40-57lb	93
Schillerstövare			6	22in / 21in	40-53lb	95
Schweizer Laufhund (small form)			6	18-22in / 12-15in	40-44lb / 33lb	96
Siberian Husky		W	GD	21-23½in / 20-22in	45-60lb / 35-50lb	98
Sicilian Hound			6	18-22in / 17-18in	22-26lb / 18-22lb	98
Slovakian Hound			5	18-20in	44-49lb	99
Smalandsstövare			6	20in	33-40in	99
Small Münsterländer			7	19-22in / 17-20in	33lb	99
Smooth Coollie	W	W	HD	18-19½in	35-45lb	100
Soft-coated Wheaten Terrier	T	T	T	18-19½in	35-45lb	101
Stabyhoun			7	209n	33-44lb	102
Stumpy-tailed Cattle Dog				18-209n / 17-19in	40-50lb / 35-45lb	103
Styrian Mountain Hound			6	16-20in	33-40lb	103
Tosa Fighting Dog			2	24in	83lb +	106
Trailhound				24in	65lb	107
Tyrolese Hound			6	16-19in	33-49lb	107
Welsh Springer Spaniel	G	SD	G	19in / 18in	35-45lb	109
Wetterhoun			7	22in	33-44lb	110
Wire-haired Pointing Griffon		SD	G	21½-23½in / 19½-21½in	50-60lb	112
Yugoslavian Herder			I	22-24in / 20-22in	55-77lb	113
Yugoslavian Hound			6	18-22in	35-53lb	113

American Foxhound

Australian Kelpie

Large Dogs (24-30in/60-76cm high)

BREED	CLASSIFICATION			HEIGHT	WEIGHT	PAGE
	KC	AKC	FCI			
Afghan Hound	H	H	CO	27-29in	58-64lb	30
Akita		W	GD	20-27in	77-88lb	31
Alano				27in	160lb	31
Alaskan Malamute		W	GD	25-28in 23-26in	85-125lb	31
American Foxhound	H	H	LH	22-25in 21-24in	65-70lb	32
Argentinian Mastiff				26in	110-130lb	34
Artésién Normand				25in	80lb	34
Australian Greyhound				28in	75-80lb	34
Auvergne Pointer			7	22-25in 22-23in	49-62lb	35
Beauceron			I	24-27½in	66-77lb	38
Belgian Pointer				25in	60lb	39
Belgian Shepherd Dog — Groenendael — Laekenois — Malinois — Tervueren	W	W	HD	24-26in 22-24in	62lb	39
Berger Picard			I	26in	75lb	39
Bernese Mountain Dog	W	W	GD	25-27½in 23-26in	88lb	40
Billy			5	24-26in 23-24in	55-66lb	40
Black and Tan Coonhound		H		25-27in 23-25in	50-75lb	41
Bloodhound	H	H	LH	25-27in 23-25in	90-110lb 80-100lb	41
Borzoi	H	H	CO	29in 27in	75-105lb	43
Bouvier des Flandres		W	HD	24½-27in 23-25½in	77-80lb 59½-77lb	44
Braco Navarro				22-26½in	60-70lb	44
Briard	W	W	HD	24-27in 23-25½in	75lb	44
Bull Mastiff	W	W	GD	25-27in 24-26in	110-130lb 90-110lb	46
Chambray			5	28in	66lb	47
Chesapeake Bay Retriever		SD	G	23-26in 21-24in	65-75lb 55-65lb	48
Chien Francais Blanc et Noir			5	26-28in	62-66lb	48
Chortaj				28in	80lb	50
Curly-Coated Retriever	G	SD	G	25-27in	70-80lb	52
Czechoslovakian Pointer			7	24-26in 23-24in	62-75lb 49-62lb	52
Doberman	W	W	GD	27in 25½in	66-80lb	54
Dogue de Bordeaux			2	24-27in	110lb	54
Dupuy Poiter			7	27in 26in	49-62lb	55
Dutch Sheepdog			I	23-25in	66lb	55
English Setter	G	SD	G	25-27in 24-25½in	60-66lb 55-61½lb	56
Eskimo Dog			2	23-27in 20-24in	75-105lb 60-90lb	57
Estrela Mountain Dog			2	23-27in	88-110lb	58
Fila Brasileiro			2	26in	110lb	58
Foxhound	H	H	LH	22-25in 21-24in	65-70lb	59
French Pointer			7	22-26in	55-71lb	60
German Long-haired Pointer			7	24-25in	55-65lb	60
German Rough-haired Pointer			7	23-25in 21-23in	55-70lb 45-60lb	60
German Shepherd Dog	W	W	HD	24-26in 22-24in	77-85lb	61
German Short-haired Pointer	G	SD	G	23-25in 21-23in	55-70lb 45-60lb	62
German Wire-haired Pointer		SD	G	23½-25½in 22in	55-70½lb 45-59½lb	62
Giant Schnauzer	U	W	GD	25½-27½in 23½-25½in	77lb 70lb	63
Gordon Setter	G	SD	G	26in 24½in	65lb 56lb	64
Grand Bleu de Gascogne			5	25-28in	71-77lb	64
Grand Gascon-Saintongeois			5	25-28in 24-26in	66-71lb	64
Grand Griffon Vendéen			5	24-26in	44-55lb	65
Great Swiss Mountain Dog			2	28in	130lb	65
Greyhound	H	H	CO	28-30in 27-28in	60-70lb	66
Hovawart			2	25-27in 22-26in	66-88lb 55-77lb	68

BREED	CLASSIFICATION			HEIGHT	WEIGHT	PAGE
	KC	AKC	FCI			
Hungarian Hound			5	22-26in	66-77lb	68
Ibizan Hound	H		CO	22-29in	42-50lb	69
Italian Pointer			7	22-26½in	55-80lb	72
Levesque			5	24-27in	66-71lb	78
Lurcher				26in approx	60lb approx	79
Magyar Agár			10	26in	60-68lb 49-57lb	79
Maremma Sheepdog			I	25½in 23½in	77-99lb 66-85lb	80
Neapolitan Mastiff			2	25-29in 23-27in	Up to 155lb	81
Newfoundland	W	W	GD	28in 26in	140-150lb 110-120lb	81
Otterhound		H	SH	27in 24in	66-77lb	83
Owtscharka				20-25in	60lb	84
Pharaoh Hound	H		CO	22-25in 21-24in	65lb	85
Picardy Spaniel			7	24-26in	60-70lb	85
Podengo (large form)			5	22-28in	66lb	86
Pointer	G	SD	CD	25-27in 24-26in	44-66lb	86
Poitevin			5	24-28in	66lb	86
Polish Hound			5	22-26in 22-24in	55-71lb 44-57lb	86
Polish Tatra Herddog			I	25-27in 23-25in	66-77lb	86
Pyrenean Mountain Dog	W	W	HD	28in + 26in +	110lb + 90lb +	90
Rastreador Brasileiro			5	26in	55lb	91
Rhodesian Ridgeback	H	H	SH	25-27in 24-26in	80lb ± 5lb 70lb	91
Rottweiler	W	W	GD	25-27in 23-25in	110lb	91
Rough-haired Vizsla			7	23-25in 21-24in	49-66lb	92
Rumanian Sheepdog				25in	80lb	92
Russian Hound				25in	55lb	92
St Bernard	W	W	GD	27½in 25½in	110-121lb	93
St Hubert Hound			5	26in 24in	88-105lb	93
Saluki	H	H	CO	23-28in	66lb max	99
Sloughi			10	27in 25½in	66-70lb	99
Spanish Greyhound			10	26-28in	66lb	102
Spanish Mastiff			2	26-28in	110-132lb	102
Spanish Pointer			7	26-29½in	55-66lb	102
Spinone			7	23-27½in 23-25½in	71-82lb 62-71lb	102
Swedish Elkhound			5	23-25in	66lb	104
Tasy				28in	75lb	105
Tibetan Mastiff			2	24-27in	220lb	105
Weimaraner	G	SD	G	24-27in 22-25in	70-85lb	107

Large Dogs (over 30in/76cm high)

BREED	CLASSIFICATION			HEIGHT	WEIGHT	PAGE
	KC	AKC	FCI			
Deerhound	H	H	CO	30in + 28in +	85-105lb 65-80lb	53
Flemish Draught Dog				30in	130lb	59
Great Dane	W	W	GD	30in 28in	120lb 100lb	65
Komondor	W	W	HD	31½in 27½in	110-135lb 80-110lb	75
Landseer			2	31in	132-155lb	77
Leonberger			2	30in 27in	88lb +	77
Mastiff	W	W	GD	30in 27½in	175-190lb	80
Pyrenean Mastiff			2	31in	155lb	90
Rampur Hound				30in	75lb	91

AFFENPINSCHER
(Monkey Dog)

The Affenpinscher is an old breed, the origins of which can be traced back to the seventeenth century. The ancestry of the breed is obscure, but it is thought that there were originally two varieties, the larger form of which is now extinct. The name 'Affenpinscher' translates from the German as 'monkey terrier'; in the United States, the breed is known as the 'Monkey Dog'. The face of the Affenpinscher is distinctly reminiscent of a primate, with relatively large eyes offset against prominent eyebrows.

Although quite a small dog, the Affenpinscher does not lack courage, nor is it a delicate breed. The coat is relatively hard and wiry, with black being the preferred color. It is not unusual for the lower jaw to be slightly longer than the upper, and this is not recognized as a fault for show purposes. The tail has to be docked, and carried high.

The Affenpinscher is currently seen less often than the Brussels Griffon, to whose bloodline it contributed. First recognized by the AKC during 1936, the fortunes of the breed declined during the Second World War, when no new stock was available, but, since then, its popularity has grown again. It remains scarce in Britain, however, and was only accredited with championship status by the Kennel Club as recently as 1980.

Affenpinscher

Afghan Hound

AFGHAN HOUND

In eastern Europe and Asia, the sport of coursing has been popular for centuries, and various types of dog have been bred to give chase to game. At Kabul, in Afghanistan, a number of such hounds were kept by the ruling dynasties. They could outpace horsemen over short distances, and they caught game independently, not in packs, running down prey ranging from hares to deer, as well as taking other predators such as wolves and even snow leopards. The hounds first located their quarry by sight and then pursued it relentlessly across the rocky terrain. Afghans still retain tremendous stamina, while their coats give protection against the climatic extremes of their native region.

Although Afghan Hounds were first seen in Britain towards the end of the nineteenth century, when they were introduced by soldiers returning home from the Afghan War, they did not attract any real attention until the arrival of Zardin, who accompanied his owner, Captain John Baff, to Britain, in 1907. Modern bloodlines date back to the 1920s when eight were imported to Scotland from the East. In Afghanistan, various localized forms of the breed were recognized, and this particular group of Afghans had the light, desert coats. They gave rise to the Bell-Murray line. In 1925, some darker, more sturdy Afghans, belonging to the mountain race, appeared in England and led to the foundation of the Ghazni strain.

Examples of the Bell-Murray strain were sent to the United States, and the first official registration of an Afghan took place there in 1927. During the next decade, following further importations, various bloodlines evolved and the breed gained in popularity. By the 1970s, over 10,000 Afghan Hounds were being registered each year.

The Afghan is undoubtedly one of the most popular and fashionable breeds worldwide, and, as a result, its shortcomings tend to be overlooked. The long, relatively soft coat, needs constant attention to maintain its attractive appearance. The hunting and chasing instincts of the breed live on in contemporary dogs, which can lead to some training difficulties. Afghans also require considerable exercise, but few breeds can rival them for elegance and individuality.

AIDI (Chien de l'Atlas)

The Aidi is a native breed of Morocco, where it is kept to help shepherds protect their flocks of sheep and goats. Lively, powerful dogs, with thick coats, they have been bred in a variety of colors. Still kept largely for working purposes, the Aidi traditionally has a docked tail and cropped ears.

AINU (Hokkaido-Ken)

Originally from the island of Hokkaido, Japan, this breed is relatively small and stocky. The coat is dense and quite short; the tail is curled. The pricked ears are another indication of its relationship to other spitz breeds. The Ainu is playful, intelligent, and responsive, and also makes a good guard dog.

AIREDALE TERRIER

The Airedale Terrier's ancestry can be traced back to the mid-nineteenth century, when the breed was established in the region of the River Aire and neighboring valleys in Yorkshire, England. The now extinct Black and Tan Tyke, crossed with Otterhounds, probably laid the foundation of the breed. At first, a variety of names, such as Waterside, Bingley or Working Terrier, were used when these dogs were exhibited at local agricultural shows. Finally, the breed's name was established at the Airedale Agricultural Show of 1879, held at Bingley in Yorkshire.

The founder of many early bloodlines of the Airedale was Champion Master Briar (1897-1906). He sired Champion Clonmel Monarch, who in turn, made a major contribution to the breed's development in the United States.

The Airedale, which is the largest of the terriers, has been used as a working dog for many years. It was trained to act as a sentry and messenger during the First World War, and the breed became a popular choice when the police started using dogs. Airedales are now widely kept as game dogs in North America, parts of Africa and India.

These terriers have also proved popular in many European countries, as both pets and show dogs. Although extremely loyal, they tend to be rather aloof with strangers, and so make good guard dogs. As a show breed, Airedales need considerable preparation. Coats must be adequately trimmed, to avoid any hint of a ragged appearance. The Airedale Terrier has proved a consistent 'Best in Show' winner, generally in the hands of experienced exhibitors.

AKITA

The qualities of the Akita are well documented in Japanese accounts dating back to the seventeenth century. The breed derives from dogs kept for hunting purposes by a nobleman who was exiled in the far north province of Akita, on the island of Honshu. Although the popularity of the breed fluctuated over the centuries, the government ensured its survival by declaring it a 'national monument' in 1931. Financial support is available for anyone who has difficulty in maintaining a champion Akita.

The forerunners of the contemporary Akita were trained to hunt in pairs, even such large animals as bears, but they were also gentle enough to retrieve waterfowl without marking the birds. Akitas resemble Chow Chows, to some extent, although they are smooth-coated

Airedale Terrier

and significantly taller. The tail should be well-curled and their ears should always be erect.

The most famous Akita in recent times was a dog called Hachiko, who accompanied his owner daily to and from the local railway station, Shibuya, near Tokyo. One evening in May, 1925, Hachiko came home alone: the professor had died at work. The dog continued going back and forth each day without fail, however, until he died nine years later. A statue, paid for by public donations, was put up commemorating Hachiko's loyalty.

The Akita was first introduced to the United States during 1937. After the Second World War, some servicemen returning from Japan brought more dogs back. The Akita Club of America was established in 1956 and the breed was first registered in the AKC studbook in 1972. It is recognized in Britain by the Kennel Club, but cannot yet compete for Challenge Certificates in shows.

ALANO

Tapestries dating back to the sixteenth century portray dogs resembling the Alano hunting wild boar and stags. This is a Spanish breed, developed around Andalusia and Extremadura. The Alano has a close affinity to both the Boxer and a Spanish breed, the Matin de Terceira, originally bred in the Azores. Mastiffs, as well as Bullenbeissers, which were kept for hunting in the region of present-day Germany, undoubtedly contributed to all three breeds.

ALASKAN MALAMUTE

Bred originally in the freezing wastelands of Alaska, these dogs were kept by a tribe of Innuits known as the Mahlemuts. Apart from their ability to pull sledges, Alaskan Malamutes worked in packs as hunters, and also defended their owners from attack. The stamina of the breed is noteworthy; teams of six dogs are capable of pulling a sleigh weighing in excess of 700lb (355kg), for distances of 50 miles (80km) or more during the course of a day.

The Malamute is not as common as similar breeds, such as the Samoyed, but seems to be gaining in popularity. These are strong dogs, but responsive to training, and, normally, quite trustworthy. They are bred in various colors, being usually either black and white, or grey, reminiscent of a wolf, and have the distinctive facial markings.

Alaskan Malamute

AMERICAN COCKER SPANIEL

A relatively small spaniel, the American Cocker was recognized as a separate breed from its English counterpart (known outside the United States as the Cocker Spaniel), in 1946. The lighter American Cocker has been evolved to cater for the differing needs of sportsmen. In the United States, quail are a favored target, yet do not occur wild in Britain, where Cocker Spaniels are trained to take larger game, such as pheasants.

The American Cocker was first registered in Britain in 1968, and is rapidly attracting a strong following, both in the show ring, and as a pet. These spaniels are usually friendly with children, and prove relatively easy to train. They have a longer coat than the English Cocker Spaniel and this is likely to require considerable attention, particularly in the case of a working gundog.

AMERICAN FOXHOUND

Early American settlers introduced Foxhounds from Britain, and these formed the basis of today's breed. The ancestors of contemporary bloodlines may well date back to the hounds which Robert Brooke took with him to the New World in 1650, a pack that remained with the family for over three centuries. Further stock was imported from France and Ireland, as well as England, during the eighteenth century, and are the foundation of today's Virginia Foxhounds.

The breed has now become divided into four basic, working categories. Foxhounds kept for drag hunting must have good pace — a characteristic shared with those which take part in field trials — as they race competitively. Gundogs should have a good voice, while the traditional pursuit of foxes by riders on horseback calls for hounds that possess a combination of athleticism and stamina, capable of operating within the framework of the pack. The American Foxhound, unlike its British counterpart, is also kept for show purposes. Although these hounds are friendly, they suffer from the stubbornness traditionally associated with dogs of this type.

AMERICAN STAFFORDSHIRE TERRIER

Another breed introduced from England, the origins of the American Staffordshire Terrier are closely linked to those of the Staffordshire Bull Terrier. Both derived from crossings

American Cocker Spaniel

American Staffordshire Terrier

of Bulldogs with English Terriers; possibly Fox Terriers. Dogs of this type had been introduced to the United States by 1870, and became known officially as the Staffordshire Terrier in 1935. The prefix 'American' was added in 1972. The breed has been developed on different lines to its British relative, being both taller and heavier in appearance.

American Staffordshire Terriers are very powerful dogs for their size, and do not hesitate to tackle larger opponents if directly threatened. As could be expected, they make good guard dogs, and are highly adaptable, soon settling down in new surroundings.

AMERICAN TOY TERRIER (Amertoy)

Various attempts have been made to produce toy terriers. In Britain, the Bull Terrier was used for this purpose but the American breeders adopted the Smooth Fox Terrier, one of the smaller breeds, as their prototype. By consistently selecting the smallest offspring, with a further input from both the English Toy Terrier and the Chihuahua, the Amertoy was created. These dogs have rather domed skulls, and are predominantly white in color. They have yet to be recognized as a separate breed by the AKC.

AMERICAN WATER SPANIEL

There is a striking similarity between this breed and the Irish Water Spaniel. The American form was probably based on an Irish bloodline, with the Curly-coated Retriever and, possibly, the English Water Spaniel also contributing to its early pedigree.

Kept almost exclusively as a working gundog, prior to being recognized by the AKC in 1940, the American Water Spaniel remains a highly efficient companion for a sportsman. The coat acts almost as a waterproof layer, making swimming more efficient, while the powerful tail enables it to steer itself in the water. Very responsive to training, these dogs make excellent retrievers of both furred and feathered game, but remain very scarce outside the United States.

ANATOLIAN KARABASH
(Anatolian Shepherd Dog)

This is an old breed, developed in Turkey, and it shares a common ancestry with other rough-coated mastiffs. Although essentially a herding dog, the Anatolian Karabash moves watchfully with herds of grazing stock, protecting the animals from predators. Not

American Water Spaniel

Anatolian Karabash

surprisingly, these dogs are hardy, powerful and alert. They tend to be pale in color, often with black markings on the face, and the coat is thick, and medium in length. In Turkey, the ears are often cropped. This breed is becoming increasingly popular, both in Britain and the United States at present.

APPENZELL MOUNTAIN DOG (Appenzellen Sennenhund)

The Swiss Mountain Dogs are divided into four separate breeds, of which the Bernese has become the most popular. The Appenzell is a relatively small dog. The breed originated in Appenzell Canton, where it worked largely with cattle. First seen in Britain during the 1930s, the breed remains scarce here, although it has become quite common in Germany. These dogs are loyal.

ARGENTINIAN MASTIFF (Dogue d'Argentine)

This breed is rather reminiscent of a white Boxer in appearance, with a similar coat, although larger in size. Its ancestry is unclear, but the dogs are essentially hunters, taking large game, such as pumas. They possess the loose folds of skin around the neck typical of fighting dogs. The breed remains almost unknown in Europe.

ARIÈGEOIS

A localized breed, coming from the Ariège region in the southwest of France, these hounds resulted from crossings of the Grand Gascon Saintongeous with the Briquet, and thus they are relatively small and finely built. Their coats are predominantly white, augmented with darker markings.

ARTÉSIEN NORMAND

The Artésian Normand is a stout, heavy hound, resembling a Bloodhound, but with a long body. It was first bred in France during the reign of Louis XIV (1638-1715). The ears are pronounced, while the head is relatively long, and there are loose folds of skin on the sides of the face. A hunting breed, the Norman Hound is often tricolored, or white offset by dark markings.

AUSTRALIAN CATTLE DOG

The first settlers in Australia relied on dogs to control the movements of their stock over the vast stretches of grazing land. A breed known as the Smithfield was originally kept for this purpose. Some time about 1830, a litter of puppies, resulting from the crossing of a Smithfield with a Dingo, was born. The puppies were red, with bob-tails, and became known as Timmins Biters, after

Australian Cattle Dog

their owner, a Mr Timmins who lived in New South Wales. Later, in 1840, two, smooth, blue merle collies were imported from Scotland by a Mr Hall, and eventually were mated to Timmins Biters; the offspring were called Hall Heelers.

The development of this breed continued and, by 1897, a standard was drawn up, at which time the dogs were known as Australian Heelers. The name was changed again to Australian Cattle Dog when the standard was revised in 1963. These are relatively small dogs, mottled in appearance, and possessing great stamina and courage. Australian Cattle Dogs are still kept for working purposes and are also valued as guard dogs. The breed has been attracting increasing attention outside Australia, and is currently exhibited in the Miscellaneous Class under AKC rules.

AUSTRALIAN GREYHOUND

The Australian form of the Greyhound was evolved to catch game that eluded many of the traditional breeds imported during the early years of settlement. In order to cope with the rough terrain, these dogs are well-muscled and relatively stocky, with sound feet. They are slightly smaller than the Greyhound kept for show purposes in Britain. The breed itself is not recognized as a separate entity by the Australian Kennel Council and appears to be in decline.

AUSTRALIAN KELPIE

A pair of Fox Collies brought from Scotland were the forerunners of this breed. They had mated and produced a litter of puppies before the ship on which they were traveling docked in Australia. The majority of the litter were black and tan, like their parents, but one puppy was red. They proved to be good sheepdogs. One of the pups was mated to a black-and-tan bitch called Kelpie; one of their litter, another bitch, also called Kelpie, formed the basis of the new breed.

Australian Kelpie

Australian Kelpies were first shown in 1908, at Melbourne. Subsequently, some completely black Kelpies were bred, and were recognized separately for a period as Barbs, although this distinction no longer exists. The Australian Kelpie has evolved into one of the best breeds of sheepdog. With a highly developed 'eye', they control sheep to a large extent by simply staring hard at them. Growing interest in the breed has led to its inclusion in the Miscellaneous Class by the AKC.

AUSTRALIAN SILKY TERRIER

This breed, derived largely from a combination of Yorkshire and Australian Terriers, has undergone considerable development during this century. Forerunners of the contemporary Australian Silky Terrier were first exhibited at the Royal Melbourne Show in 1872, when they were known as Broken-coated Terriers. The close relationship with the Yorkshire Terrier was monitored by the Victorian Silky and Yorkshire Terrier Club, which laid down distinctions between the two breeds in 1900. With growing interest in the breed around Sydney, the Sydney Silky Club came into existence, but only in 1959 was a standard established for the renamed Australian Silky Terrier, by the Australian Kennel Council.

The chief distinctions between this breed and the Yorkshire Terrier are that the Australian Silky is bigger overall, with a shorter coat which does not reach to the ground. The coat color is bluish and tan, with darker shades being preferred. The terrier's spirit is still very much in evidence, as the Australian Silky is a competent hunter of vermin, if the opportunity presents itself. Attractive-looking, the Silky is also a loyal guard dog. Outside its native land, the breed has a strong following in New Zealand, and is increasingly popular in the United States, where it is known as the Silky Terrier; it is also popular in Britain.

Australian Terrier

Australian Silky Terrier

Australian Terrier

AUSTRALIAN TERRIER

The origins of the Australian Terrier date back to the late 1860s. At first, it was known under a variety of names, reflecting the large number of terrier breeds that had contributed to its development. While the original forerunner of the Australian Terrier was the Broken-haired Terrier, the impact of the Dandie Dinmont, the Skye, and the Old Scotch Terrier can all be recognized in the contemporary breed. At first, these terriers are blue and tan in color, but crossings, involving the Cairn Terrier, introduced red.

The Australian Terrier is a truly versatile dog, and an ideal small companion in the home. Although one of the smallest terriers, they are strong and long-lived as a general rule, and caring for their coats is not difficult. These terriers are also alert and bold as guard dogs. It is no surprise therefore, that the breed has become popular worldwide, being recognized in countries as far apart as Mexico, India and South Africa.

AUSTRIAN HOUND
(Corinthian Brandlbracke)
The old Black and Tan Hounds, formerly widely kept through much of Europe, were the progenitors of various contemporary breeds which have a much more localized distribution. The Austrian Hound is one example; it is a smooth-coated breed with a thick, glossy coat showing black and tan markings, with white on the lower parts. The ears are relatively long and the body is medium-sized.

AUSTRIAN PINSCHER (Oesterreichischer Kurzhaariger Pinscher)
Although dogs of this type have been kept in Austria for centuries, they remain virtually unknown elsewhere. The Austrian Pinscher is a relatively small, short-haired breed, resembling other pinschers in appearance. The tail is short, and curls naturally if left undocked.

AUVERGNE POINTER
(Braque d'Auvergne)
There were originally two forms of this pointer, a local breed from the Auvergne region of France. The Grand Braque was the larger type, while the Braque Bleu had a more balanced, refined appearance. The breed today retains a relatively heavy physique, showing less influence from English stock than other pointers. Black and white, with black markings around the head, Auvergne Pointers have a reputation for working well. Although not as fast as some related breeds, they are easy to train, intelligent and quiet.

BALKAN HOUND
(Balkanski Gonic)
The Balkan Hound is a composite breed which was developed in an area centered on the old trading routes of the Mediterranean. Dogs brought from other countries, such as Egypt, contributed to its ancestry. Today, Balkan Hounds are predominantly reddish in color, with black markings above the

Basenji

eyes and a black saddle on the body. These hounds are both trackers and hunters, and have industrious natures.

BARB
The Barb evolved with the Australian Kelpie, and the distinction between the two, based on color, no longer exists. Barbs were simply black Kelpies, taking their name from the first dog of the type, which was called Barb, after a famous racehorse of the 1870s.

BARBET
The Barbet is believed to be one of the oldest French breeds, and has given rise to contemporary favorites, such as the Poodles, Bichon and various sheepdogs. By the turn of the present century the Barbet itself had become very scarce, but thanks to dedicated enthusiasts, the breed was saved, and has enjoyed increasing support during recent years.

A popular dog for wildfowlers, the hardy Barbet is undeterred by icy waters; it may be related to the old English Water Dog. The coat is thick and wooly; it is a powerful dog for its size.

BASENJI
The Basenji bears a striking resemblance to dogs portrayed on Ancient Egyptian artefacts. Certainly, the breed has been kept for centuries in central Africa, where it was trained to hunt in packs, driving game into waiting nets.

A pair were exported to England in 1895, but succumbed to distemper soon afterward. In 1937, the breed was exhibited in London at Crufts Dog Show, and a pair were taken to New York, where they bred successfully. Unfortunately, both the parents and the puppies were again afflicted with distemper and only the original male, called Bois, survived. A single bitch was then obtained and was mated with Bois, producing the first litter of Basenjis reared successfully in the United States. Others were imported and, in 1942, the Basenji Club of America was founded.

The Basenji, also sometimes known as the 'Barkless Dog' because of its lack of voice, is a very distinctive dog. It has an intelligent, alert appearance with pricked ears, dark eyes and a broad, wrinkled forehead. The fine, silk-like coat of the Basenji emphasizes its sleek

appearance. It is reddish-brown in color — chestnut-red being the preferred shade — with white markings on the feet, chest and tip of the tail, which curls over to one side of the back. Basenjis are obedient and friendly, their only drawback is a tendency for individuals to challenge each other when kept together, as happens naturally in wild packs of dogs. Once such skirmishes are over and an order of dominance is established, serious disputes are rare.

BASSET ARTÉSIAN NORMAND
The description 'basset' seems to have been first applied to dogs in a book on hunting by Fouilloux, published in France in 1585. The word itself is derived from the French *bas*, meaning 'low'. Much of the pioneer breeding of Bassets was undertaken by the friars of St Hubert's Abbey, using other French hounds. The major difference between this basset, and the better-known Basset Hound, is that the former is both lighter and less stocky. In common with other bassets, these dogs are friendly yet stubborn, and retain their hunting instincts.

BASSET BLEU DE GASCOGNE
These bassets were bred from the Petit Bleu de Gascon, and do not have any direct connection with Gascogny. They resemble the Artésian Normand, but have shorter legs and a more elegant appearance. They remain rare outside France.

BASSET D'ARTOIS
Derived from the Chien d'Artois, this breed of basset has a relatively long and powerful body. It may have contributed to the development of the Basset Hound in Britain, as these dogs are relatively stocky compared to other related French breeds. The Basset d'Artois possesses a short, thick coat, and is normally tricolored. Once again, this form is not often seen outside France.

BASSET FAUVE DE BRETAGNE
These bassets were ignored by British breeders when they first started to experiment with other basset breeds at the end of the nineteenth century, for two major reasons. The breed was concentrated in the Brittany area away from Paris, and its appearance is not similar to that of other bassets. The short coat is neither smooth like the Basset Artésian Normand, nor rough like the Basset Griffon Vendéen, but of an intermediate texture. The coat should be a single

Basset Griffon Vendéen

Basset·Hound

color; white markings are penalized. Even today, the breed remains confined to France.

BASSET GRIFFON VENDÉEN

This distinctive basset has a rough coat and is predominantly white, with darker markings. When these dogs were first seen in Britain, they were not considered as a separate breed, and were referred to as Griffon Bassets. The breed gained recognition in its own right when more were brought to Britain, about 30 years ago. The Basset Griffon Vendéen is one of the largest forms of basset, with relatively strong and straight legs, having a shoulder height of as much as 16in (40cm). They are similar to other members of the group in temperament.

BASSET HOUND

The Basset Hound was bred to accompany hunters on foot, rather than on horseback. Serious interest in the breed in Britain was kindled by Sir Everette Millais, who imported some dogs from France in 1874. It had already been bred in Britain, but had aroused little enthusiasm. Sir Everette set out to ensure that a large number were exhibited for the first time at the Wolverhampton Show of 1880. The public became fascinated by the unique appearance of these hounds, and the breed received a further boost when Queen Alexandra acquired some.

A number were sent during the 1880s to the United States, and the first examples of the breed were registered in 1885. Since then, the breed has flourished, as a hunting, show and pet hound. These dogs are normally either tricolored, or lemon and white, and their short coats are easy to maintain in good condition.

The Basset Hound is so naturally tenacious that it is a difficult breed to train and, once on a scent, these hounds are not easily deterred. They are very friendly, however, and tolerant with children. Basset Hounds are active dogs and need adequate exercise coupled with sensible feeding to keep their weight down. In cases of severe obesity, the penis of a male dog may actually suffer direct trauma from the ground.

BAVARIAN SCHWEISSHUND (Bayerischer Gebirgs-Schweisshund)

Breeders seeking an agile dog, capable of hunting red deer in the mountains of Bavaria, developed the Bavarian Schweisshund. A cross between the rather more ponderous Hanoverian Schweisshund and the light Bavarian Hound, the breed is still kept today almost totally for the purpose of catching deer. The Bavarian Schweisshund is about 20in (50cm) in height, and has a dense coat and powerful legs.

Beagles

BEAGLE

Hunting with packs of hounds has been a popular pastime ever since the time of the ancient Greeks. Specific breeds have been developed in order to pursue particular prey and beagles are no exception to this rule, although their origin is obscure. They were probably derived from larger hounds in the sixteenth century and were kept for hunting rabbits and hares. Packs of beagles are still used for this purpose in many countries of the world today.

A miniature version of the Beagle, less than 10in (25cm) in height to the shoulder, was popular up to World War I. Known as the Pocket Beagle, it has since faded into obscurity. There was also a rough-coated variety in existence for a period. Today, apart from hunting, the Beagle is popular both as a show dog and household pet. In common with other hounds, beagles can prove disobedient having found a scent, and are gluttons for food, yet their friendly, vivacious manner provides more than adequate compensation for such tendencies. The Beagle is an active, even-tempered hound, and makes a good guard dog, possessing a surprisingly loud bark for its size.

BEAGLE HARRIER

Kept almost exclusively in France for hunting hares, the Beagle Harrier, as its name suggests, is derived from a combination of Beagle and Harrier bloodlines. These hounds are up to 17in (42.5cm) in height, with short, generally tricolored, coats.

BEARDED COLLIE

One of the oldest British breeds, the Bearded Collie was originally kept to work with sheep. They still fulfill this purpose in parts of southern Scotland, acting as both sheepdogs and drovers. Pictorial evidence of the breed goes back to 1771, when Gainsborough included a Bearded Collie in his portrait of the Duke of Buccleigh, but some suggest that similar dogs may have been in existence as long ago as the Roman invasion.

Bearded Collie

Although Bearded Collies were often seen at shows in Peebleshire, in Scotland, there were no show standards established and, by the 1930s, the breed had seriously declined in numbers. It was rescued by a Mrs Willison, who owned the Bothkennar Kennels. Her endeavors led to the foundation of the Bearded Collie Club in 1955. Some of these collies were sent to the United States several years later, although no litters were produced there until 1967. Their future now seems assured on both sides of the Atlantic.

BEAUCERON
(Berger de Beauce)
One of a group of related breeds kept for herding sheep, the Beauceron was first bred in the area around Brie, and not Beauce as its name suggests. These short-coated dogs resemble the German Shepherd Dog in appearance. They are responsive to training, yet can be aggressive, an advantage to those seeking a guard dog. The Beauceron is not a common breed, however, and has failed to make the same impact as the Briard outside France.

BEDLINGTON TERRIER

The origins of this breed can be traced back to 1820, when Joseph Ainsley obtained a bitch called Coates Phoebe from Alnwick, near Bedlington, in Northumbria. She was mated to a Rothbury Terrier in 1825, and Ainsley named the offspring Bedlington Terriers, after the town where he was living. Subsequent crosses with the

Bedlington Terriers

Belgian Shepherd Dog

Whippet, contributing speed, and the Dandie Dinmont Terrier, which left its mark on the appearance and character of these dogs, have led to the emergence of the breed seen today.

The Bedlington Terrier is bred in two recognized colors, blue and liver. Although the latter predominated during the early years of the breed, blue has become increasingly common lately. Bedlingtons are fearless dogs, quite willing to tackle badgers, otters and foxes; they also become devoted to their owners. The extensive trimming required for an exhibition Bedlington has deterred many from showing their dogs, but advice can be obtained from an experienced dog groomer.

BELGIAN POINTER
(Braque Belge)
The Belgian Pointer is one of a number of gundogs which have been selectively bred from French stock and has a restricted distribution, still being kept predominantly for working rather than exhibition purposes. The coat color is a combination of slate-grey with brown markings, while the fur itself is short and dense. A strongly built dog, the Belgian Pointer's head is relatively broad compared to those of other pointers.

BELGIAN SHEPHERD DOG
The Belgian Shepherd Dog is both a guard dog and herder. There are four recognized varieties.

The Laekenois, probably the least common form, originated close to Antwerp, and it was kept to guard linen placed outside for bleaching. Fawn with black markings on the face, it has a rough coat that is relatively hard to the touch, in contrast to the Groenendael, which it resembles in type.

The Groenendael has a distinctive black coat. These dogs were first seen in the United States in 1907, where they were kept as police dogs. During the First World War, they acted as sentries and messengers. They make good companions, in addition to their working abilities.

The Tervueren is closely related to the Groenendael, although they are now recognized as separate breeds. The distinction is based largely on grounds of color. The hairs of the Tervueren are tipped with black, creating a dark effect. The coat must not be as black as that of the Groenendael, however, nor too pale. The darker markings are more pronounced around the facial area and forequarters, and at the tip of the tail.

The Malinois can be easily distinguished from other Belgian Shepherd Dogs by its smooth coat. Its appearance suggests a close relationship with the better-known German Shepherd Dog. The Malinois was first seen in the United States in 1948, but has made little impact on Britain to date. Like other Belgian Shepherd Dogs, they adjust well to a family environment but remain wary of strangers. Bitches are invariably smaller than males.

BERGER DE LANGUEDOC
There are five distinct breeds grouped under this description, each named after the area in Languedoc, France, where they were developed. These dogs range in height from 16-20in (40-50cm), and have brownish to black coats of varying lengths. Known as the Grau, Farou, Larzac, Carrigues and Carmargue, all five breeds are kept as working sheepdogs and guard dogs on the farms where they live.

BERGER PICARD
Thought to have been introduced to northern France as long ago as the ninth century, the Berger Picard has been kept almost exclusively as a working sheepdog since that time. It is a large, hardy breed, about 26in (65cm) high, with a thick, protective coat. The Berger Picard is easy to train and makes a good watchdog.

Berger Polonais de Vallée

Berner Laufhund

BERGER POLONAIS DE VALLÉE

This breed is believed to have been developed by the Huns in the eighth century AD in the area that is now Poland. The Berger Polonais de Vallée is tough and hardy, rather reminiscent of the Old English Sheepdog, but smaller in size. The tail of the breed has largely been bred out, but if present, it is docked at an early age. Generally of one color, some individuals also show white markings. They retain their herding instincts and also make good guard dogs.

BERNER LAUFHUND

The Berner Laufhund is a typical example of one of the many breeds of hound that were developed in Switzerland. The individual characteristics of these have been maintained by the Swiss Hound Club, which was founded in 1931. The Berner Laufhund is generally black and white in color, sometimes with tan markings, or tricolored. Both smooth- and rough-coated forms are bred, as in a variety with shorter legs. In common with other Laufhunds, the Berner has long, folded ears and a narrow skull.

BERNESE MOUNTAIN DOG

An old Swiss breed, the Bernese Mountain Dog is thought to have been introduced by the Romans. By the end of the last century, the breed had declined and was virtually lost until, in 1892, a breeder called Franz Schertenleib started to rekindle

Bernese Mountain Dogs

Bichon Frise

interest. The Bernese differs from the other three Swiss Mountain Dogs because it has a long silky coat, although it is similar in color, being jet black with brown areas on the legs. There must also be white markings on the chest and spots above the eyes.

Bernese Mountain Dogs were kept largely as a working breed in the Canton of Berne, and were trained as drovers and guard dogs. They respond well to human attention and show great loyalty in return.

BICHON FRISÉ

There were originally four recognized forms of the Bichon, developed from the Barbet, in the area just around the Mediterranean. Such dogs as these were frequently traded, became popular in Tenerife, but virtually disappeared from Europe. They were re-introduced to Europe during the fourteenth century, and were especially favored as pets in Italy. Interest in the breed spread to Spain as well as France, where, during the reign of Henry III (1574-89), such dogs were highly pampered by their wealthy owners.

Towards the end of the nineteenth century, the Bichon's status had declined, to the extent that it had become a popular companion for organ grinders and acted as a show dog in circuses. Eventually, following much dedicated work by breeders, a standard was established for the breed in France in 1933. Up until that date, the breed was known as either Bichon or Tenerife; the present name was coined by Madame Nizet de Leemans, who was then President of the FCI.

The breed was first seen in the United States following the emigration of a Monsieur Picault and his wife from France in 1956. Their bitch, named Etoile de Steren Vor, produced the first litter of Bichons Frisés seen there. Other breeders obtained further stock, and registration was granted by the AKC in 1972. The Kennel Club in Britain recognized the Bichon Frisé two years later, and it has since become a very popular member of the Toy group, with its pleasing appearance and lively personality rapidly attracting a strong following. These dogs have white, curly coats.

BILLY

A descendant of the old breeds of pack hounds, dating back to the reign of Louis XII (1462-1515), the Billy was developed by Hublot du Rivault, in Poitou, France. They are large hounds, with a distinctive body coloration, a combination of white, and orange or lemon. Like their ancestors, Billies are kept for hunting deer in packs, relying on scent to track their quarry.

BLACK ELKHOUND

The numbers of this breed have declined to the point where its continued survival must be in doubt. It is now largely restricted to Norway, although it used to be seen in other parts of Scandinavia as well, but has been surpassed by the more popular grey Elkhound. The Black variety is both lighter and smaller than its grey relative, but remains a typical spitz dog nevertheless, possessing the usual curled tail, pricked ears and thick coat. Black Elkhounds have proved to be hardy, resourceful dogs and, although kept originally for hunting large game, they also make good guard dogs.

BLACK AND TAN COONHOUND

Although only recognized by the AKC in 1945, the Black and Tan Coonhound is thought to be descended from the Talbot Hound, which was being bred in Britain during the eleventh century. More recently, Bloodhounds and Foxhounds, as well as Virginia Foxhound stock established in the United States, were used to develop the breed. The Virginia Foxhound itself was known as the 'Black and Tan', and these Coonhounds were bred selectively, with regard to color, from them. 'Cooners' of other colors are also known.

As their name suggests, these hounds hunt racoons, but they will also take large quarry such as bears and deer, being both powerful and fast in pursuit. The close relationship with the Bloodhound is clearly evident when the Black and Tan Coonhound is following a scent, as it works with its nose close to the ground, only baying when the quarry is spotted. The breed has retained its identity as a working dog, with the standard drawn up by the AKC specifically mentioning this quality.

BLOODHOUND

The Bloodhound is undoubtedly the most effective member of the group of hounds that hunt by scent. Dogs possessing this ability can be traced right back to the third century AD, and it is likely that the Bloodhound itself was being bred before the Middle Ages. It was developed from St Hubert Hounds brought back from the Holy Land after the Crusades. There were then two recognized color forms, white and black, with the black form being seen in England. By the twelfth century, such dogs were highly prized for hunting, and

Black Elkhound

Bloodhound

kennels were often established at monasteries. As a mark of their pedigree, they were described as 'blooded hounds', which may have provided the basis for their current name.

Partly as a result of its name, however, the Bloodhound acquired an unjustified reputation as an aggressive dog. In the United States, they were used to track down escaped slaves, which lent credence to the brutal tales told about them. In reality, the Bloodhound is an extremely gentle dog, happiest when just following a scent. Working Bloodhounds have been kept for this purpose by police forces in many parts of the world. One famous dog, called Nick Carter, succeeded in following a scent that was over four days old, which led to the capture and subsequent conviction of a wanted criminal.

While the scenting ability and power of the Bloodhound may be advantageous in the field, these qualities can lead to problems when training a dog to become part of a household. They require considerable exercise, and are likely to be sidetracked by an interesting scent, rather than returning when called. Bloodhounds are also very sensitive, a trait that further complicates training. They make great companions despite their drawbacks and prove most affectionate, especially with children. While Bloodhounds are not as common as some breeds in the show ring, separate scenting trials are often organized, ensuring that this talent is not allowed to diminish over successive generations.

BOLOGNESE

These small dogs were being bred in Italy as long ago as the fifteenth century and were first seen in Britain three centuries later. It is thought that they may be descended from European Water Dogs; the breed is now regarded as a member of the Bichon group. The curly coat of the Bolognese is predominantly white in color, with shorter fur around the mouth. The breed is still largely confined to Italy.

BORDER COLLIE

The intelligence and working capacity of the Border Collie has been acknowledged for centuries, especially in the border district of Scotland, yet, only recently has the breed been accepted for showing by the Kennel Club. It has competed at working dog trials for a much longer period of time.

The original ancestor of the Border Collie is likely to have been the Persian Sheepdog, while in recent times, the development of the breed has been

Border Collie

monitored by the International Sheepdog Society. Very responsive to training, the Border Collie is an active, enthusiastic worker, and does not settle very well in the normal domestic environment, where it has little or no opportunity to use its talents. The breed is generally black and white in color, and both rough- and smooth-coated forms have been bred.

BORDER TERRIER

Another of the breeds developed around the Cheviot Hills, bordering England and Scotland, the Border Terrier is a tough, uncompromising individual. These terriers were popularized by the Master of the Border Hunt during the nineteenth century, and were kept to pursue foxes in the company of riders. Border Terriers readily go to earth and battle with foxes or even otters. They can get fearfully injured in the ensuing struggle, yet never buck a challenge. The hardiness of the breed is assisted by their wiry coats, which help them survive outside in the cold climate.

The breed first started to receive recognition in England shortly after the First World War. The Border Terrier Club came into existence during the early 1920s; recognition of the breed by

Border Terriers

the Kennel Club followed. Although popular in Britain both as show and working dogs, as well as making active pets, Border Terriers are only just becoming appreciated in the United States.

BORZOI
(Russian Wolfhound)

The Borzoi is one of the breeds of hound that hunt by sight, rather than by following a scent. It has all the elegance of the sight hounds — long legs, a gracefully curving back with a long neck and tapering head. Hounds of this type were in existence in Russia as long ago as 1260, and by 1650 the first standard for the Borzoi had been established. This differs remarkably little from contemporary requirements for the breed.

Repeated outcrosses during the latter part of the nineteenth century led to a overall decline in type; in 1873, the Imperial Association was formed in Russia in an attempt to preserve the traditional appearance of these hounds. Many contemporary United States bloodlines were developed from the stock held by the members of this association.

The Borzoi Hound was first exhibited in Britain by the Prince of Wales in 1889, and the breed was seen in the United States during the following year. In 1903, Joseph Thomas travelled to Russia and obtained stock to take back to the United States from the famous Perchino Kennels, owned by the Grand Duke Nicholas, and also from the Woronzova Kennels. During the same year, the Russian Wolfhound Club of America was founded, and did much to popularize the breed.

Borzois have retained the speed which enabled them to outrun wolves, and they are still kept for coursing in some areas. They require a considerable amount of exercise to keep them fit, and must be allowed to run free off the lead. Their coats also need constant care and attention to maintain the truly aristocratic image of the breed.

BOSTON TERRIER

A dog called Judge, obtained about 1870 from England by a Robert C. Hooper, was the forerunner of this breed. Judge was the result of a cross between a Bulldog and an English Terrier, and was, in turn, mated to a white bitch known as both Gyp and Kate. By 1889, these terriers had become sufficiently numerous for 30 breeders to form the American Bull Terrier Club. In the face of heated opposition from Bull Terrier owners, the name of the breed was changed to Boston Terrier, after the

Borzois

Boston Terrier

town where it was developed.

The AKC finally recognized the breed in 1893; since then its popularity has spread throughout the United States and overseas. The Boston Terrier is also well represented in Britain. These dogs have kept the characteristics of both the original breeds which contributed to their ancestry. Boston Terriers, while making reliable guard dogs, revel in human company and are generally good-natured.

The breed is often seen in the show ring. Preparation is not very difficult, and the short coat requires relatively little care to be seen at its best. Color and markings are both important considerations. White areas must be clearly delineated, extending up the head and from the neck down on to the chest, while all the feet must also be white. In profile, the shape of the body is reminiscent of a terrier.

BOURBONNAIS POINTER
(Braque de Bourbonnais)
A relatively ungainly form of pointer, the Bourbonnais, was developed at the end of the last century in Bourbonnais, central France. It has remained scarce even in its homeland, although the breed is not untalented as a working dog. Slow but conscientious, and gentle by nature, these pointers can be taught to retrieve game. They are invariably white with pale brownish markings, and have a thick water-repellant coat.

BOUVIER DES ARDENNES
This breed, which never achieved the popularity of the Bouvier des Flandres, is now considered extinct. It was bred primarily as a working sheepdog, but was also used for guarding stock and property.

BOUVIER DES FLANDRES
The Bouvier des Flandres was originally developed in northern France, and southwest Flanders, where it acted as a cattle dog. The breed was first shown in 1910; a standard was established two

Bouvier des Flandres

Boxer

years later when a breed society was formed. Despite the decimation of their native region during the First World War, the hardy Bouvier des Flandres survived, and during the 1930s was introduced to the United States. Its popularity there increased significantly with the success of Champion Marios de Clos Cerbeus in the show ring.

The breed is currently making a considerable impact on the British show scene, and breeders are going to great lengths to ensure that the power, strength and speed of these dogs is not lost through indiscriminate matings. Bouvier des Flandres are lively dogs, loyal and trustworthy with established acquaintances, but wary of strangers.

BOXER
The Boxer, which evolved primarily from the German Bullenbeisser, is of mastiff descent. Attempts to create the breed began in the 1830s, and involved crosses with other breeds such as the English Bulldog, which is credited with the introduction of significant areas of white to the coat of the Boxer. Present standards insist that such markings must be restricted; the AKC specifies that a maximum of a third of the coat should be white.

The breed was only slowly accepted in the United States, although the first Boxer was registered in 1904. The importation of International Champion Check von Hunnenstein into the United States by the Cirrol Kennels in the 1930s, marked the turning point in public interest. This dog was the first Boxer to win an American 'Best in Show' award. Other German Boxers were subsequently imported; the Boxer has since become one of the most popular breeds worldwide.

Boxers are active and lively, respond well to training and were among the first breeds used for police work. Character is still regarded as an important feature and their attributes include loyalty, intelligence and courage. They are not generally aggressive, and prove to be good with children, although they are sometimes too boisterous in a home where there are young toddlers. Their short coats require the minimum of attention and it is traditional for their tails to be docked. Unfortunately, the most distressing aspect of owning a Boxer is the high susceptibility of the breed to many types of tumor. Why this should be the case is at present unknown.

BRACO NAVARRO
(Braco Carlos VIII)
A breed kept almost exclusively for hunting, the Braco Navarro was first developed as a gundog in southwestern Spain nearly two centuries ago, and may have descended from herding stock. They are powerful dogs, and have short white coats with brownish markings.

BRIARD
The Briard is an old working breed, whose ancestors are portrayed in tapestries dating back to the eighth century. They were kept initially to guard sheep against wolves and other predators, but gradually their role changed to that of herder. It is unclear whether the breed originated in the province of Brie; it has been suggested that the 'de Brie' component of their native names is simply a corruption of 'd'Aubry'. In the fourteenth-century legend of Aubry of Montdidier, a dog similar to the Briard features prominently in the story.

Briard

Bulldog

The first standards for the Briard were laid down at the end of the nineteenth century and the breed society, known as *Les Amis du Briard*, was founded a short time afterward. American soliders encountered the breed during the First World War and, by 1920, it had been introduced to the United States.

It is only during recent years that the Briard has made an impact in Britain, but it has rapidly proved popular. They are extremely loyal dogs, rarely straying far from their home territory. Training can prove difficult, since the breed has a strong, independent streak. Breeders are working hard to preserve the unusual characteristics of these dogs, such as the double dew claws on the hind feet, and increasing numbers are now being shown, especially at major British events. Regular grooming is essential.

BRITTANY SPANIEL
Although it has been kept in Europe for over a century, and was introduced to the United States as long ago as 1931, the Brittany Spaniel was only first seen at the Crufts Dog Show in 1984. Dogs of this type were being bred in the region of Brittany in France by 1850, when a separate standard was established for them. The Brittany Spaniel remains primarily a working dog, commonly seen at field trials in the United States, rather than shows, although its appearance at the latter has increased over the past few years.

The Brittany Spaniel looks more like a setter than a spaniel, compared to the contemporary short-legged British breeds, and also resembles the setter in its working style. They are usually a dark orange or liver, offset against white, and are friendly by nature.

BULLDOG
Descended from ancient mastiff stock, the Bulldog has become inextricably linked with Britain. Here, prior to 1835, such dogs were bred to take part in bull-baiting contests. In such competitions, a bull would be staked and the dogs encouraged to attack its nose. The unfortunate bull defended itself as far as possible, while the onlookers wagered on the outcome of the contest. The major requirement was for courageous dogs; their appearance was of little significance.

After bull-baiting was banned, the Bulldog lost ground to the Bull Terrier as a fighting dog, and only after the breed club was founded in 1864 did the future of the breed become more assured. Since that time, a great deal of emphasis has been placed on actual appearance. Any trace of their former aggressiveness has been removed, but their courage remains.

Bulldogs are solid, muscular dogs with powerful jaws, which can prove difficult to part if the need arises. They have become friendly and affectionate by nature, and, while certainly not a graceful breed, the Bulldog still attracts many devotees. It is, however, often one of the more expensive breeds to buy.

Brittany Spaniel

Bull Terriers

BULL MASTIFF

Mastiffs of various types have been common in Britain for centuries. A type known as the Bandog was kept for guarding property during the thirteenth century. Policing large country estates during the 1800s was the responsibility of gamekeepers, but it was a dangerous occupation; they were often attacked and killed by poachers in the course of their duties. Gamekeepers looked to dogs to be alert and defend them against such assaults, and to serve this purpose the Bull Mastiff was developed from crossings of Mastiffs with Bull Terriers. The breed was recognized by the Kennel Club in 1924, and the sturdy appearance and nature of the Bull Mastiff has ensured its use as a guard dog in many other countries.

Bull Mastiff

BULL TERRIER

The old English White Terrier, crossed with the Bulldog, laid the foundation of this famous breed. Developed initially for ratting and as a competitive fighting dog, the long-nosed white form was produced in Birmingham by a dog dealer called James Hinks. These dogs were generally more refined than the Staffordshire Bull Terrier, which also contributed to their origins. The supporters of the Staffordshire scoffed at the new breed until a challenge was arranged between one of their terriers and a white bitch of Hinks' called Puss. Puss vanquished her opponent in less than half an hour, and managed to escape sufficiently unscathed to win at a dog show the next day.

Further refinement of the breed has since been carried out and, while the majority of Bull Terriers are not agressive, they prove very determined guards and refuse to back away from a fight if threatened. As long ago as 1863, Bull Terriers were grouped by size for show purposes, and it is no surprise that a miniature form was developed. There may be considerable variation in the weight of individual puppies in a Bull Terrier litter, and selective breeding, using the smaller members, laid the foundation for the miniature strain. Under 14in (35cm) high, such dogs are now recognized by the Kennel Club as a separate breed.

CAIRN TERRIER

Before the Cairn Terrier was seen as a show dog at the beginning of the century, the breed had been kept for many years as a working dog on the Isle of Skye. Although the Skye Terrier was better known, the Cairn was a highly valued dog in the local community, used to drive foxes and other vermin from hiding places in rocks. It takes its name from the Gaelic word for a pile of stones. At this stage, there was no emphasis placed on the coloring or particular type and, in fact, quite a variety of local strains were recognized.

Standardization then followed, but the hardy, active nature of the Cairn Terrier was retained. In 1909, at the Inverness Show, the breed was initially exhibited as the 'Short-haired Skye Terrier'. Following recognition by the Kennel Club, the popularity of the Cairn now almost matches that of the West Highland White. The coat remains an important feature of the contemporary Cairn, and must consist of a double layer of hair. The Cairn is a sensitive breed, which does not react well to harsh treatment. Willing and loyal, Cairns are alert and keen of hearing.

CANAAN DOG

The Canaan Dog is rather reminiscent of a smooth Collie in appearance, although it is more solid and has a curly tail. It is thought to have been descended from the various Pariah Dogs which once ranged throughout the Middle East. The breed has now become closely linked with Israel and only a few individuals have actually been exported elsewhere. Both brave and intelligent, Canaan Dogs are said to be very responsive to training.

CANE DA PASTORE BERGAMASCO

An old breed of herding dog kept in the mountainous parts of northern Italy, the Cane da Pastore Bergamasco bears some resemblance to both the Briard and the Puli. It possesses the qualities found in many of the other herding dogs, and is said to have been kept by man for over 2,000 years.

Cairn Terriers

CATALAN SHEEPDOG
(Gos d'Atura)
These unusual dogs evolved in the region of Catalonia, descending almost certainly from mastiff stock, and have since become popular throughout Spain. The long-haired variety works with sheep as well as cattle, while the short-haired form is more widely seen at shows, and is kept as a pet. The breed was used as a guard dog and messenger during the Spanish Civil War in the 1930s.

CAVALIER KING CHARLES SPANIEL
This breed is a reconstruction of an older type of toy spaniel, and was developed during the 1920s in the United States when a Mr Eldridge from Long Island, New York, set out to encourage a return to the type of toy spaniels portrayed in old paintings. The Cavalier King Charles Spaniel has a more pronounced nose and a longer tail than the King Charles, and is recognized as a separate breed.

Although the Cavalier is to this day classified in the Miscellaneous Class by the AKC, it has become one of the most popular toy breeds in Britain. A Cavalier won the 'Best in Show' award at Crufts Dog Show in 1973, confirming the success of the recreation of the breed. They are bred in the same colors as the King Charles Spaniel.

Cavalier King Charles Spaniel

Cesky Terrier

The Cavalier is a very active dog, requiring more exercise than most of the other toy breeds. They are generally affectionate, although some individuals can prove to be rather withdrawn and nervous. Such problems are often related to their early life; a puppy properly reared should not prove a disappointment in this respect.

CESKY TERRIER
This breed was developed in what is now Czechoslovakia and is becoming more and more common in various European countries as a show dog. It was originally developed to go to ground and fight foxes and badgers, work that called for a strong yet short-legged dog with plenty of courage. The Cesky Terrier was bred using Scottish and Sealyham Terriers, but has now become slightly bigger than either of these breeds. Their coat, less wiry than that of other terriers, is wavy and slightly glossy in appearance. The breed has retained the terrier character of its ancestors, and as such makes an exceptionally good family pet.

CHAMBRAY
One of the French breeds of hound, the Chambray is tall and powerful, although it lacks the pace of some breeds. It is lemon and white in color, with the coat becoming paler as the dog ages. The hair is soft, fine and short.

CHESAPEAKE BAY RETRIEVER

The origin of these retrievers can be traced back to 1807, when an English ship floundered off the coast of Maryland. The American vessel *Canton* was nearby, and picked up the crew as well as the two Newfoundland puppies that had been on board. One was red and was named Sailor; the other, a black bitch, was called Canton, as a gesture of thanks to the rescuing crew. These dogs remained with the *Canton* and their retrieving ability was noted. Outcrosses with various other breeds eventually led to the development of a breed of a recognizable type by 1885. It is likely that the Flat-coated, and possibly the Curly-coated Retrievers, both contributed to the bloodline. The breed has been named after Chesapeake Bay where, working in cold choppy waters, these dogs can retrieve as many as 300 ducks during a day's shooting.

The coat of the Chesapeake Bay Retriever is an important feature of the breed. It is a brownish color, which becomes paler during the summer. The combination of a thick undercoat, coupled with the oily top coat, provide insulation in freezing waters, and only a shake or so is required to dry out the coat afterward.

The Chesapeake Bay Retriever, while greatly appreciated by the wildfowler, is not frequently seen at shows, probably because it lacks the aesthetic appeal of similar breeds. It also remains uncommon outside the United States. These are nevertheless friendly and intelligent dogs, yet not particularly sociable with other dogs.

CHIEN COURANT DE BOSNIE À POIL DUR

Descended from the old Celtic Hound, this breed remains largely confined to Yugoslavia. They are powerful hounds of medium size, with good stamina, and have been used to hunt wild boar, as well as lesser game such as hares. They vary in color with white, through fawn, to grey, showing other markings as well. While the undercoat is soft, the long outer coat is characterized by particularly long guard hairs.

CHIEN COURANT DE LA VALLÉE DE LA SAVE

A Yugoslavian breed first registered in 1955, these hounds are similar in size to the Chien Courant de Bosnie, but are yellowish-brown or reddish in color, with white markings on the head, around the neck, and on the underparts. They have a loud, baying call, rather reminiscent of a bell, and are used to pursue small game.

CHIEN D'ARTOIS

One of the original breeds from which many of the contemporary hunting dogs of France are descended, the Chien d'Artois is descended from St Hubert Hound. They bear more resemblance to the Foxhound than many of the French breeds and are tricolored, with a saddle area of grey or fawn. These hounds are still largely unknown outside France.

CHIEN DE TRAIT (Matin Belge)

This breed is now considered to be extinct. It is thought to have been the darker type of French hound which contributed to the development of the Bloodhound, and was similar to the St Hubert Hound.

CHIEN FRANCAIS BLANC ET NOIR

In the early years of this century, there were as many as 300 separate packs of hounds in France. Each was jealously guarded, and it is no coincidence that many localized breeds evolved as a result. The survival of the majority was dependent on the estates where they were kept, and, as these declined in

Chesapeake Bay Retriever

numbers, the breeds were often lost.

The Chien Francais Blanc et Noir is a breed which is still extant from that period. It is one of the larger varieties, kept for hunting big game, such as wild boar and deer. Color is the distinctive feature. As its name implies, these hounds are white with black areas forming a mantle. Red markings are allowed on the legs, while pale reddish-brown areas under the ears, on the head and at the base of the tail are also permitted.

CHIEN FRANCAIS TRICOLORE

These hounds are another large breed which has survived to the present day. They were kept originally to hunt deer in particular, with their relatively slender body giving them considerable pace and stamina. During the reign of Louis XV (1710-74), cross-breeding with English Foxhounds was undertaken to improve their speed.

The long, slightly folded ears of the Chien Francais Tricolore reflect their ancestry, which traces back to the old Celtic Hound. They are consistently tricolored white, black and tan. As with other hounds of this type, the Chien Français Tricolore remains virtually unknown outside France.

CHIHUAHUA

The Toltec Indians, who lived in what is now Mexico, kept a breed of dog known as the Techichi as long ago as the ninth century. These dogs were small with long coats, and mute. Their ancestry may have extended back as far as the Mayan civilization of the fifth century AD. Evidence can be seen in carvings at the Monastery of Huejotzingo, where a study of a head, as well as a portrait, showing a breed very similar to the contemporary Chihuahua, have been discovered.

The Chihuahua is thought to have arisen from crossings of the Techichi with a hairless breed introduced from Asia. This breed was probably similar to the Chinese Crested Dog, and contributed to an overall decrease in their size. After the Aztecs overran the Toltecs, Chihuahuas were highly valued; blue individuals were thought to be sacred. Columbus, in a letter to his patron the King of Spain, recorded finding small, mute, domesticated dogs on the island now known as Cuba.

The first Chihuahuas, named after a Mexican state, were seen in the United States in about 1850. A relatively small number, perhaps as few as two dozen, formed the basis of the breed. The Chihuahua was recognized by the AKC

Long-coated Chihuahua

in 1904, and the Chihuahua Club of America was established in 1923. The smooth-coated form is most common, but the long-coated variety is rapidly increasing in numbers. This division was accepted for show purposes in the United States in 1952; 13 years later in Britain. The breed was first seen in Britain as recently as 1934 and only became popular after the Second World War. They have since become greatly valued, both as show dogs and pets.

Chihuahuas are unusual in preferring the company of other dogs of the same breed, and often resent outsiders; the short-coated variety tends to be most definite in this respect. They are not nervous by nature, making alert and surprisingly noisy guards.

CHINESE CRESTED DOG

Various hairless breeds have been recorded. In the early years of the present century, the Chinese Crested Dog was grouped with the Mexican and African Hairless forms. Two distinct types of Crested Dog were then known. One had long legs, resembling a Whippet and the other form was a short, relatively stocky dog with hair on the neck and between the toes, and a tufted tail. This type is currently undergoing a resurgence in popularity.

Smooth-coated Chihuahuas

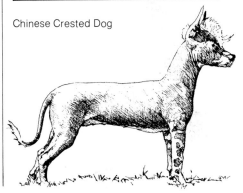
Chinese Crested Dog

Chow Chow

Such dogs never fail to attract attention when they appear and, with their unique appeal, may soon become more firmly established.

CHINESE HOUND

Descended from a breed of long-coated dogs native to Kashmir, these hounds are similar to Greyhounds, although considerably heavier. Dark brown in color, their thick, short coat forms a slight ridge along the back. They were originally bred to hunt in packs, with large game such as wild boar being their quarry. It is not certain whether the Chinese Hounds still exist in any number; at least 50 years ago the breed was in decline.

CHORTAJ

The Chortaj was firmly accepted as a pure Russian breed at the Cynological Congress which took place in Moscow in 1952 and, since then, efforts have been made to ensure its survival. Heavier than a Greyhound, the Chortaj is nevertheless a coursing breed, with the long neck and rather curved body typical of this group of dogs.

CHOW CHOW

The origin of the Chow Chow is obscure, but the breed is certainly very old, and can be traced back 2,000 years. It has

been suggested that the Chow Chow is a descendant of the Tibetan Mastiff, crossed with the Samoyed of Siberia. Although the Chow Chow shares common characteristics with both these breeds, it is unique in possessing a bluish-black tongue, and could itself have been an ancestor of the Samoyed and related spitz dogs.

Despite their regal appearance, Chow Chows have been considered as utilitarian dogs. Their fur was valued in the cold region of Manchuria, while farming the breed for meat was not uncommon in various parts of China.

The name 'Chow Chow' is not Chinese but was a term used by sea captains to describe the artefacts brought as cargo from the Orient. The Reverend Gilbert White describes a pair that were shipped back from Canton during 1780, but serious interest in the breed did not occur until as much as a century later, when Queen Victoria started keeping these dogs.

At about the same time in the United States, the Chow Chow came to public attention. In 1890, a dog called Takya was shown in the Miscellaneous Class at the Westminster Kennel Club Show in New York, and took third prize. They have since become popular in both countries, making good show dogs and frequently winning top awards. One Chow

Chow has the notable distinction of winning the greatest number of Challenge Certificates of all breeds.

Young Chow Chows are extremely appealing, but often prove very difficult to train successfully, so that this breed is normally absent from obedience classes. These dogs can also be rather temperamental, especially when strangers are present, but are likely to be affectionate with people they know well.

CLUMBER SPANIEL

The origins of this breed can be traced back to the eighteenth century, when the 2nd Duke of Newcastle acquired some spaniels of this type from the Duc de Noailles. They became known as Clumber Spaniels, taking their name from the Duke's estate, Clumber Park.

It was not until 1859 that classes were staged for these spaniels in Britain. They are heavier and less mobile than other related breeds, as they were developed at a time when game was plentiful and a skilled scent-hunting dog was generally considered most desirable. The breed was first registered in 1883 in the United States, but Clumber Spaniels do not have a great following in either country today, despite their unusual appearance and their attractive lemon and white coloration. They are quieter than most other spaniels. Reliable retrievers, they could readily be classed as dual-purpose gundogs.

COCKER SPANIEL

Spaniels, as a group, date back to at least 1368. 'Spanyells', as they were known, were subsequently divided into two distinct groups: water spaniels and land spaniels. A further sub-division of the latter group occurred, with the smallest breeds becoming known as 'toys'. The rather bigger, working spaniels were separated into two categories, on the basis of the working styles: the 'starters' flushed out game for purposes of falconry, while 'cockers' were evolved especially to hunt woodcock.

Localized breeding gave rise to different types, but slowly the breed known as the Cocker developed in Wales and also in southwest England. Recognized by the Kennel Club in 1892, at first Cockers fell behind other breeds such as the Sussex in numbers, yet by the 1930s they had become the most popular breed in England.

When working as a gundog, the Cocker should investigate the area in front of the gun, and having flushed out the game, must sit, so as not to distract the hunter. On command, the Cocker will retrieve the game, venturing into water if necessary.

Clumber Spaniel

Cocker Spaniel

Cocker Spaniel

Curly-coated Retriever

In the show ring, Cocker Spaniels have achieved great success, with the Ware stud being especially renowned. Unfortunately, Cockers' coats can grow rather curly, reflecting the trace of Water Spaniel blood in the breed, and this is penalized under both the Kennel Club and AKC standards. They have been bred in an extremely wide range of colors, traditionally self (solid) combinations, with white restricted to the chest area alone. Combinations such as black and white, or even three colors are also permitted.

These spaniels adapt well to a domestic environment, but they will benefit from good periods of exercise. A close watch should be kept on their long, thick-coated ears, since infections in the ear canals are relatively common. In the United States, a slightly smaller form of the Cocker has also been bred and is now recognized separately as the American Cocker Spaniel.

COTON DE TULEAR
This toy breed, belonging to the Bichon group, was developed in the Malagasy Republic (which was formerly known as Madagascar). Ancestors of the Coton de Tulear were brought to the island of Bourbon by troops during the seventeenth century. A similar breed, called the Chien Coton, developed on the neighbouring island of Reunion, and was used in crossings. New blood has also been introduced from the Maltese. The coat of these dogs is fluffy and white, often distinguished by yellowish markings. A number have been exported to Europe especially France; they appear to be rare in Malagasy now.

CROATIAN SHEEPDOG
An old breed, kept originally for herding stock, the Croatian Sheepdog has since become much more popular outside its native Yugoslavia. Two forms are recognized by the FCI; the Kraski Ovcar is distinguished from the Hrvatski Ovcar on grounds of size, being 4in (10cm) taller. Both types have long coats and are of typical sheepdog build. They are predominantly black with paler markings on the chest extending down to the legs.

CURLY-COATED RETRIEVER
The old English Water Spaniel is thought to have been one of the main ancestors of this breed. The Irish Water Spaniel is also likely to have contributed to its development, and possibly the Newfoundland. Further crossings with Poodles were carried out in the 1880s, apparently in order to ensure that the coat was tightly curled.

About this time, some Curly-coated Retrievers were sent to New Zealand, where they were trained to retrieve ducks; in Australia, they became popular for the same purpose in the vicinity of the Murray River. The breed was first seen in the United States in 1907. Curly-coated Retrievers have not attracted the same following as other similar breeds, partly because of their reputation for being relatively 'hard-mouthed' when retrieving game. Their main feature is the distinctive coat, black or liver in color and a mass of small curls. These dogs are hardy and readily take to water.

CZECHOSLOVAKIAN POINTER (Cesky Fousek: Bohmisch Rauhbart)
The Czechoslovakian Pointer was very nearly lost as a breed during the First World War, but some careful breeding between the wars has ensured that it still remains a valued gundog. It is similar in appearance to the German Rough-haired Pointer. The coat is unusual in that it is much thinner during the summer, when the thick undercoat is molted and not replaced. There are also long individual hairs in the top coat, which convey an overall impression of bristles. These pointers are brown or brown and white in color.

D

Dalmatian

DALMATIAN

The origins of this breed have been lost, but it has been known as the Dalmatian since the mid-eighteenth century. Such dogs were common companions of travelling romanies in Britain, while in Austria, Dalmatians acted as watchdogs on the borders of the province of Dalmatia. During the latter part of the nineteenth century, Dalmatians were commonly kept around stables, where they accompanied riders and carriages. Their popularity decreased with the advent of motorized transport. They are more than just decorative dogs: they make reliable guards with their deep bark.

Dalmatians are reserved and wary of strangers. Puppies are born pure white, with the characteristic spots appearing later. Two color forms are recognized: black or liver brown spots on a white background. It is considered a fault for both colors to be present on the same dog, while the spots themselves must be both circular in shape and well defined, with no trace of overlapping. The short coat itself requires very little attention, even during a molt.

DANDIE DINMONT TERRIER

Sir Walter Scott was responsible for bringing this breed to the attention of

Dandie Dinmont Terrier

people outside the Border area of Scotland, where it first developed. It was named after a character in Scott's novel *Guy Mannering*, which was first published in 1814.

Bred from native terriers in the area, these small dogs were kept for hunting both otters and badgers. Although no longer regarded as a working breed, the Dandie Dinmont has remained a tough, hardy dog with great character. They are strong-willed, with an independent streak which can lead to some difficulties during training. Dandie Dinmonts nevertheless make good pets, and are both intelligent and affectionate. They tend to be one-person dogs, however, and although devoted to their owners, are not trustworthy with other dogs.

The coat requires considerable care, particularly in the case of show dogs. Dandie Dinmonts are either pepper or mustard in color, and the hair must be plucked to prevent it becoming too long and faded. While the breed does not regularly win top awards, it always attracts attention.

DEERHOUND

All dogs that were kept for coursing were initially called 'greyhounds'; in Scotland, a special breed was developed with the speed and power to run down the large red deer. This breed has since become known as the Deerhound. At first, by law, such dogs could only be kept by members of the aristocracy, to guard against poaching.

The appearance of the breed has changed little from their depiction in Landseer's paintings of the last century. The breed still remains relatively uncommon, however, since Deerhounds require a considerable amount of feeding as well as plenty of exercise. While friendly in home surroundings, these hounds are ruthless in their pursuit of game when the opportunity presents itself. They make impressive show dogs, and are now being seen in increased numbers at British events.

Deerhounds

Dobermans (brown variety)

Dogue de Bordeaux

DOBERMAN

In 1870, Louis Doberman set out to produce a new breed of dog, using Rottweilers and German Pinschers as the bloodstock. Later, as the breed developed, German Shepherd Dogs and Black and Tan Terriers were introduced to add refinement.

The Doberman has been a working breed for many years, both as a guard dog and with army and police forces. The temperament of the breed has occasionally proved questionable and, in the United States particularly, great emphasis was placed on overcoming aggression in those used for show stock. Unfortunately, this lead has not been followed so determinedly elsewhere, and it is important to choose a Doberman from a trustworthy blood-line. Dogs of this breed can become dominant, unless firmly trained from an early age. They are strong individuals, and likely to prove a liability unless fully controllable. Their attractive sleek appearance is a reflection of their muscular body, and Dobermans need regular exercise to keep their trim proportions.

Dobermans (dark variety)

DOGUE DE BORDEAUX

An extremely solid breed, the Dogue de Bordeaux is descended from old mastiff stock, extending as far back as the Molussus of ancient Rome. Originally centered around the region of Bordeaux, these dogs are not common outside France. They used to be pitted against wolves and bears, and are certainly fierce when roused. The most usual coat color is a striking shade of pale yellow.

DREVER

The combination of Swedish hound stock and Dachshund-type dogs from Germany around the turn of the century, has given rise to the Drever. It is a

Dunker

DUTCH SHEEPDOG

These sheepdogs are concentrated in north Brabant, and have been kept largely for working purposes. Three distinct forms exist, distinguished by their coats. The wire-haired type is reminiscent of the Bouvier des Flandres and has proved suitable for many tasks, including some police work. The smooth-coated Dutch Sheepdog is similar to the Belgian Shepherd Dogs and a long-haired version is also known. A breed club was formed at the end of the last century, but these dogs are only now being seen regularly at European shows.

E

popular breed in Sweden, where it is kept for hunting purposes, driving game toward guns. Because they are relatively slow, Drevers are especially useful in the pursuit of deer, since their pace does not alarm the deer and cause them to break away. The breed was first recognized in Sweden in 1949. The Drever possesses the long body typical of the Dachshund, but otherwise has a traditional hound-like appearance. The white markings are said to make it more visible in dense forest.

DUNKER

Named after the man responsible for developing the breed, the Dunker originated in Norway. Wilhelm Dunker used the Harlequin Hound, of Russian descent, and other similar breeds to produce a hunting dog capable of tracking hares by scent. The most distinctive feature of the Dunker is its appearance, since it is either black or blue on a white ground, augmented with brown markings. These hounds are not commonly exhibited in Norway, and are extremely rare elsewhere.

DUPUY POINTER
(Braque Dupuy)

A member of the group of French pointers, the Dupuy Pointer is more closely related to its English counterpart than other Braques. Introduction of English Pointer blood to the now extinct Old Braque gave them a more elegant

appearance, as well as improving the working abilities of the Dupuy. Predominantly brown and white in color, with some physical similarity to the Greyhound, these pointers are valuable companions for sportsmen, but have been largely ignored for show purposes and remain confined to France.

DUTCH HOUND (Steenbrak)

Local farm dogs from Brabant in Holland formed the basis of this breed in the seventeenth century. The contemporary Dutch Hound, crossed with various hounds, especially those of German origins, still reflects its teutonic ancestry. Relatively small and light, with pendulous ears, it is bred in the usual hound colors.

DUTCH PARTRIDGE DOG
(Drentse Patrijshond)

This breed has changed little down the course of the centuries. Early examples featured in sixteenth-century paintings. These dogs were developed in Drentse, northeast Holland, close to West Germany. Despite its name, the Dutch Partridge Dog will retrieve all types of game, even hare. It is intelligent and easily trained. Kept largely as a working dog and pet, it has not attracted much attention from show breeders to date. Unlike some other fairly localized breeds, however, the Dutch Partridge Dog is being seen increasingly in Britain and in the United States.

EGYPTIAN
SHEEPDOG (Armant)

The Egyptian Sheepdog evolved around the settlement of Armant in Egypt, and is thought to be descended from dogs introduced by Napoleon's armies. They work largely as sheepdogs, guarding stock, and are not exhibited. A few have been seen in Europe, and the breed was briefly introduced to Britain in the twentieth century by an Egyptian ambassador, Professor Nachat Pascha. Bred in a variety of colors, they have coarse, long coats and are medium-sized.

ELKHOUND

Immortalized in Viking tales and sagas, the Elkhound is one of a number of similar breeds developed in Scandinavia

Elkhound

primarily for hunting. Remains of such dogs have been discovered in Norway dating back to 5000BC. These hounds were used to pursue elk, the fierce native deer of Scandinavia, and also hunted bears, lynxes and mountain lions.

It is only relatively recently that the Elkhound has been considered an exhibition breed. The Norwegian Hunters Association organized a show in 1877, and a studbook and standard followed. The breed has since become widely known outside Scandinavia, popular for their friendly, sensitive natures, and intelligent, responsive ways.

The grey coat is an important feature, giving adequate protection in adverse weather. Around the neck, extending onto the chest, is a long ruff. This fur is shed when the dog is molting.

ENGLISH SETTER

As long ago as the sixteenth century, there were dogs that located game by means of a combination of scent and sight and then sat, waiting for their next command. These became known as setting (sitting) dogs, later simply as setters. Some early engravings show considerable similarities between these setters and spaniels, and it is almost certain that both the Springer and Water Spaniels, as well as the Spanish Pointer, have contributed to the early pedigree of the English Setter. At this time, the heads of setters resembled those of spaniels, and their coats also had a tendency to curl, especially in the region of the thighs.

The development of the modern English Setter can be traced back to 1825, when Edward Laverack obtained a dog and bitch from the Reverend A. Harrison, who had kept a pure strain of the breed for more than three decades. Laverack continued this work, and in 1874, a pair were sold onto Charles Raymond in the United States. Here, Purcell Llewellin obtained further dogs from the Laverack stock, and this gave rise to the famous Llewellin line.

The English setter was first shown in 1859. Over a century later, the breed attracted a great deal of attention when Champion Silbury Soames of Maidavale won 'Best in Show' at Crufts Dog Show in 1964. English Setters are relatively slow to mature, compared with other breeds, such as terriers, and young dogs often suffer accordingly in the mixed competitions. They show well despite this, and make good companions, but require adequate space for exercise and are best suited to life outside city areas. Friendly and quiet by nature, this form of setter is quite trustworthy.

English Setter

ENGLISH SPRINGER SPANIEL

When working spaniels were divided into two distinct groups, the description 'springer' was given to the taller, larger dogs, distinguishing them from the 'cocker' form. The Duke of Norfolk was one of the first to keep a kennel of Springers, and, as a result, these dogs were known as Norfolk Spaniels for a period. Their function was to 'spring' quarry, flushing it out from its hiding place.

The Springer was only recognized as a distinct breed in 1902. Although the original aim of the Sporting Spaniel Society was to ensure that the Springer remained a working dog, there is now a noticeable difference between sporting and exhibition dogs. Those kept for working purposes are smaller and stockier than their show counterparts, and the head is not as fully developed. Springers remain excellent companions in the field; they have a wider range than similar breeds, and prove very good retrievers, ready to enter water if necessary. Their coats need relatively little attention for show purposes. They are essentially friendly dogs, although they can be slightly suspicious of strangers.

English Springer Spaniel

ENGLISH TOY TERRIER

During the latter half of the nineteenth century, there was a trend towards the miniaturization of some of the dog breeds. The Manchester Terrier, probably crossed with the Italian Greyhound, was used to form the basis of the English Toy Terrier breed. There is also likely to have been deliberate selection, using the smallest offspring in each litter to further the development of

English Toy Terrier

the toy form. The breed was clearly in existence by 1881, but recently its popularity has declined for a combination of reasons. Certainly, foreign toy breeds have attracted increasing attention in Britain, but, perhaps more significantly, the overall conformation of the English Toy Terrier has suffered at the expense of other requirements such as color. For exhibition purposes, a particular emphasis is placed on this feature, as well as the actual distribution of markings.

ENTLEBUCH MOUNTAIN DOG (Entlebucher Sennenhund)

One of the lesser-known Swiss breeds, the Entlebuch were kept by traveling stockmen, and carried out guarding and herding duties, as well as hunting. The continuing existence of the breed was ensured by Herr Herm, who, in association with the Swiss Kennel Club, classified the different types of Mountain Dog at the start of the present century. The Entlebuch is, in fact, the smallest member of the group, which also includes the Bernese Mountain Dog, and although reasonably common in Switzerland, it is rare elsewhere. The breed does not differ in temperament from other Mountain Dogs.

Entlebuch Mountain Dog

EPAGNEUL FRANÇAIS

This breed resembles the English Springer Spaniel both in type and color and has the same characteristic head and ears. It is French in origin, and was classified for a period at the start of the century as a setter. There was a time when the continuing existence of the Epagneul Français was in doubt, in the face of increasing popularity of other spaniels and British gundogs, but its

survival is now assured. They are versatile dogs in the field, and can be trained without difficulty.

EPAGNEUL PONT-AUDEMER

Developed during the latter part of the eighteenth century in Pont-Audemer, Normandy, this breed is a combination of various French Spaniels and other gundogs. These spaniels resemble the English Springer, with their curly coats but have a very distinctive crest of fur on the head. Water Dogs or Irish Water Spaniels probably contributed to their ancestry and, not surprisingly, they are completely at home in water, working especially well with wild duck. In colouring, the Epagneul Pont-Audemer is either chestnut or chestnut and grey, set against white markings. Numbers have declined in recent years and the breed is quite scarce, even in France.

ERZ MOUNTAINS DACHSBRACKE

As their name suggests, these hounds evolved in the Erz Mountains which form part of Bohemia; they were then introduced to Austria. They are especially valued for hunting hares and foxes, and are currently concentrated in Corinthia, although the breed is not common. The Erz Mountains Dachsbracke is always

black and tan, or red, which makes it distinguishable from the related German form, the Westphalian Dachsbracke.

ESKIMO DOG

A variety of breeds have been termed 'eskimo dog', but the genuine Eskimo Dog was first bred in Greenland. It is the oldest breed known in the Arctic region, and was named 'Kingmik' by the Innuits, an Eskimo tribe of northern Canada. These dogs were an integral part of the lives of the tribe. They pulled sleighs, acted as guard dogs and hunted; puppies were kept as pets around the settlement. Eskimo Dogs were able to survive on meagre rations, and, as the early explorers soon discovered, they were the only means of transport in the region.

The Eskimo Dog was first accepted as a distinct breed by the Canadian Kennel Club prior to 1900 and, although they are not often needed for transportation, these dogs are still raced and have become more widely known. They are hardy, friendly dogs, never failing to make an impact at shows.

ESTONIAN HOUND

One of a number of old Russian breeds of scent hound, the Estonian survived the demise of hunting as a pastime, after the revolution, unlike some other similar

Eskimo Dog

breeds. The Estonian displays a number of traits inherited from the St Hubert Hound, with long, folded ears and tri-colored coat. Black is most often the predominant color. These dogs are fast, eager hunters, whether working singly or in packs.

ESTRELA MOUNTAIN DOG
(Cao Serra da Estrela)

These dogs were originally known as Portuguese Mountain Dogs when they were first seen in Britain, although their name was subsequently altered to reflect the original locality where the breed was first developed. Origins are unknown, but the breed is probably related to the Spanish Mastiff. Originally kept as guard dogs, they are correspondingly strong, needing adequate training when young to ensure that they remain fully manageable later. Portuguese Mountain Dogs have become more widespread on the show scene during recent years.

EURASIER

The Eurasier is a relatively modern breed, introduced during the 1950s. A breeder called Wipfel of Weinheim set out to establish a breed similar to the old German Wolf Spitz, using the Chow Chow and Samoyed as basic stock. His efforts were rewarded with recognition of the breed by the FCI and the German Kennel Club. The breed name reflects the link between Europe and Asia in its development. The Eurasier is still based in the Weinheim region. It is clearly of spitz-type, possessing a relatively short coat, showing the musculature.

Estrela Mountain Dog

FIELD SPANIEL

The Field Spaniel was originally bred from a combination of the Cocker and Springer stock. At first, black dogs were distinguished from other colors, and designated as Black Spaniels. About the turn of the century, however, the type of the Field Spaniel altered drastically. The result was a breed of spaniels with very short legs and long bodies, virtually useless in the field.

Field Spaniel

The vogue for spaniels of this type rapidly faded and only through the efforts of a few breeders did the Field Spaniel survive this period. It is now undergoing a revival in popularity, after being bred back to its original type. These spaniels are keen, eager workers, and do well in domestic surroundings with access to the countryside.

FILA BRASILEIRO
(Cao de Fila)

When Central America was conquered by Spain and Portugal during the sixteenth century, it was natural that some European breeds would be introduced to the new territories. Mastiff-type stock from Europe interbred with native dogs and the Fila Brasileiro is one breed that has arisen as a result. These dogs are powerful and fierce; they are kept to guard stock and property, and also act as drovers. Although friendly with those in their immediate circle, they have proved extremely courageous when they are challenged. The breed remains unknown in Europe.

FINNISH HOUND
(Finsk Stövare)

This is the largest existing breed of Scandinavian Hound. It has a composite ancestry: Foxhounds, German and French hounds, and various of the native breeds have all contributed to its development. The Finnish Hound is primarily a hunting dog, and is attracting a growing number of followers in its native country. Friendly and trustworthy by nature, this breed can also be stubborn, like the majority of hounds that hunt by scent.

FINNISH SPITZ

The Finnish Spitz, developed from other native breeds of hound, was first recognized in Finland in the latter part of the nineteenth century. It possesses a distinctive, reddish coat, with the mane being a particular feature of male dogs. Finnish Spitz have a lively disposition and a high-pitched bark, making them useful as guard dogs. The breed is not commonly seen at shows despite its undoubted appeal and, while recognized in Europe, it has yet to be accorded championship status by the AKC.

FLAT-COATED RETRIEVER

This breed originated in Newfoundland, and was developed from Newfoundland stock, but it has since become very popular in Britain. The first Flat-coated Retriever seen in Britain, Wyndham, attracted considerable interest when exhibited at the Birmingham Show in

Foxhounds

Finnish Spitz

Flat-coated Retriever

1860. The breed was originally called the Wavy-coated Retriever, but the subsequent introduction of setter blood gave rise to a more elegantly proportioned dog, with a flat coat. Two men in particular were responsible for establishing these retrievers. S.E. Shirley, who helped to found the Kennel Club in 1873, did much to popularize the breed, while H.R. Cooke developed a strain of Flat-coated Retrievers at his kennels over a period of 70 years.

The breed went into a decline during the First World War, but it remained a popular choice with gamekeepers. Since the early 1960s, it has undergone a revival. Up until recently, only black individuals were acceptable under the breed standards, but now liver-colored dogs can also be exhibited. Flat-coated Retrievers have phlegmatic, intelligent natures, and do well both as show dogs and in the field.

FLEMISH DRAUGHT DOG
(Vlaamsche Trekhond)
As the name itself suggests, this breed, developed from dogs kept for driving stock in Belgium, was kept originally for the purpose of pulling carts. These dogs are very powerful and easily trained, characteristics that make them ideal for their traditional work. They are also very good guard dogs. Flemish Draught Dogs are predominantly greyish in color, with darker markings on the face.

FOXHOUND
The history of the Foxhound is well documented in the records of individual hunts, but its origins are uncertain. Greyhounds crossed with northern hounds may have contributed to the very early development of the breed. The ancestry of many bloodlines can be traced back in the studbooks of the Masters of Foxhounds Association to the eighteenth century, several decades before the Kennel Club was founded. By

1880, there were 7,000 hounds in 150 packs in Britain alone.

Foxhounds had been sent to the United States long before this time, and ultimately a separate breed evolved there. The English form remains a stockier, larger dog than its American counterpart. Foxhounds are still kept primarily for hunting purposes, and are very unlikely to be seen in a British show ring. They are not suitable as pets, since they require considerable exercise, have big appetites and possess strongly independent, yet friendly, natures.

FRENCH BULLDOG

In England, there was a race of toy Bulldogs in existence during the 1860s, but such dogs were generally not very popular so that many were exported to France. Here, trial crossings with other breeds led to the emergence of a strain known as Boule-Dog Français. There was at first little standardization, and not all individuals showed the upright bat-shaped ears characteristic of the breed today, a trait that was established by breeders in the United States. In Europe, the 'rose' ear of the traditional Bulldog was originally more popular. The dispute led to the foundation of the French Bulldog Club of America at the end of the last century, and promoted a rapid rise in the popularity of these dogs. The most important dog of the period was Champion Nellcote Gamin, which had a great influence on the breed's development in the United States.

The French Bulldog should have a more alert, lively expression than its Bulldog ancestor. They are relatively small dogs, and usually have a good temperament. Their short coats do not need much attention, and the breed has much to recommend it, both as a pet and show dog. They are intelligent and quiet, rarely barking, unless roused.

French Bulldog

French Pointer

FRENCH POINTER
(Braque Français)

These pointers have changed little in appearance since the early nineteenth century. They are one of the oldest French breeds, and have contributed to more recent bloodlines. There are two distinct varieties, with the Braque Français Petite Taille being smaller than the Braque Français. Their coats are short, and a combination of chestnut and white in color. Both forms have broader heads than English pointers, while the Petite Taille also has smaller ears, and a less pronounced muzzle.

GERMAN HOUND
(Deutscher Bracke)

There used to be a number of breeds of hound in Germany, but now only the Deutscher Bracke remains. It has much in common with other scent hounds, resembling the Harrier in size and the Stövare of Scandinavia in appearance. After the 1951 meeting of the breed club at Olpe, where a standard was drawn up, these hounds have also been described as Olpe Hounds. They are not exhibited, but are kept in packs for hunting.

GERMAN HUNTING TERRIER
(Deutscher Jagdterrier)

This terrier breed was developed in Bavaria during the present century, and was the result of a quest for a fearless, strong dog with terrier characteristics. The breeders concerned decided to cross Fox Terriers with old terrier breeds of the region, in order to restore the working abilities of the native dogs. They felt that the emphasis which had been placed on producing show dogs, had weakened the natural talents of their terriers. They started with a dog of Broken-coated Terrier ancestry in combination with a Welsh Terrier, before introducing some Fox Terrier blood. The resulting breed, although small, matched their requirements, and possessed powerful jaws and a thick, dark coat. These terriers will go to ground readily, and will also retrieve.

German Hunting Terrier

GERMAN LONG-HAIRED POINTER
(Deutscher Langhaar Vorstehund)

A combination of the Water Spaniel with French spaniel breeds gave rise to these pointers; various setters were later used in the breed's development. In appearance, the German Long-haired Pointer is reminiscent of the Irish Setter, although the coat is liver in color, sometimes augmented with white markings. First used to accompany hawks, these pointers have since proved very valuable as independent gundogs.

The German Long-haired Pointer has gained a reputation as a bird dog, but can work equally well with other game. The breed is much less common than its short-haired equivalent outside Germany, despite its many attractive qualities. These dogs are easy to train.

GERMAN ROUGH-HAIRED POINTER
(Deutscher Stichelhaar Vorstehund)

The German Rough-haired Pointer is a working bird dog and is similar to the Pointing Griffon, although smaller in size. Brown is usually the dominant color of the rough coat, which may also be white in parts. This breed has never gained the following of the other German Pointers, and nearly became extinct during the middle of the last century. Saved largely by the efforts of an individual German breeder, they are not kept outside their native country.

German Shepherd Dog

GERMAN SHEEP PUDEL
(Deutscher Schafpudel)
The Pudel was bred from Barbets and Water Dogs, and, in turn, was probably one of the main ancestors of the modern Poodle. The German Sheep Pudel, or Schafpudel, is still kept for working rather than for showing. These are quite big dogs, predominantly white, with thick undercoats and a shaggy outer coat. With a reputation for being both intelligent and easily managed, the Pudel also makes a reliable guard dog.

GERMAN SHEPHERD DOG (Alsatian)
Few breeds have inspired such a conflict of opinion as the German Shepherd Dog, also known for a period as the Alsatian. The ancestry of the breed traces back over a century, when it evolved from various working breeds in Germany.

German Shepherd Dog

The German Shepherd Dog was first shown at Hanover in 1882; the breed club was founded in 1899. German Shepherds now rank among the most popular dogs in the world.

Character is a very important feature. The German Shepherd Dog is highly intelligent. They are able to work as herding dogs, often with relatively little training, while their guarding instincts have been refined for use in both military and police work. They are also trained as guide dogs for the blind, and often excel in obedience competitions.

The bad publicity the breed receives is more often the fault of the owners, rather than individual dogs. A trained German Shepherd Dog is an obedient, loyal companion, but when encouraged to be aggressive in defence of persons or property, they will act accordingly. They are well-proportioned, powerful, yet agile dogs, with a natural trotting gait that has been emphasized to give them an apparently effortless, bounding motion.

Puppies may not have the typically upright ears of the breed until the age of six months or so. The coat is composed of a double layer of hair, which helps to insulate the body and provides sufficient waterproofing. Color is not a crucial feature of the breed, but white German Shepherd Dogs are generally unacceptable for showing.

GERMAN SHORT-HAIRED POINTER

Regarded by some authorities as the most versatile gundog of all, the German Short-haired Pointer is able to work both as a pointer and as a retriever, and is at home both on land and in the water. The breed has a mixed ancestry, probably descended in part from the German Bird Dog, which itself came from the Spanish Pointer; many of the local breeds of hunting dog once extant in Germany also contributed to its pedigree. Some of these were almost certainly scent hounds.

Dogs of this type were probably known by the seventeenth century, but it was the establishment of a studbook in 1870 that provided the stimulus for further improvement. Particular emphasis was then laid on the working ability of the breed. English pointer stock was introduced to improve both the style and technique of these dogs, and also made them more biddable.

First registered by the AKC in 1930, field trials were held for this breed in 1944, and are now a regular feature at many events. The German Short-haired Pointer is an all-weather dog, tough and hardy as well powerful and tenacious. The breed is popular in the show ring but is too active to settle well as a pet.

GERMAN SPANIEL
(Wachtelhund)

The Water Dog is believed to have been involved in the development of an old type of spaniel once seen in many parts of Europe, and resembling the present-day German Spaniel in its appearance. The breed died out to a large extent, and was nearly lost in Germany, but a dedicated group of breeders started a campaign to save it in 1897 and the German Spaniel was the result.

The German Spaniel has become one of the most valued sporting dogs in Germany. Breeders have even refrained from showing them, fearing that this might encourage characteristics that would compromise their working ability. Apart from their scenting skills,

German Short-haired Pointer

these spaniels can also be trained as retrievers, and will enter water freely. They are smaller than a Springer Spaniel, yet very strong and will act as guard dogs if needed. Their coats are relatively long and wavy, while their overall type clearly reflects their relationship with other breeds of spaniel.

GERMAN SPITZ (Wolf Spitz)

This breed has been known ever since the early seventeenth century, and the miniature form, developed largely in the region of Pomerania, has become better known in Britain and the United States as the Pomeranian. These dogs were originally white, with other colors emerging later in Britain.

The German Spitz Club was responsible for laying down standards for these dogs. They are grey with a distinctive mane, and resemble a wolf in these respects, hence their alternative name of Wolf Spitz. A black form, kept around the vineyards of Württemberg as a guard, was also known for a period. The German Spitz has a lively temperament and is effective as a watchdog.

GERMAN WIRE-HAIRED POINTER

The German Short-haired Pointer was the basis for this breed, along with various other breeds. The characteristic rough, wiry coat has always been considered a very important feature of these

German Wire-haired Pointer

pointers, especially as they are expected to work in all weathers. It also serves to shield the body when the dog is surrounded by dense undergrowth. The bearded lips and bushy eyebrows help protect vulnerable areas of the head. The undercoat is pronounced in winter, but is shed completely during the summer months.

The German Wire-haired Pointer had evolved into a distinctive breed by the 1870s, and was introduced to the United States in 1920. It has been slow to establish a following in Britain, in the face of competition from traditional gundog breeds. An energetic and sturdy breed, it is very similar to the German Short-haired Pointer in general temperament.

GIANT SCHNAUZER

These dogs were originally kept both as working cattle dogs and guard dogs around breweries. The breed is thought to have been bred initially in the region of Swabia, in southern Bavaria, possibly from the Standard Schnauzer crossed with local dogs, as well as the Bouvier des Flandres. When cattle driving declined, the breed found another role as a police dog.

The Giant Schnauzer has not achieved any significant degree of popularity in either the United States or Britain. The coat needs a great deal of attention if the dog is to be shown, and will have to be trimmed considerably to create the best effect.

GLEN OF IMAAL TERRIER

This breed of terrier was developed in County Wicklow, Ireland, in the Glen of Imaal. Bred initially to tackle badgers underground, these terriers proved so tough that they were often pitted against other dogs in competitions.

The Irish Kennel Club staged the first classes for the breed in 1933, but it has not achieved any great level of support, even in Eire itself. Glen of Imaal Terriers are sometimes seen at major events, however, and have the typical terrier spirit, delighting in hunting.

GOLDEN RETRIEVER

These beautiful dogs were first bred in Scotland, on the Guisachan estate owned by Lord Tweedmouth. It was claimed for a period that the ancestors of the breed were a group of performing dogs from a Russian circus, but the true origins of the breed are less romantic.

The first Yellow Retriever acquired by Lord Tweedmouth, called Nous, was obtained from the Earl of Chichester. The estate at Guisachan was on the River Tweed, and here dogs known as Tweed Water Spaniels had been bred, largely for retrieving purposes. It was to one such dog, called Belle, that Nous was mated in about 1867. Four yellow puppies resulted. The development of the breed from this point onward is well documented in the gamekeeper's records at Guisachan. Further Tweed Water Spaniel crosses, as well as the introduction of Irish Setter blood, took place; some of the offspring were given to other breeders.

The Yellow or Golden Retriever, as the breed became known, rapidly gained in popularity in England at the end of the nineteenth century. A field trial was won by a Golden Retriever in 1904, and the breed was first shown as Flat-coats (Golden) in 1908. Five years later, they were grouped separately; shortly after,

Giant Schnauzer

Golden Retriever

Gordon Setter

the Golden Retriever Club was first formed.

Dogs of this type were seen in the United States as long ago as the 1890s, but were not registered as Golden Retrievers until 1925. Prior to this date, they were simply classed as retrievers, with a note made on their color.

Darker-colored individuals are still preferred today. The rise in interest in these retrievers has been phenomenal, with registrations in Britain alone running at nearly 10,000 a year. The Golden Retriever is an excellent show dog, easy to prepare, and usually well-behaved once in the arena. The breed's working abilities have not been neglected either, and it is consistently represented both at field trials and in obedience classes. Their natural intelligence has made them an obvious choice for guide dogs for the blind, and for narcotics detection. The Golden Retriever is a gentle breed, however, and quite trustworthy with children.

GORDON SETTER

Setters of this type were first kept during the late eighteenth century by the 4th Duke of Gordon, for hunting grouse. Shortly afterward, they became known as Black and Tan Setters, although those in the Gordon kennels were predominantly tricolored. The breed was relatively unrefined at this stage, having a fairly heavy appearance, until crossings with the Irish Setter contributed a more sleek outline. When such dogs were first registered by the Kennel Club, the name was changed back to the Gordon Setter.

Two of the Duke's Gordon Setters were exported to the United States in 1842, and other members of the breed soon followed. Interest in the Gordon Setter has been rekindled in recent years, through the endeavors of the Gordon Setter Club of America. Attempts have been made to introduce greater pace into the breed, without compromising steady, reliable retriev-

ing qualities. They are ideal companions for the solitary sportsman, and remain the largest member of the setter group. No clear division has been made between working and show stock. They are relatively slow to mature, and prove very loyal to their owners.

GRAHUND

One of the group of spitz-type breeds that have evolved in Scandinavia, the Grahund's name simply means 'grey dog'. It is smaller and less stocky than the better known Elkhound, but remains muscular, and is of similar coloration. Indeed, the Grahund possesses the usual characteristics associated with spitz breeds, such as the curly tail and the pricked ears. It was first recognized as the Noisk Elghund by the Swedish Kennel Club in 1891, but remains essentially a Swedish, rather than Norwegian, breed, and is rarely seen outside its native country.

GRAND BLEU DE GASGOGNE

Another French breed of hound, the ancestry of this breed probably dates back to the St Hubert Hound, via the Grand Chiens Courants. The colour and markings are a particular feature of the Grand Bleu de Gasgogne, with the black ticking on white hairs creating a blue effect overall. Tan or red areas are confined only to the head, forelegs and hindquarters. These dogs have friendly, but rather stubborn dispositions. Further refinement is seen in the smaller Petit Bleu de Gasgogne.

Grand Bleu de Gascogne

GRAND GASCON-SAINTONGEOIS

These hounds resulted from crosses of Gascon and Saintongeois breeds. They are large, and unusual in possessing loose folds of skin on the head as well as the neck. Their characteristic markings, small areas of brown fur on both hindlimbs just above the hock joints, are officially known as the *marques de chevreuil*. The coat is black and white, often with extensive areas of ticking. The Grand Gascon-Saintongeois is kept for hunting roe deer, in packs, and remains confined to France, where it is still quite a popular breed. A smaller variety, the Gascon Saintongeois Petit, has also been developed for catching hares.

GRAND GRIFFON NIVERNAIS

The Griffons are a group of old French hunting dogs, rather reminiscent of the Otterhound in appearance. This particular breed was kept largely in the province of Nivernais, for hunting wild boar. It is often darker in color, and with a more elongated body than the Vendéen breed. These hounds range from black to fawn, although grey is the most common color, and have long, shaggy coats. Friendly and energetic by nature, these Griffons have not become popular anywhere else in Europe. A miniature form, called the Griffon Nivernais de Petit Taille, is also kept in some areas.

Grand Griffon Nivernais

GRAND GRIFFON VENDÉEN

This breed is the best-known member of the Griffon group. The Grand Griffon Vendéen has shorter legs than the Grand Griffon Nivernais. They are predominantly white or yellowish in color, with a rough outer coat and a dense undercoat.

Friendly by nature, they have long, furry ears and a large head compared to the rest of the body. The Basset form of this breed is more common outside France, while a smaller version, called the Briquet Griffon Vendéen, is also in existence.

GREAT DANE

One of the most instantly recognizable breeds, the Great Dane is elegant and graceful, despite its enormous size. The ancestry of these dogs may go right back to the Molossus of Roman times, and the Alaunt. The breed certainly descends from mastiff stock, and has probably

been in existence for at least 400 years. Similar dogs are described in Chinese literature dating back to 1121 BC.

German breeders were responsible for laying the foundaton of the modern Great Dane. These dogs were originally kept for hunting wild boar; in 1880, at a conference of breed judges, it was agreed that these dogs should be called *Deutsche Dogge*. In Britain, however, the

Great Dane

breed was called the Great Dane and this name stuck, while in Italy, where the breed has a strong following, it is known as *alano*, meaning 'mastiff'. The standard established in Germany in 1891 has been adopted throughout Europe, as well as in the United States, despite these differences of terminology.

As might be expected, Great Danes have large appetites, especially when they are growing. They are relatively easy to train, and do best in spacious surroundings where they can have adequate exercise. The size of the Great Dane is likely to make it unsuitable for a home with small children, although the breed is not untrustworthy as a rule. Their short coats are easy to keep in good condition.

GREAT SWISS MOUNTAIN DOG (Grosser Schweizer Sennenhund)

Although slightly bigger, these dogs are very similar to the Bernese Mountain Dog, and have smooth, thick and shiny coats which provide protection in bad weather. The Great Swiss Mountain Dog is a powerful breed, which was kept

Great Dane

Great Swiss Mountain Dog

originally for pulling carts and mountain rescue. Descended from the Alpine Mastiff, the breed faded in popularity around the turn of the century. Following its recognition in 1908 by the Swiss Kennel Club, however, the breed once more attracted attention. They have much to recommend them as pets, being easy to train, affectionate and alert guards. These dogs remain extremely scarce outside Switzerland.

GREEK GREYHOUND

A Greek coursing hound, working with deer and hare, these greyhounds closely resemble the Saluki in appearance, with their powerful, thin legs. They are adept at working either on flat or in mountainous terrain. The most common coloring is black and tan, sometimes augmented with white on the chest, while the coat itself is short, and slightly hard to the touch.

GREENLAND DOG
(Gronlandshund)

A northern breed required for pulling sledges in arctic regions, the Greenland Dog is closely related to the Eskimo Dog, and is sometimes grouped with it. Only the Canadian Kennel Club will recognize the Eskimo Dog, however, while in Europe, the FCI only acknowledges the Greenland Dog. The Greenland Dog is kept for guarding and for transportation. They are very strong, muscular dogs, with a hard outer coat and a dense layer of fur beneath for withstanding freezing temperatures. They can be black, grey or white and often show brownish markings.

GREYHOUND

Greyhounds have changed little in appearance throughout the centuries. Dogs, recognizably of this particular type, are represented on Egyptian tombs dating back to 2900 BC. The Roman writer, Ovid, described the breed in minute detail, while Greyhounds were certainly known in England by the ninth century AD. A manuscript of this period shows Elfric, Duke of Mercia, accompanied by two Greyhounds.

The breed was probably introduced to the Americas by Spanish explorers in the sixteenth century. General Custer kept a pack of Greyhounds, some of which took part in a race immediately before the ill-fated expedition to the Big

Horn River in 1876.

The coursing instinct of the breed is present in the track-racers of today. The mechanical 'line' was devised in 1912 by O.P. Smith in the United States, and Greyhound track racing began in the 1920s. The natural quarry of the Greyhound is hare, but they have been recorded as taking a variety of game, ranging from deer to foxes. The most famous meet is the Waterloo Cup in Britain, which first took place in 1836, and has been an annual event ever since, apart from 1917 and 1918.

Many Greyhounds are sold as pets once their racing careers are over. They are lively, affectionate dogs, but are not ideal if space is limited. Greyhounds are best muzzled when they are allowed off the lead, as they retain their coursing instincts and may chase smaller dogs. They do not require a great deal of exercise, however, often choosing just to run fast in wide circles until they tire, which they do quite quickly.

GRIFFON À POIL LAINEUX

A breeder called Boulet created this breed by crossing Wire-haired Pointing Griffons with Barbets. The resulting breed was called Grand Boulet for a period. These dogs have not become as popular as their Wire-haired ancestors, but have proved to be keen and versatile gundogs. Training shows the Griffon à Poil Laineux to be intelligent. The distinctive coat is long and flattish, occasionally wavy but not curly. Brown should be the predominant color, but some white is permitted.

GRIFFON BLEU DE GASCOGNE DE PETITE TAILLE

This breed of Griffon resembles the Grand Bleu, but is smaller in size. It possesses a rough rather than smooth coat, and has longer hair on the head, a characteristic of the Griffon. It is bred in the same colors as other Griffons. The neck is relatively thin and the longish ears show no signs of folding. Lively and affectionate by nature, the Griffons remain an exclusively French breed.

GRIFFON BRUXELLOIS

The Affenpinscher, which was crossed with Belgian mongrels, laid the foundations for this distinctive and plucky breed. The Griffon Bruxellois may not be the most attractive dog but has great character. In the early days of the breed, these dogs were frequently seen accompanying Brussels cab drivers. Other breeds, including the Yorkshire Terrier, were subsequently bred in to give rise to the contemporary Griffon Bruxellois.

Greyhound

Griffon Bruxellois

Hamiltonstövare

Crossbreeding with Pugs resulted in a smooth-coated variety described as the Brabançon.

They are sensitive dogs, and this character trait may account for their absence from the show ring, since they can be nervous in such surroundings. The Brabançon is usually worse than the Griffon Bruxellois in this respect. Neither take readily to strangers, but are highly intelligent and readily trained. Some dogs may not take easily to being walked on a lead, and it is advisable to teach them this lesson early in life.

GRIFFON FAUVE DE BRETAGNE
Fast and strong, these Griffon hounds were kept originally to hunt wild boar and foxes in Brittany. The coat of the Griffon Fauve de Bretagne is rough to the touch, and fawn in color, although some black is allowed. They are not the friendliest of breeds and are rarely seen outside France.

HALDENSTÖVARE
This breed is the largest of the four Stövare-type hounds. It was developed near Halden, a town in southeast Norway, not far from Sweden. Essentially a native breed, it has been improved by crosses with other hounds from Germany, Sweden and Russia. Bloodstock from France and Belgium may also have been introduced.

Kept primarily to hunt alone rather than as a member of a large pack, the Haldenstövare, with its broad chest, long legs and powerful body, is ideally adapted to work in thick snow. These hounds are predominantly white with areas of black and brown markings on the head. They are lively and friendly, but are not common, even in their homeland, despite their striking appearance.

HAMILTONSTÖVARE
The creator of this breed, a Swede called Hamilton, set out to produce a utility hound, breeding from the Herderbracke and the Holsteiner Hound (now extinct), as well as the Curlandish Hound. Although kept essentially as a hunting breed, the Hamiltonstövare has also become a popular show dog. Classes were set up for the breed in 1886, and it is now often the most popular scent hound at Scandinavian shows.

The breed has also been seen in Britain, where it was first known simply as the Swedish Foxhound. As various Swedish breeds could fit this description, the name was finally altered. The Hamiltonstövare will probably become increasingly popular. It has a lively, energetic nature, yet does well in the show ring, thanks to its good proportions and elegant appearance.

HANOVERIAN SCHWEISSHUND
The origin of this breed dates back to the beginning of the nineteenth century. It developed from crosses between the Bracke, which resembled the St Hubert Hound, and a lighter breed developed in the region of the Hartz Mountains. The breed still possesses the heavy head and skin folds around the head and neck typical of the St Hubert Hound. The original function of the Schweisshund was simply to track game, held on a lead. Lighter hounds would then be brought in to pursue the quarry.

The breed is still kept for tracking and has remained relatively small compared to a number of other hounds. Hanoverian Schweisshunds are very like the Bloodhound in temperament.

HAPPA DOG
These small dogs resemble the Pekingese, although they have short coats. Developed in China, the breed was first brought to Britain in 1907, where it was exhibited by the Honourable Mrs Lancelot Carnegie. These dogs were

described as being black and tan in color, slightly similar to the Bulldog, although very much smaller. The breed has not been seen outside China for many years and very little is known about it.

HARLEQUIN PINSCHER
(Harlekinpinscher)

The FCI only recognized this breed in 1958, and it is the latest of the German Pinschers to be given such status. The breed takes its name from its coloration, which is a contrasting pattern of black and white markings. These pinschers are intermediate in size, larger than the miniature form and typical of the group in appearance, with short hair and pricked ears. The Harlequin Pinscher has a terrier character; it enjoys hunting small animals, and makes a faithful and loyal guard dog. It remains largely confined to Germany.

HARRIER

Hounds have been used to hunt hares for centuries, with various breeds being developed specifically for this purpose, but the origins of the Harrier remain a subject of much discussion among sportsmen. The breed was probably introduced to Britain by the Normans. Sir Elias de Midhope owned the very first recorded pack, known as the Penistone, in 1260, a pack that continued to be maintained for over five centuries. The breed has been known in the United States since the early days of European settlement, and now appears to be gaining in popularity as a show breed, after recognition by the AKC. At present, the Harrier is commonly not shown in Britain.

HAVANESE

A member of the Bichon group, there is some dispute as to whether the breed was developed in the Philippines, or Cuba. The original stock came from the Mediterranean region, and may well have included the Maltese. Like other Bichons, the Havanese is a small breed, with a curly, soft coat. The basic color is white, combined with darker colors or chestnut. The breed was seen in France during the early years of the century, but is now almost unknown in Europe.

HOVAWART

The original Hovawart strain was first developed over 500 years ago to act as guard dogs, and was called 'Hofewart', meaning 'warden of the estate and farmyard'. The breed then declined and became extinct during the last century. In the early 1900s, however, it proved

Hungarian Pulis

possible to recreate dogs from local German breeds, which were very similar in appearance to the original Hofewart. The breed was adopted under its current name by the German Kennel Club in 1936.

The Hovawart is reminiscent of the Flat-coated Retriever in some respects. These dogs are either black or gold, or a combination of these colors, and apart from proving good guards, they make great companions, being intelligent, affectionate and obedient.

HUNGARIAN HOUND
(Erdélyi Kopo)

A hunting breed, which can also act as a retriever, the Hungarian Hound occurred originally in the eastern part of the country. Two forms used to exist, but the smaller variety, kept for the pursuit of foxes and hares, is now extinct. It was red in color, whereas the larger type is predominantly black, with brown on the legs and head. Some white markings may also occur on the feet and chest. These dogs are similar to Swedish hounds in appearance. Their longish ears also suggest a French influence, despite the fact that the skin folds of the St Hubert Hound are absent.

HUNGARIAN PULI

The ancestors of the contemporary Puli were brought by the Magyars into the country now known as Hungary, about a millenium ago. It is thought that the breed may be related to the Tibetan Terrier, which was also kept as a sheepdog.

Pulis were the smallest of a trio of Magyar breeds used for this purpose, although the bigger Komandor and Kuvasz may well have been more valued for guarding the stock, rather than actually controlling the movements of a flock. 'Puli' means 'driver'.

The Puli is usually black, although grey and even white individuals are acceptable, providing no other markings are evident on the coat. The black coat of the Puli is dull, lacking both depth and the reflective sheen associated with this color in other breeds. The unusual coat, tufted at first, gradually becomes matted on top, as the dog grows older, with the thick, soft undercoat forming distinct cords all over the body, obscuring the eyes.

During the Second World War, Pulis became known outside Hungary as refugees fled, taking their dogs with them. Although its numbers declined for this period, they rapidly built up afterward. First seen in the United States during the 1930s, Pulis were recognized there in 1936, but their impact in Britain has been much slower. Apart from their distinctive appearance, Pulis are hardy, active dogs with friendly, intelligent natures.

HUNGARIAN VIZLA

Another of the breeds thought to have been introduced by the Magyars, the Vizla has established a reputation for itself as a versatile gundog in recent years. The landscape dictated some of the characteristics of the breed; there was little natural cover, so that speed and cunning were required. The Vizla developed into a combination of pointer and retriever, possessing a keen sense of smell.

Hungarian Vizla

Between the wars, the breed did not flourish and some reconstruction was necessary. When hostilities broke out again, prior to the Russian invasion, refugees and emigrants took their dogs with them to European countries. Other Vizlas managed to find their way to Czechoslovakia and Russia. The breed was recognized by the AKC in 1960, and it has also become increasingly common in Britain during recent years. The aristocratic appearance of these dogs, coupled with their attractive brownish-gold coats and working abilities, are only part of their appeal. Their obedient, affectionate natures make them well worth considering as pets.

HYGENHOUND
(Hygenstövare)

The Scandinavian hounds bear quite a close resemblance to each other, because of their common ancestors. This particular breed was developed about the middle of the last century in Norway by F. Hygen, who used Holsteiner Hounds as the basic stock. The Hygenhound is also closely related to the Dunker, and was shown with it in the same classes until 1934. The muzzle of the Hygenhound is more pointed than those of similar breeds, and it is usually yellow with some areas of white on the body. These hounds do not differ significantly from others of their type in temperament, and hunt alone, rather than in packs. Even in Norway, however, they are not common.

Hygenhound

Ibizan Hound

I

IBIZAN HOUND

The appearance of the Ibizan Hound has changed little since the time of the Egyptian pharaohs, 3,400 years ago. The ancient god Anubis, the 'watchdog of the dead', who is represented in the tomb of Tutankhamen, bears quite a striking resemblance to both the modern Ibizan Hound and to its close relative, the Pharaoh Hound. The coloring of the artefacts is more suggestive of the Ibizan Hound, however. These are hunting dogs, able to locate prey by both scent and sight, although their facial characteristics are more suggestive of scent hounds.

The breed takes its name from the island of Ibiza, where the Phoenicians are believed to have introduced the breed. The Ibizan Hound is also common on the Spanish mainland, and while the breed itself is often shown in southern Europe, the long-haired variety still remains largely confined to

Irish Setter

Irish Terriers

Spain. Ibizan Hounds were first seen in the United States in 1956, and were officially recognized by the AKC at the end of 1978. Great care has been taken to ensure that the breed remains pure.

ICELAND DOG
These dogs have been bred in their native country for hundreds of years. First exported to Britain at the start of this century, the breed did not prove popular there and was allowed to die out. It is a typical spitz-type breed with its curled tail and pricked ears, similar to the Elkhound but smaller in size and often with a multicolored coat. As a working breed, the Iceland Dog makes an ideal stock dog, and can be used for driving and herding horses as well as sheep.

Iceland Dog

IRISH SETTER
The Irish Setter, the most popular setter breed, first appeared in the nineteenth century. Its ancestors were most probably spaniels, pointers and other setters, particularly the English and Gordon breeds. The Irish Setter is often referred to as the 'Red Setter', but in the early days of the breed dogs were more often red and white, rather than solid red. The Earl of Enniskillen was prominent in developing the latter form. At first, some dogs showed black markings, but the presence of this color is now considered a very serious fault. White markings, to a limited extent are, however, still permitted, but the overall color must be rich chestnut.

Despite its striking appearance, this breed was essentially developed as a gundog. It was first brought to the United States for this purpose during the latter part of the nineteenth century. It is not surprising, however, that the breed has since become so popular as a show dog and a pet. Although these dogs have acquired something of a reputation for being wayward and unresponsive, such characteristics are more likely to reflect inadequate training than innate deficiencies. Irish Setters are one of the most demanding gundogs to train, but once the lessons have been learned, they are obedient and trustworthy companions.

IRISH TERRIER
One of the most distinctive members of the terrier group, the Irish Terrier appears to have no close relatives, and is rather more reminiscent of the Irish Wolfhound in profile than other terriers. They can range in color from bright low, through to a yellowish-red, with small areas of white occasionally present on the feet and chest.

Classes for Irish Terriers were first established in Dublin in 1874, but it was a number of years before these dogs were ever seen outside Ireland. Used as messengers in the First World War, they were highly valued for their courage. They make versatile companions for any sportsman. They like to hunt, and will retrieve, even in water. The breed is not common today and appears to be declining in numbers.

As a show dog, the Irish Terrier can prove difficult to handle, resenting other competitors and frequently picking quarrels with them. These terriers are very loyal, and make alert guards; their hardy natures ensure that they can adapt to a variety of conditions.

IRISH WATER SPANIEL
As long ago as the seventh century AD, dogs of this type were being reared in Ireland. Two forms were known originally, the North and South Water Spaniels, which probably evolved from the old European Water Dog. The history of the breed in recent times can be traced back to 1849, when Boatswain, a dog that would have a great impact on the breed, was bred by Justin McArthy. Classes for the Irish Water Spaniel were first held in 1859; seven years later Boatswain's grandson, Doctor, won at the Birmingham show. From this point onward, the breed became increasingly popular, and it was seen in the United States by 1873. Fashion changed, however, and the Irish Water Spaniel had begun to decline in numbers by the end of the century. There was even a

Irish Water Spaniel

lightly. The breed is slow to mature, and puppies, themselves larger than adult dogs of other breeds, can be very demanding and destructive. The size of the Irish Wolfhound dictates that it must be kept in spacious surroundings, and provided with adequate exercise. It is one of the most sensitive breeds, requiring a great deal of attention, and must never be considered as a guard dog because of its trusting, affectionate nature. For the show ring, the rather wild, unkempt appearance of the Irish Wolfhound must not be spoiled by clipping or trimming the coat.

ISTRIAN HOUND

Two forms of these Yugoslavian hounds are recognized. The short-haired type is known as the Kratkodiaki; the long-haired form, which gave rise to the Styrian Mountain Hound, is known as the Resati. Both forms are white in color, with areas of yellow and orange, especially on the head. Istrian Hounds resemble the French breeds in appearance, with their relatively long ears and pointed heads. They have a reputation for being lively yet hard workers, but are not well known.

period when the survival of the breed was in doubt, but recent revival means the breed is now being seen more often.

These spaniels do not differ from related breeds in their working nature, despite their unique appearance. The curly coat offers great protection against both water and cold, and they have proved their hardiness by retrieving waterfowl from dangerous tidal waters during winter. The coat is difficult to condition for show purposes; experienced exhibitors will often let their dogs get thoroughly soaked beforehand, and then allow the hair to dry naturally. Their oily furs helps to weatherproof the coat, and may have a slight odor. The Irish Water Spaniel is always dark liver in color, with the coat having a purplish bloom referred to as 'puce liver'.

IRISH WOLFHOUND

These friendly giants were first kept for hunting wolves and elk. Dogs of this type may have been sent to Rome from Ireland as long ago as 391AD. At a much later date, the mass export of Irish Wolfhounds, following the extinction of its native quarry, almost led to the breed's disappearance. From 1862 on, however, a Scot, Captain George A. Graham, set out to re-establish the breed, and it has since flourished.

The decision to acquire one of these distinctive dogs should not be taken

Irish Wolfhounds

ITALIAN GREYHOUND

More than 2,000 years ago, a small greyhound-type breed existed in various parts of the Mediterranean region; by the sixteenth century, these dogs had become fashionable among the Italian ruling class. These greyhounds were soon associated with royalty all over Europe, and often featured in portraits and paintings. They enjoyed a great following during the latter half of the nineteenth century, but later declined in numbers.

As can happen with miniaturization, the soundness of the breed was compromised for a period, which had an adverse effect on its popularity. In Scandinavia, however, the breed's coursing ability was actively encouraged and, although these dogs may have been slightly larger in size, they remained

Italian Greyhounds

sound. The average weight of the breed is now about 8lb (3.6kg).

These greyhounds have a very fine, soft coat and are more sensitive to the cold than many other breeds, so it is advisable to provide them with coats for walks during wintry spells. The Italian Greyhound has a delightful temperament, but can be rather reserved with strangers. The appetite of the breed is generally quite small, and they can be selective over their food, but exercise should encourage them to eat well.

ITALIAN HOUND

This old breed has characteristics in common with both the Celtic and the St Hubert Hound. It can be dull black, brown or tricolored, and has been bred in both rough and smooth-haired varieties. It makes a good individual gundog or pack member.

ITALIAN POINTER

Native hounds of Italy were combined with gundogs to produce the Italian Pointer, which was first recognized as a separate breed in the early years of the eighteenth century. It possesses the relatively large head characteristic of the older hound breeds, while its gundog ancestry is reflected in the appearance of its body. The coat of the breed is short, and white with brown or orange markings. The Italian Pointer remains largely confined to Italy, where it is most common. In temperament, it shows traits of both hounds and gundogs.

JACK RUSSELL TERRIER

This popular breed was the end result of attempts to recreate the older type of English Terrier, as the modern Fox Terrier, in the view of many breeders, had developed an artificial appearance. The breed was named after the Reverend J. Russell, who was very instrumental in establishing the Fox Terrier. A number

Jack Russell Terrier

of terriers are all described as Jack Russells, and up to now this has hindered the attempts of breeders to persuade the Kennel Club to recognize these dogs as a distinct breed, although they are now a common variety in many countries, as well as in Britain. While some individuals can be of uncertain temperament, the majority are spirited hunters.

JAPANESE CHIN
(Japanese Spaniel)

One of the oldest of the toy breeds, the Japanese Chin was, in fact, first bred in China; subsequently, some stock was given to the Emperor of Japan. These dogs belonged to the nobility, and were awarded to those who had served their country well. Commodore Perry was given a pair in 1853, when he started to trade with Japan, and Queen Victoria was then presented with the breed. Others arrived in the United States, and sailors soon appreciated that there was a good profit to be made from smuggling such dogs out of Japan. However, the breed did not prove long-lived and earth-

Italian Hound

Japanese Chin

Japanese Chins

quakes in Japan significantly reduced the numbers of breeding stock. The Japanese Chin is now slightly smaller in size, but soundness is rated more highly.

The breed is represented throughout much of Europe, including Britain, where it was recognized by the Kennel Club as long ago as 1894. Originally known in the United States as the Japanese Spaniel, its name was changed in 1977 to Japanese Chin. These dogs do not present any special problems with regard to care, and now achieve the normal lifespan expected for this type of breed. They are bright and lively, and are happy in relatively cramped surroundings, such as apartments.

JAPANESE
MIDDLE-SIZED DOG (Sanshu)
These dogs are very similar to the Akita, although smaller in size. They have the typical appearance of a member of the spitz group. They are bred in a variety of colors, and are just as loyal to their owners as the Akita. The breed may well have been brought to Britain during the early years of the present century. It was then believed to have come from Cambodia, and was known as the Phu Quoc Dog.

JAPANESE
SMALL-SIZED DOG (Shiba Inu)
The Japanese Small-Sized Dog is closely related to the Japanese Middle-Sized, and is distinguished mainly by its size. They are also of spitz stock and were kept as hunting dogs, pursuing small game in the mountains of Japan. It is believed that such dogs were introduced to Japan centuries ago from the Pacific. They are relatively powerful in view of their size, with a rough coat and a softer underlayer of fur.

JAPANESE SPITZ
While the name of Japanese Spitz is often applied to the group of related Japanese breeds, it is also used in connection with one specific breed. These dogs are white in color, and rather reminiscent of a Samoyed with their longish coats. The Japanese Spitz may have arisen as a cross between other native breeds and the German Spitz, which is also white. Already known in Britain, as well as other countries, including Sri Lanka, these dogs are likely to be seen more frequently, since they are attractive show animals and make good pets.

JAPANESE TERRIER
(Nihon Terrier)
A localized breed, the Japanese Terrier has arisen from crosses of native dogs with either the Smooth Fox Terrier or

Japanese Spitzes

the Amertoy. They are quite small, with a coat which is either black and white or tan and white. The ears are pricked.

JURA LAUFHUND
The region of the Jura Mountains, where these hounds originated, is close to the Swiss border with France and, as a result, the Jura Laufhund shows a closer resemblance to French hounds than to other Swiss breeds. It is similar in appearance to the St Hubert Hound with its large head, wrinkled forehead and long ears. The coat is short, thick and black and tan in color, often with a small area of white on the chest. Kept essentially for hunting game such as foxes and hares, the Jura Laufhund makes an excellent tracker, possessing a good voice when pursuing quarry. A short-legged variety has also been developed for the same purpose.

K

KANGAROO HOUND

Early Australian settlers controlled the numbers of kangaroos and wallabies with the aid of these hounds. The task required a very powerful, fast dog, and the Kangaroo Hound was developed by crossing Deerhounds with Greyhounds. Subsequently, however, other methods of control have been implemented, and, although the Kangaroo Hound is still found in remote areas of the country, its continuing existence must be in serious doubt. These hounds are not shown, nor is the breed known in other countries.

KARELIAN BEAR DOG (Karelsk Björnhund)

Developed as a guard dog as well as a hunter, the Karelian Bear Dog has the typical appearance of a spitz breed, with its thick, black and white coat. With the decline of the bear populations in the Arctic region, the Bear Dog has been used to hunt other potentially dangerous animals such as elk. These are brave yet aggressive dogs; recently, attempts have been made to breed out their quarrelsome tendencies without compromising their hunting skills. The breed is often exhibited at Finnish shows and is becoming more popular in other parts of Scandinavia. It is also known in Russia.

KEESHOND (Dutch Barge Dog)

Developed in The Netherlands from Wolf Spitz stock which originated in Germany, this breed has been in existence for over 200 years. They are thought to be named after Kees de Gyselaer and Kees de Witt, the leaders of *Patriotlen* ('Patriots'), the opposition party to the House of Orange. In the eighteenth century, this breed became the party's mascot.

Keeshonden were often kept on *rijnaken*, small boats plying their trade along the River Rhine. The breed suffered as a result of its links with the *Patriotlen*; when the Prince of Orange took power, few wanted to own such a symbol of opposition. The river boats also became larger during this period, with space for bigger dogs. Both these factors brought about a sharp decline in the popularity of the breed.

Keeshound

Modern interest stems from 1920, when Baroness van Handenbrook decided to launch a campaign for the breed's revival. Perhaps surprisingly, the breed had survived virtually unchanged in a few localities, and its numbers grew quite rapidly. Keeshonden were seen in Britain in 1925, and have remained quite popular ever since. They are not hunting dogs and settle well in a domestic environment, where they can be relied upon to detect the presence of any strangers. Keeshonden have a distinctive bark, with a bell-like quality.

KERRY BEAGLE

The numbers of these hounds have declined to the point where only one pack is in existence, although other single individuals are known. Originating from, and concentrated in, southern Ireland, they are thought to be descended from larger hounds originally kept for pursuing deer. The name 'Beagle' is rather misleading, since these hounds are in fact significantly bigger than the true Beagle. Kerry Beagles have relatively long ears and are rather reminiscent of the French hounds in appearance, except they are black and tan in color. They resemble other breeds of this type in temperament.

KERRY BLUE TERRIER

It was in the mountainous area of County Kerry, southern Ireland, that the Kerry Blue Terrier was first bred, over a century ago. The breed remained isolated for a number of years, and was kept exclusively as a working dog. Only later were these terriers actually considered for competitive showing; since then, they have won top awards at some of the major shows.

The color and coat are important features of the breed. Puppies are all black when they are born and gradually lighten to the desired shade of blue, sometimes retaining black points. This change may be detected as early as nine

Kerry Blue Terrier

months of age, but often those that change color later prove to be the deeper, more desirable shade of blue. Brown tints are not uncommon, but only permitted in young dogs. The coat itself is naturally soft and wavy, and can grow unsightly unless it is trimmed back, although this practice is discouraged in Eire. The Kerry Blue Terrier is not a temperamental dog and makes a good companion, and an alert guard dog.

KING CHARLES SPANIEL
(English Toy Spaniel)

These toy spaniels were great favourites with King Charles II (1630-85), who often exercised his dogs himself in St James's Park, London. Although it has been suggested that in 1613 Captain Saris of the Royal Navy brought the breed back from Japan as a gift for James I (1566-1625), from the Emperor, these spaniels were most certainly known in England from the previous century. The breed was originally black and tan, but those spaniels particularly favored by King Charles were black and white and had been introduced by Henrietta of Orleans from France.

Other colors were developed later. The variety known today as the Prince Charles is tricolored, while the Ruby,

King Charles Spaniel

as its name suggests, is chestnut red. The Blenheim is a combination of ruby and white, and was developed by the 1st Duke of Marlborough, who moved to Blenheim Palace in 1702. Blenheims soon became highly valued for work with woodcocks. The King Charles Spaniel varies in size, and has suffered quite significantly in popularity in Britain at the expense of the Cavalier King Charles, having gained a reputation for being an unsound breed.

KOMONDOR

A large breed of sheepdog known as the Racka was brought to Hungary by the Magyars during their phase of settlement in the ninth century AD. These

dogs resembled the present-day Komondor, and were kept for both guarding and herding. The Komondor developed from this breed. With changes in agriculture, however, smaller breeds found favor and one of the traditional roles of the Komondor was lost. Pulis became used for controlling the movements of the sheep, with the Komondor acting as guard dog.

The breed was first seen in the United States about 1933, and has recently appeared in Britain, where its unusual appearance has attracted much attention. The coats of these dogs naturally become matted unless they are carefully groomed. The individual strands of hair form cords, and these must be separated if the coat becomes wet to prevent matting. The Komondor is an intelligent breed, but may need firm control until adequately trained.

KRAMFORHLÄNDER

After the Second World War, a small dog, most probably a Griffon Fauve de Bretagne, was given by a group of American soldiers to a Frau Schliefenbaum, who lived in Siegen, West Germany. It mated with her Wire-haired Terrier bitch, and Frau Schliefenbaum thought that the resulting puppies were so attractive that she set out to fix their characteristics in a new breed. Her quest was successful, and resulted in the Kramfohrländer, which was recognized by the German Kennel Club in 1953, and subsequently by the FCI. These dogs are rough-coated, preferably with an area of white forming a saddle. They are becoming increasingly popular, and are good companions and watchdogs.

KUVASZ

The name of this breed is derived from the Turkish word *karvasz*, meaning 'armed guard of the nobility', and indeed ownership was at first restricted to members of the royal circle. The Kuvasz actually originated in Tibet, but has been developed in Hungary.

The Kuvasz went into a serious decline in the early decades of the present century, but some dogs had reached the United States by the 1930s. Here, the breed was recognized by the AKC in 1935 and attracted considerable interest. The breed is now also frequently seen on the European mainland, but has not yet made any great impression in Britain. Kuvasz are very striking dogs, with white, glossy coats that are significantly shorter in summer than in winter. The breed is sensitive and highly intelligent and must be treated accordingly. They possess a strong instinct to protect children.

Komondor

L

LABRADOR RETRIEVER

At the beginning of the nineteenth century, a distinctive breed was brought to Britain from Newfoundland. These dogs were black, with short coats. The Earl of Malmesbury owned a number of them and was responsible for the breed becoming known as the Labrador Retriever. In Newfoundland, however, where a high tax was imposed on all dogs, the numbers of the breed declined, while British quarantine restrictions made the importation of stock very difficult.

Labradors were crossed with other retrievers until a standard was drawn up for the breed in 1903. In the early years, most Labradors were black, but later yellows became increasingly common. The standard specifies that other self (single) colors are also permitted, and some chocolate individuals have recently been exhibited.

Labradors are commonly kept by gamekeepers and sportsmen, and have been trained to assist in the detection of drugs; they also work as police dogs and as guide dogs for the blind. Bitches are particularly suitable. There is no significant difference in working ability between dogs of different colors.

Labrador Retrievers

In the show ring, the breed has achieved a strong following. Under Kennel Club rules, championship status can only be given to dogs who prove themselves both in the field and in show competition. The title 'Show Champion' is awarded to Labrador Retrievers that qualify only in the show ring. The gentle, friendly temperament of the breed makes these dogs ideal as family pets, and they will also prove alert guards. Unfortunately, they have a tendency to run to fat; regular exercise and a sensible feeding routine will prevent this problem arising.

LAIKA

Laika is the name of various related breeds kept for working, and which have been developed largely in Russia. They were originally sporting dogs, trained to work with birds, but are also used for other duties.

The smallest form is seen in the area close to the Finnish border and, although larger than the Finnish Spitz, resembles this breed in appearance. Colour ranges from fawn, through grey to black. Laikas from northern Russia are more reminiscent of the Samoyed, whereas the big eastern race, a powerful dog, used for pulling sledges, shows a closer affinity to other native breeds of this area. Other Laikas are kept as guard dogs and the breed has also been used in the Russian space program.

LAKELAND TERRIER

In the Lake District, in northwestern England, hunting has always been important, as much from necessity as sport. The region supported a high population of sheep, and control of foxes was vital in reducing losses, especially at lambing time. Terriers were often kept, along with packs of hounds, for this purpose. The old English Black and Tan Terrier, which was rough-coated, contributed to the development of the Lakeland breed, the physical qualities of which were considered much more significant than its color. Many tales of the Lakeland Terrier's bravery were told; one dog, owned by Lord Lonsdale, ran an otter to ground; when freed by explosives three days later, it emerged

Lakeland Terrier

Landseer

completely unharmed from its experience. Other dogs are reputed to have survived underground for 12 days.

There were various local names for the breed, including Elterwater Terrier, but Lakeland Terrier was finally adopted as the official name in 1912. A standard was drawn up nine years later. These terriers are now seen fairly often at shows around the world, but retain close links with their native Cumbria. Regular trimming will keep the coat in a good show condition. Lakeland Terriers are alert to strangers and have the typically lively nature of terriers.

LANDSEER
The Newfoundland is bred in a variety of colors, but classification of the black and white form varies according to the country concerned. The FCI recognizes such dogs as a separate breed, called Landseer after the nineteenth-century artist who frequently portrayed them, notably in his painting entitled *A distinguished member of the Humane Society* (1838). The black and white form has become lighter in body than the other Newfoundlands, but it has a very similar temperament and is just as powerful a swimmer.

LAPINPOROKOIRA
(Laponian Vallhund)
By using breeds such as the Collie and the German Shepherd Dog, and crossing them with the Lapphund, Finnish breeders produced a dog that was able to control the movements of livestock and was also effective as a guard. These dogs are very tough, but lack any hunting traits, which makes them ideal for the work. The resemblance to spitz breeds remains obvious, but the tail is not usually permanently curled over the back. The breed's dense undercoat and longer topcoat makes it well able to survive in the cold northern climate. It was recognized in 1946 by the FCI, but is not widespread outside Scandinavia.

LAPPHUND
(Lapinkoira, Swedish Lapp Spitz)
Kept originally in the far north for herding reindeer, the Lapphund is another spitz-type breed which has become closely linked with Sweden. They are now employed by the Swedish army as guard dogs. Despite their relatively small size, Lapphunds are fearless, although they are not hunters by instinct. The breed is not common in other parts of Europe.

LARGE MÜNSTERLÄNDER
The usual process of miniaturization was actually reversed in the case of the Münsterländer, since this large breed resulted from a small variety developed in the area of Westphalia. Bigger specimens were paired together until breeders finally obtained recognition from the German Kennel Club for the new dogs. Large Münsterländers have a strong following in both Germany and The Netherlands and are currently making a considerable impact on the British show scene. The breed possesses the characteristics of other gundogs, being easily trained, loyal and affectionate.

LEONBERGER
While in the care of a certain Herr Essig of Leonberg, a St Bernard bitch was impregnated by a Newfoundland. The animal was subsequently returned to the Hospice of St Bernard, where many St Bernards had been recently wiped out by an avalanche and a severe epidemic of distemper.

Using the resulting litters, Herr Essig aimed to produce a breed that would resemble the heraldic lion painted on the Leonberg city crest. The Leonberger was first exhibited at a Paris show in 1907, and was also introduced to Britain in the same year, where it had rather a mixed reception. The breed is now represented at most European

Large Münsterländer

shows, but has never been seriously considered as a working breed, unlike its ancestors.

LEVESQUE

Interbreeding between English Foxhounds and hounds of French origin was not uncommon, and the Levesque is one breed resulting from such liaisons. It is a combination of Saintongeois, Gascon and Foxhound blood. The Levesque is a large breed with a smooth coat that is predominantly black and white in color, with small areas of brownish fur near the hock joints. These hounds are friendly, but have a stubborn streak.

LHASA APSO

Despite their rather exotic appearance, this small breed is both hardy and tough. These dogs originated in Tibet, where they are called 'Apso Seng Kye', meaning 'Black Lion Sentinel Dogs'. Traditionally, they were kept inside dwellings in the sacred city of Lhasa, while Tibetan Mastiffs guarded outside. The Lhasa Apso is an alert, intelligent breed, well able to distinguish friend from stranger. They are very responsive to training, and playful by nature.

The breed was first introduced to Britain by Colonel Kennedy who had been working in the East as a medical officer. His two dogs were shown in London in 1929 and a breed club was founded shortly after, in 1933. The Lhasa Apso has since become the most popular of the four Tibetan breeds. To keep these dogs looking their best, considerable time must be spent caring for their long, flowing coats, which actually trail along the ground.

Long-haired Dachshund (miniature)

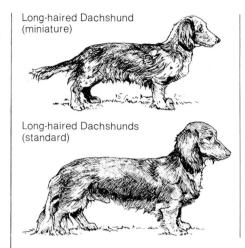

Long-haired Dachshunds (standard)

LONG-HAIRED DACHSHUND

The name 'Dachshund' means 'badger dog' in German. Hunting breeds have been developed to work in particular environments, and the Dachshund is no exception. In the thick, dense forests of Germany, it was impossible to pursue foxes and badgers riding on horseback. Dogs were developed to go down the burrows of such creatures, fighting under conditions where there was little space and a shortage of air. Courage was a vital attribute of the breed, since their opponents were formidable adversaries, often weighing more than the dogs themselves.

Lhasa Apso

The original breed, which in turn has given rise to the six types of Dachshund now recognized, was known as the Teckel. The traditional form of the breed was short-haired, but spaniel blood introduced the long-haired characteristic. Today, the Long-haired Dachshund remains one of the least fashionable members of its group, perhaps because it is relatively shy. There is usually a fair difference in temperament between the various Dachshund types, probably as a result of the different breeds which have been used to contribute individual features. Long-haired Dachshunds make good house dogs, and have a bark which sounds like that of a much bigger dog. The miniature form of the Long-haired Dachshund, recognized as a separate breed, is more popular than the standard variety. Despite their size, these are still essentially hounds.

LÖWCHEN

The Löwchen, sometimes referred to as the Little Lion Dog, was first given championship status by the Kennel Club for the 1976 Crufts Dog Show. The popularity of the breed, both as a show dog and household pet, has continued to increase since that time. The Löwchen has a very pleasant disposition and is impressive in the show ring. Their dark eyes convey their intelligent, kindly natures and they are active, playful and friendly.

Dogs of this type were known by the turn of the century, and may have been kept in Malta as long ago as 1840. They are thought to be related to both the Barbet and the Bichon, but their ancestry is unclear. In the early 1900s the breed was scarce, and only since the Second World War has it undergone a revival. The Löwchen's name is derived from the leonine trim of its coat, which includes a pom-pom of hair at the end of its tail.

Löwchens

Lurcher

LUNDEHUND

Devised to work in a specific, hazardous environment, the Lundehund is one of the smaller spitz-type dogs. They were originally bred on the island of Vaerog, near Norway, to catch puffins, a favored food of the local people for centuries. The breed had to be nimble enough to climb safely up the rocky outcrops where the birds were found. Lundehunds caught and retrieved the puffins and could locate nests during the breeding season so that the eggs could be harvested.

The Lundehund is currently only recognized in Scandinavia. They are tough, working dogs, despite their small size. They have muscular bodies and well-developed feet with double dew claws.

LURCHER

The traditional type of Lurcher is a Collie-Greyhound cross, a popular hunting dog of the Irish romanies. Often used for poaching, Lurchers are very stealthy workers, taking their quarry with hardly any noise before returning discreetly to their owner. They keep away from strangers, especially when hunting, and are usually darker in color, which helps them to remain undetected. At present, there is no standardization of the Lurcher, or its various forms, but attempts are being made to introduce some degree of uniformity.

LUZERNER LAUFHUND

The Swiss hounds divide into two groups. Light, mobile breeds were favored, some of which were in turn mated to short-legged dogs, such as the Dachshund, to yield similar offspring. The Luzerner Laufhund is one typical example of this and bears a resemblance to French hounds, with the profile of the St Hubert Hound and the color of the Grand Bleu de Gascogne. The smaller variety is known as the Niederlaufhund. Both types are white, with black and blue markings, while some individuals also show tan areas.

MACELLAIO HERDING DOG (Cane di Macellaio)

A native breed of Sicily, the short-coated Macellaio Herding Dog resembles the Rottweiler, having a similar head and powerful body. The ears are normally cropped; the coat is often black with brownish markings, although brindled individuals are not unknown. Apart from their herding abilities, the breed also makes a useful guard dog.

MAGYAR AGÁR

A coursing breed, the Magyar Agár may well have been kept in Hungary since the ninth century AD. Today, as a result of crossings with imported stock, these dogs closely resemble Greyhounds. Fleet of foot, they hunt by sight, lacking any scenting ability. The Magyar Agár is not exhibited or known outside Hungary, but is very similar to the Greyhound in temperament.

MALTESE

Dogs of this type may have lived in Malta during the days of the Roman Empire. Maltese dogs were first introduced to Britain at the beginning of the sixteenth century and quickly became popular. Dr Caius, the physician to Elizabeth I (1533-1603), noted that the breed was kept largely by women as companions. These pets are supposed to have changed hands for vast sums of money.

At the time of the early dog shows, toward the end of the nineteenth century, the success of a breeder called Manderville with the breed, increased public interest. Maltese dogs were first seen in the United States during the early years of this century, but in Britain, they gradually declined in numbers in the face of competition from new toy breeds.

The Maltese is a very attractive dog, but its long, flowing white coat needs considerable grooming, and sometimes washing, to keep it in the peak of condition. These dogs make extremely good house pets; they have kindly natures and delight in attention and affection from their owners.

Maltese

Mastiff

MANCHESTER TERRIER

The Black and Tan Terrier, a traditional British breed, was a fiery, stocky dog kept for working and fighting. Competitions were held to find the terrier which could dispatch the largest number of rats in a set period of time. A dog called Billy is reputed to have dealt with no less than 100 rats in only six minutes, 13 seconds!

When a breeder called John Hulme wanted to create a similar type of dog, which could catch rats and also hold its own when coursing, he used a crossbred Black and Tan Terrier, paired with a Whippet for speed; the breed today has a sloping (or roach) back, which is a characteristic not normally associated with terriers. The breed was first called the Manchester Terrier during the 1860s, then the Black and Tan Terrier for a period, until the Manchester Terrier Club of America was founded in 1923 and Manchester Terrier became the official name.

The toy variety was developed from the larger form and classified separately until 1959. Both are shown together now, and have virtually merged completely. The quest for markings and color temporarily led to a deterioration in the overall soundness of the breed but all these problems have now been over-

come. Although the Manchester Terrier is not as common as it once was, the breed still enjoys a dedicated following.

MAREMMA SHEEPDOG
(Cane de Pastore Maremano Abruzzese)

The history of this breed dates back centuries; its ancestors were probably kept by the Magyars. It evolved in the region of Maremma in Italy and, while some members of the breed were kept exclusively for working with stock, others acted as farm guards. This division gave rise to two distinctive types, although only one form is now recognized.

The Maremma Sheepdog was first seen in Britain during the latter years of the last century, but was in decline until the beginning of the 1930s. The breed is now represented at major shows but is still rare. These sheepdogs are rather aloof in temperament, but are excellent guards.

MASTIFF

The term 'mastiff' also applies to a group of dogs, apart from this one, specific breed. Dogs of this type can be found on Egyptian monuments of 3000 BC. They were certainly known in Britain at the time of the Roman invasion. Julius Caesar wrote of their courage,

and records show that some were taken to Rome from Britain, where they were pitted against various other animals, and even gladiators.

At the Battle of Agincourt (1415), Sir Peers Legh, Knight of Lyme Hall in Cheshire, went into battle accompanied by his favourite Mastiff. He fell, mortally wounded,. but the bitch remained alongside until soldiers carried her master from the scene of the fighting. The Mastiff was eventually taken back to England and is reputed to have laid the foundation of the famous Lyme Hall bloodline, which has been bred right down to the present day.

The overall features of the breed declined sharply in Britain during the Second World War, but it fared better in the United States, with stock returning across the Atlantic afterward. These majestic giants do not rank among the most popular show breeds, but for owners with adequate space, few dogs prove more faithful and gentle, and certainly deter unwelcome visitors.

MEXICAN HAIRLESS
DOG (Xoloizcuintli)

Different breeds of virtually hairless dogs exist in various parts of the world. It has been suggested that they all originated in Africa and were sub-

Neopolitan Mastiff

careful breeding in more recent times, although a few individuals retain the fighting instincts of their ancestors. The breed is maintained in Italy by a few breeders and is uncommon elsewhere. Over the last few years, several have been brought to Britain and the breed may be developed here as a result.

NEWFOUNDLAND
Various stories are told about the origins of the Newfoundland, but it is generally accepted that the breed developed from dogs brought by sailors to New-

Newfoundland

foundland from Europe. Crosses with North American breeds may also have contributed to the emerging bloodline. They soon gained a reputation for hardiness and showed a natural affinity for water. Many tales relate how devoted Newfoundlands have saved the lives of drowning sailors. These dogs also worked on fishing boats, where they helped to pull in the nets.

The breed was introduced to England, and had been exhibited by 1860. The standard still reflects the working nature of the breed. Newfoundlands must have coarse, dense, water-resistant coats and powerful bodies, with strong hindquarters to aid swimming. They must also be intelligent, as well as gentle and docile in temperament. In some countries the black and white form is classified separately as the Landseer, and may show a slight difference in type.

The numbers of the breed suffered badly during the Second World War; it is doubtful whether more than a dozen individuals survived this period in England. It was largely due to the efforts of the Newfoundland Club of America that the breed was resurrected successfully. The breed is now common in many countries, including Australia, and also in Scandinavia.

sequently introduced to other countries, including China, where the similar Chinese Crested Dog developed. After this time, traders are thought to have taken such dogs to the New World.

The Mexican Hairless Dog attracted much attention when it was first seen in Britain at the beginning of this century. While clearly unable to survive the climate of northern Europe without adequate protection, they have proved to be lively dogs, and have been known to catch both rats and rabbits. This breed is not as common as the Chinese Crested.

MINIATURE PINSCHER
'Pinscher' means 'terrier' in German, and the Miniature Pinscher is believed to have descended from the old large form. Development of the breed began in earnest following the foundation of the breed club in 1895, when a standard was established. In the United States, the Miniature Pinscher became increasingly popular during the late 1920s; today it is represented in many countries of the world. These dogs bear a superficial resemblance to the Doberman, although they are smaller and are not directly related. Miniature Pinschers are fearless, which makes them extremely good watchdogs. They also have very alert and intelligent natures.

MUDI
The Mudi is of Hungarian origin, bred primarily to act as a guard dog rather than a herder of stock. The coat of this breed is not corded like that of other native dogs such as the Puli, but wavy, and of mixed coloration. They are powerful dogs and reputedly easy to train, and prove both brave when threatened, yet affectionate with their owners. The Mudi is, however, rarely seen outside Hungary.

NEAPOLITAN MASTIFF
(Mastino Napoletano)
Descended from the old Molossus of Roman times, these mastiffs have particularly large heads, which give them a ferocious appearance. They are not normally aggressive, however, thanks to

NORBOTTENSPETS

One of the smaller members of the spitz group, the Norbottenspets was first developed in northern Sweden. Its origins are unknown, although it is possible that German and Arctic Spitz blood may have contributed to its ancestry. There is also a similarity with the Lundehund, a native of the same area.

These dogs have thick protective undercoats and are white with cream, red or black markings. They are kept largely as household pets and guard dogs in Scandinavia. The breed was almost lost earlier this century, but has recently undergone a revival as a result of a growing interest in traditional native breeds.

NORFOLK TERRIER

These cheerful, sturdy terriers were first bred in the region of East Anglia during the early years of the present century. Frank 'Roughrider' Jones established the breed using terriers that he took from around the towns of Cambridge, Norwich and Market Harborough; the breed gained acceptance from the Kennel Club in 1932. There was still controversy over the correct appearance of these terriers and both drop-ear and pricked-ear dogs were

Norfolk Terrier

classed together. In 1964, the Kennel Club finally decided to separate them, with the former retaining the name Norfolk Terrier, and those with erect ears being called Norwich Terriers.

Such terriers were often known affectionately as Jones Terriers in the United States, after the founder of the breed. The distinction employed in Britain was insisted upon by the AKC in 1979, dividing the breed on the basis of the ear carriage. These terriers have very appealing personalities, and are not quarrelsome. They are hardy and loyal, and, despite their size, should not be considered as typical toy dogs, since they have strong working instincts.

NORTH EASTERN SLEIGH DOG

Kept largely in northeastern parts of Siberia, as well as Manchuria, the North Eastern Sleigh Dog is similar to the Eskimo Dog, although smaller in size. These are very powerful dogs, with muscular legs and thick, water-repellant coats. In the Arctic region, they provide a valuable means of transport by pulling sleighs across the frozen landscape. They are bred in various colors, but are most often black and white.

NORWEGIAN BUHUND

The spitz dogs are classified as a distinct group in Scandinavia, irrespective of size. The Norwegian Buhund is one of the working spitz breeds that originated in Scandinavia, probably bred from Elkhound stock. They are fast, agile dogs, and remarkably strong for their size. The breed is kept both for guarding and herding. Norwegian Buhunds are seen occasionally outside Scandinavia, and a number are kept in Britain, although the breed has not achieved any great level of popularity. They make striking show dogs and, while color is not one of their most important features, self-colored individuals — normally ranging from red to wheaten — are preferred.

Norwich Terrier

NORWICH TERRIER

This breed is distinguished from the Norfolk Terrier by the erect carriage of its ears.

NOVA SCOTIA DUCK TOLLING RETRIEVER

A lesser-known breed, which is again attracting attention in its native Canada, the Nova Scotia Duck Tolling Retriever is similar in appearance to the Golden Retriever, but is pale red or fawn in color. White markings are permitted, but not really considered desirable. The retrieving ability of these dogs in water is assisted by their thick, protective undercoat; the webbing on the feet also makes them powerful swimmers. Quiet and easily trainable, this retriever makes a good household pet as well as a working dog.

Norwegian Buhund

OLD DANISH POINTER
(Gammel Dansk Househund)

This particular breed of pointer was developed during the seventeenth century, largely from the Spanish Pointer. The similarity between the breeds is still very much in evidence, since the Old Danish Pointer possesses the wide, heavy head of its Spanish ancestor and is also bred in the same combination of white and brown. These dogs are useful gundogs and work well in flat surroundings. The breed was nearly lost at one stage, but its numbers have again built up, and it was finally recognized in 1962 by the Danish Kennel Club. They are still rare outside Scandinavia.

OLD ENGLISH SHEEPDOG

The Old English Sheepdog has become a very popular breed during recent years, largely as a result of its use in various advertising campaigns. It was probably developed in the west of England in the early nineteenth century, yet its actual origins are obscure. The breed might be related to the Bearded Collie, and possibly even to the Russian Outchar.

The Old English Sheepdog was first kept as a drover's dog, for driving stock to market. As a working breed, these dogs were not subject to tax. Their tails were docked to make this distinction clear, and this tradition is still observed today. The coat should be shaggy, without actually curling, profuse and hard in texture. Any traces of sable or brown markings are penalized at shows.

The Old English Sheepdog was first recognized by the AKC in 1888, and the breed caught public attention when Champion Slumber won 'Best in Show' at the Westminster Show in New York in 1914. At first, there was a tendency for American breeders to aim for dogs with excessively profuse coats.

Part of the appeal of the Old English Sheepdog stems from its unusual gait, which is rather reminiscent of a bear's padding action. In temperament, they are very affectionate and intelligent, yet rather boisterous, especially so when young. The active nature of the breed makes it unsuitable for a home with little

Old English Sheepdog

space for exercise, and the coat needs regular attention in order to look its best.

OTTERHOUND

A breed of dog kept essentially for hunting otters was in existence as long ago as the fourteenth century, and apparently resembled a cross between 'a hound and a terrier'. Otter hunting became a very fashionable pursuit in Britain during the latter half of the nineteenth century, when there were about 20 packs of dogs which were kept for this purpose.

Otterhound

The Hawkstone pack was the most notorious, killing 704 otters over a 20-year period starting in 1870. Another pack was owned by Squire Lomax of Clitheroe, and trained to such a degree that they would respond simply to a gesture of the hand. Most of these hounds died suddenly over the course of a single year, however, and the squire did not attempt to rebuild the pack, feeling that he had insufficient time to accomplish the same level of training before he died.

The Otterhound is believed to be descended from French stock, as it has such a close resemblance to the Griffons Vendéens in both type and coat. Blue and white has always been the preferred colour; the coat is rough, with a thick, water-repellant undercoat. These hounds are very persistent once on the trail of their quarry, over land or in water, and their webbed feet assist in swimming.

In recent years, Otterhounds have become relatively scarce in Britain, but have retained a strong following in the United States, where they were first seen about the turn of the century. The breed is loyal and affectionate; as well as proving to be dedicated workers, these hounds can also make valuable guard dogs.

OWTSCHARKA

These are four related breeds, kept in various parts of Russia for both herding and guarding stock. None are currently represented outside Russia, although some were seen in Germany during the latter part of the 1930s.

The Owtscharka is one of the smaller members of the group, and is found in southern parts of the country. It resembles the Gos d'Atura in appearance, and is reputed to respond well to training. The North Caucasian is another smaller dog of this group, possessing a short coat compared to the large Transcaucasian. Coloring is of relatively little significance and, in the case of the Mid-Asiatic, the fourth member, any color apart from pure black may be seen. The Mid-Asiatic has a coat of intermediate length and is a powerful guard dog.

PAPILLON

Papillons were popular companions for the ladies of the courts of Europe as long ago as the sixteenth century, and were being portrayed with their owners in paintings by such artists as Rubens and Boucher. The fashion for Papillons started in Spain, and soon spread to France and Italy. These dogs fetched high prices, and were often sold by dealers who traveled from country to country on mules.

The breed was first known as the Dwarf Spaniel because of its big, drooping ears. Gradually this feature changed, and the ears became erect, resembling butterfly wings, a characteristic that gave rise to the contemporary name of Papillon. Dogs of both types may still occur in the same litter; those with very drooping ears are called Phalenes or Epagneuls Nains, although they are not recognized as a separate breed.

Despite their size, Papillons are tough dogs, and not above hunting vermin, often harrassing a rat to exhaustion before finally dispatching it. The breed is also not affected to the same extent by the obstetrical problems encountered in many of the toy breeds. They make lively companions and are easy to train.

Papillon

PEKINGESE

During the eighth century AD, these dogs were considered sacred in China, where they were first bred, and their theft was treated as a capital offence. Pekingese remained the exclusive property of the Imperial family for centuries, until the Palace at Peking was taken by British troops in 1860. Four Pekingese were removed from the quarters of an aunt of the emperor, and brought to Britain. Each was a different

colour: the fawn and white Peke was presented to Queen Victoria (1819-1901), while the Duke of Richmond and Lord Hay kept and bred from the remaining three.

These dogs attracted considerable attention, especially following the exhibition of the breed for the first time in 1893, at Chester. Other Pekingese were subsequently imported, and one dog called Boxer, obtained at the time of the Boxer uprising of 1900, made a particularly significant contribution to successive bloodlines. They also proved to be very popular in the United States.

Three separate types of Pekingese were recognized in China and these distinctions remain today. Sun Dogs are golden-red; Lion Dogs have big manes and sloping hindquarters. Very small Pekes were called Sleeve Dogs because they could fit into the flared sleeves of Chinese garments.

Pekingese are both stubborn and dignified in character, with a rather pompous air. They are normally very calm and unaggressive, but can react fiercely if challenged. Care must be taken with their eyes to prevent injury.

PERDIGEIRO PORTUGUES

The Portuguese word *perdig* means 'partridge', and the Perdigeiro Portugues has gained a reputation as a bird dog. It is descended, like most Portu-

Pekingese

guese breeds, from Spanish stock, and is relatively small in size. The color of these dogs can range from red to cream, offset against darker patches and, sometimes, white markings; the coat is short and rough. They are popular, both as house pets and gundogs, but are rare outside Portugal.

PERRO DE PRESA
(Mallorquin)

A breed that was developed in the Azores, the Perro de Presa is descended from a combination of Spanish and Portuguese stock introduced to the islands by sailors, and is clearly of mastiff origin. These dogs resemble the Alano, as they are large and heavy with a short, predominantly yellow coat. The breed remains confined to the Azores, and is probably fairly rare.

PHARAOH HOUND

Few breeds have made such an impact within such a short space of time as the Pharaoh Hound has in Britain. In 1970 these dogs were barely known outside Malta and none were registered with the Kennel Club. Yet, within just five years, the Pharaoh Hound had increased in numbers to such an extent that it was granted championship status by the Kennel Club, and was being exhibited in the Miscellaneous Class of AKC shows.

The breed is similar to the Ibizan Hound, with which it shares its ancestry. The Pharaoh Hound has a sleek, short, reddish-tan coat, which helps emphasize the elegant outlines of its body. Certain white markings are permitted, and a white tip at the end of the tail is actually desirable. A hunting breed, they have the unusual distinction of being essentially a sight hound, yet able to pursue quarry also by scent. This attribute is probably the result of Egyptian Hound blood. Pharaoh Hounds are good, friendly pets, but need adequate space for exercise.

PICARDY SPANIEL
(Epagneul Picard)

The Picardy Spaniel closely resembles contemporary setter breeds, especially the Gordon, rather than other spaniels. It is an old breed, centered in the region of Picardy, in France, and is still kept as a hunting companion, working in the woods and marshland, where its intelligence and responsive behavior are greatly valued.

The Picardy Spaniel is a tall, powerfully built dog with big feet. The coat is longish, thick and quite hard. Two color variants are known to occur: the Picardy is predominantly dark blue roan, with some traces of red which are

Pharaoh Hound

Picardy Spaniel

more pronounced on the lower parts; the spaniels with red only on the feet and head are sometimes known as the Epagneuls Bleus de Picardy.

PINSCHER

The Pinscher has a considerable history. Descended from medieval hunting stock, they evolved into dogs of medium size with short coats, and were used in the development of both the Doberman and the Miniature Pinscher. Like other terriers, the Pinscher is a keen killer of vermin, and has a sporty disposition. First recognized in 1879, they do well in the show ring, but have made little impact outside Germany.

Pinscher

PODENGO

These hunting dogs, bred in three recognized sizes, remain largely confined to Portugal. The bigger form is normally worked singly or in pairs, with hares as their quarry. The two smaller varieties usually hunt in packs, pursuing rabbits. They have a very mixed ancestry; successive attempts have been made to try to improve their hunting ability through crossbreeding. The Podengo is very popular in Portugal, especially in country areas, and is commonly exhibited. These hounds are also highly valued as pets, where they prove alert companions. Bred in a variety of colors, particularly tan and fawn, the Podengo is a short-coated breed.

POINTER

Dogs of this type were first kept with Greyhounds for hare coursing. They located the hare and remained quietly observing its position until the Greyhounds were brought along to flush out the quarry. Later, certainly by the start of the nineteenth century, Pointers had become valued companions for sportsmen, and were trained to find and indicate the position of the game until a gun could be fired.

Various breeds contributed to the development of the Pointer, including the Greyhound itself. Foxhounds and Bloodhounds were also used to in-

troduce the desired qualities of speed, stealth, stamina and scenting ability. It is likely that Pointer breeds evolved almost simultaneously in various European countries. The Spanish Pointer was introduced to the British bloodline at an early stage, but, being a heavy, slow dog it contributed little to the emerging English breed apart from a strong pointing instinct; its faults also proved difficult to eradicate over the successive generations. Setters were very popular crosses during the nineteenth century, used partly to overcome the natural fierceness of the breed, and to make it easier to train successfully. From this stage onward, Pointers were worked in pairs in order to ensure a close fix on the location of the quarry, thereby taking over the role of the beaters who had been such a feature of hunting on large country estates in the nineteenth century.

The breed today is still clearly a working dog, with puppies showing pointing instincts often by the age of two months. Although not as glamorous as some dogs, the Pointer has a physique well suited to its work. Type has not been separated from working ability in these dogs, and they also do well in the show ring, adopting the frozen stance that is a typical feature of their work in the field.

Pointer

POITEVIN

Hounds of this type were common during the eighteenth century in the Haut Poitou area of France, but were nearly wiped out by an epidemic of rabies, which swept through the region in 1842. A few individuals survived, however, and, using English Foxhounds, the breed was saved, with the Poitevin predictably showing a much closer affinity to the Foxhound than any other French hound. They are normally

tricolored, like the Foxhound, with a more balanced profile and fewer skin folds than French breeds. The Poitevin is friendly and intelligent.

POLISH HOUND (Ogar Polski)

An old Polish breed, this hound is used primarily for hunting wild boar, and also as a guard dog. Although not very large, these dogs are sufficiently powerful to hunt bears. They need firm training from an early age, and prove keen, dedicated hunters, baying loudly when following a scent. Polish Hounds are black with tan markings, and have short, hard coats. Numbers have declined seriously during the present century, largely as a result of the world wars, but the Polish breed has been carefully nurtured since 1945, and is now recognized by the FCI.

POLISH TATRA HERDDOG
(Owczarek Podhalanski)

Kept in the border areas of Poland to herd sheep and guard against wolves, the Polish Tatra Herddog is a large, white breed resembling the Kuvasz in its appearance. Bitches are taller than the male dogs. A standard for the breed was first drawn up during the interwar years, but the Second World War almost led to the breed's complete destruction. A small number survived, however, and the breed was then recognized in 1967 by the FCI.

POMERANIAN

A miniature form of the sleigh dogs of the far north, the Pomeranian is the smallest member of the spitz group. Much of its development took place in Germany, specifically in the area around Pomerania. At first Pomeranians were quite large dogs, invariably white in color; such individuals are now recognized separately as the Japanese Spitz.

The Pomeranian did not become widely known until the end of the last century. The Kennel Club first recognized the breed in 1870, and it was then exhibited in the Miscellaneous Class of the AKC in 1892. Pomeranians rapidly attracted attention, but at this stage, they were still much larger than the breed today. Queen Victoria (1819-1901) obtained a number of greyish Pomeranians in 1890, and the Pomeranian Club was founded in Britain in the following year.

With white Pomeranians being considered too large, other colors became fashionable, and darker-colored Poms are now most common. One of the most spectacular of the early colors was a pure orange dog called Champion Mars, whose color was probably a throwback

Pomeranian

Standard Poodle

Miniature
Poodle

Toy
Poodle

Miniature Poodle

to the breed's ancestors — related breeds such as the Finnish Spitz can be of similar coloration.

Their sturdy build, coupled with their good temper and lively nature have ensured that Pomeranians have become very popular pets. While in the show ring, the breed has acquitted itself very well, often winning 'Best in Show' in the face of stiff competition.

POODLE

Although three breeds of poodle are recognized, they differ in size only, and they are all closely related. The largest form, the Standard Poodle, is the oldest variety. This breed was once used as a retriever, often working in water. Its coat was clipped to assist its swimming abilities and from this the various clips seen today have arisen. The breed is believed to have originated in Germany, where it was called 'Pudel', which means 'splash in water'. Poodles have since become closely associated with France, however, where they are popularly referred to as 'duck dogs'.

The smaller forms of the Poodle have become more and more popular. The Miniature Poodle is the medium-sized variety, and may have been closer to the original Poodle than the present Standard Poodle. It was first called the Toy Poodle, but its name was changed when the smallest form was recognized.

The ancestors of the Poodle were undoubtedly dogs that worked partially in water. The old Rough-haired Water

Standard Poodle

Poodle Pointer

Dog, bred in England, was very similar to an unclipped Poodle, while the Irish Water Dog also bears a distinct likeness to the breed.

Poodles are bred in a very wide range of colors, with corresponding skin coloration. The coat is an important feature, and has proved ideal for styling. There are various types of clip; the style usually varies from country to country. The Lion (or English Saddle) clip is favored by the Kennel Club, whereas the AKC permit the Puppy, English Saddle and Continental clips. Experienced exhibitors or trimming parlors will be able to advise on this aspect of show preparation.

The Poodle's intelligence has long been exploited in circuses, especially in France — these dogs soon master basic tricks. Poodles are lively dogs, with active and friendly dispositions. Whatever their size, they can make compentent guard dogs.

POODLE POINTER
(Pudel Pointer)
In Germany at the end of the last century, it was decided to cross Poodles with Pointers to produce a breed of dog

that combined the Pointer's working skills with the Poodle's intelligence and retrieving ability in the water. The result was the Poodle Pointer.

These dogs more closely resemble the German Wire-haired Pointer than they do Poodles, and are brownish in color. Their strength and working abilities have won them much support in the United States, but the breed is not currently represented in Britain. Only the Poodle Pointers that have proved themselves in field trials are actually given championship status in Germany, where they are popular game dogs.

PORCELAINE
The elegant appearance of these French hounds may have been the inspiration for their name. They are lighter than other hounds, with the relatively thin legs of racing Greyhounds. Their long, pendulous and folded ears reveal their ancient lineage. The breed was originally kept for hunting hares and smaller types of deer.

The Porcelaine has remained a pure breed for centuries, and is predominantly white offset against orange markings, which are often circular in shape. Like many other French hounds, they remain confined to their native country.

PORTUGUESE CATTLE
DOG (Cao de Castro Laboreiro)
A breed that has been developed in the cattle areas in Portugal, the Portuguese Cattle Dog is solid and heavy. Descended from various native dogs of that region, they are dark in color, usually greyish, with a short, water-resistant coat. Portuguese Cattle Dogs do not readily accept strangers, and so make alert guard dogs. As the breed is now being exhibited more frequently and a standard has been prepared, numbers may well begin to increase.

PORTUGUESE SHEEPDOG
(Cao da Serra de Aires)
These dogs are similar to Bearded Collies, but they are smaller and lack the 'beard' of the collie. Portuguese Sheepdogs were bred from local dogs, for the purpose their name suggests, and color is therefore a relatively insignificant feature. They are hardy, with a long, slightly wavy, water-repellant coat. The hair shows no cording, as occurs in the Hungarian Sheepdog, which might possibly share a common ancestry. The Portuguese Sheepdog is not seen outside its native country.

PORTUGUESE SHEPHERD
DOG (Cao Rafeiro do Alentejo)
The ancestors of this large breed of

herding dog were of mastiff stock. Portuguese Shepherd Dogs originated in the Alentejo province, to the south of Lisbon. They were guard dogs as well as sheepdogs, being extremely alert. The short, thick coat reflects the breed's outdoor existence, and is a combination of dark or black areas with white patches. The Portuguese Shepherd Dog, which can be aggressive, is not kept for show purposes at present.

PORTUGUESE
WATER DOG (Cao de Agua)
Although the origins of this breed have been lost, it is almost certainly related to the Old Water Dog which was once common in Europe. Portuguese Water Dogs were known in Britain almost 400 years ago. This is confirmed by a sixteenth-century portrait of a Portuguese Water Dog called Bungy, which belonged to Sir John Harrington. This painting is believed to be the oldest surviving English pet portrait. Today, these dogs accompany Portuguese fishermen on the Algarve coast, acting as retrievers; on land they guard property.

Numbers had seriously declined at the turn of the century, but the breed has since undergone a revival in popularity and is now usually represented at the larger Portuguese shows. The working nature of the breed has not been lost, however, and it will not adapt to a truly domestic existence.

Portuguese Water Dog

PUG
Although many toy breeds descend from terrier or spaniel stock, the Pug is of mastiff origin. Dogs of this type were known in the Orient as long ago as 400 BC. They spread from China and Tibet to Japan and thence to Europe, where they became great favorites in royal circles. William of Orange adopted the breed as the official dog of the House of Orange; it is said that a Pug warned him of the approaching Spanish army, saving his life. He introduced the Pug to England, when he became king. Later, Josephine

Pug

acquired a Pug called Fortune, which was supposed to have nipped her husband Napoleon on their wedding night. The term 'pug' was probably first used during the early eighteenth century when marmoset monkeys were fashionable as pets, since monkeys were popularly known as 'pugs' and the dogs bore an uncanny resemblance to them.

The popular black form is thought to have originated in Japan and was introduced to England by Lady Brassey, who brought some back from a world cruise in 1877. The Pug has changed little in appearance since the turn of the century, and, although the popularity of the breed has declined somewhat from its peak, it remains one of the most popular toy dogs. The short coat needs relatively little attention, while the friendly temperament of the Pug makes it an ideal family pet. Care should be taken to prevent any injury to the prominent eyes and their compacted noses may cause a degree of snuffling when they age.

PUMI

This breed dates back to the seventeenth century, when the Puli, which was native to Hungary, was crossed with droving dogs introduced from both Germany and France. The resulting Pumi was, however, only recognized as a distinct breed at the beginning of the present century. It has a long, slightly corded coat reflecting the contribution of the Puli, while its highly active nature and raised ears are a reflection of the European component in its bloodline.

Pumi

They are small, yet quite fearless, even when dealing with the most difficult cattle. The Pumi is noisy, and possesses some hunting skills, essentially those of a scent dog. It will never hesitate to kill vermin and may even attack larger creatures if provoked. Self-colored dogs are only permitted for show, with grey being most common.

Pyrenean Mountain Dog

PYRENEAN MASTIFF
(Mastin de los Pirineos)
Both the Pyrenean Mastiff and the Pyrenean Mountain Dog originated from the Tibetan Mastiff. The Pyrenean Mastiff is now slightly smaller than its near relative, but is still bulky in shape. It was initially developed to tackle dangerous predators in the mountains, and to herd stock. Despite their size, these dogs are easy to train, loyal and intelligent.

PYRENEAN MOUNTAIN DOG
The Pyrenean Mountain Dog, descended from mastiffs, was originally kept for guarding sheep, especially against attacks by wolves. Their thick, heavy coats provided protection in combat, and they were often provided with spiked iron collars as further defense. The breed contributed to the development of the Newfoundland breed in North America. With the decline in the number of wolves in Europe, however, the future of the Pyrenean Mountain Dog was seriously in doubt until the turn of the century when Herr Dretzen and other breeders obtained sufficient stock to set up a breeding program. Both the size and the correspondingly large appetite that these dogs have has prevented them from becoming established in Britain when they were introduced.

The breed was first recognized by the AKC in 1933, and by the Kennel Club 11 years later. Since that time, the breed has become more popular. Its aggressive instincts have been very carefully eradicated over successive generations and the breed is now generally quite trustworthy. The double dew claws on the hindlegs still remain an important characteristic and must not be removed if the dog is to be shown.

These dogs look very impressive in the show ring, partly because of their size. They have retained the powerful physique that enabled them to pull laden sledges in the snowy winters of the Pyrenean mountains, and they are also ideal guard dogs, in view of their bulk and fierce bark. Pyrenean Mountain Dogs do best in spacious surroundings.

PYRENEAN SHEEPDOG
(Berger des Pyrénées)
A breed kept for herding in the Pyrenees, these sheepdogs have never achieved the wider following of the Pyrenean Mountain Dog. They are still kept essentially as working dogs and both long- and short-coated varieties are bred; at least five separate types are recognized. The Pyrenean Sheepdog is rather reminiscent of a small Collie. They are hardy and industrious, but do not accept strangers readily.

R

RAMPUR HOUND

The Rampur Hound originated in north-west India, where it was kept for pursuing jackals. It is a big, rather inelegant hound, greyish or black in color, with yellow eyes and a roman nose. This breed was first seen in Britain during the early years of the present century, but never attracted much support, probably because of its doubtful temperament.

RASTREADOR BRASILEIRO

Various breeds, including the German Shepherd Dog and the Foxhound, were crossed to produce a dog capable of hunting jaguars, one of the bigger South American wild cats. The Rastreador Brasileiro still resembles the Foxhound in appearance, and is reputed to have a strong and courageous nature.

RHODESIAN RIDGEBACK
(African Lion Hound)

Named after the distinctive ridge of fur running along its back, the Rhodesian Ridgeback is the traditional breed of southern Africa. Hottentots kept the ancestors of the breed and these dogs were subsequently crossed with dogs brought from Europe. European settlers required a tough dog, for hunting and guarding, which could survive climatic extremes, scarcity of water and prove resistant to the ticks, endemic in the

Rhodesian Ridgeback

Rottweiler

region. The Boers were largely responsible for developing the Ridgeback to meet these demands. The first standard, established for the breed in Rhodesia in 1922, has changed little as Ridgebacks became popular around the world.

Rhodesian Ridgebacks are easy dogs to control and prove exceptionally loyal, but will not tolerate trespassers. Their alternative name, 'Lion Hound', derives from the period when they were used to hunt these big cats. While not physically capable of overpowering a lion, the Ridgeback would chase and harry its quarry until it came within the range of a hunter. The breed will also tackle smaller game, taking it off balance by knocking the animal over.

ROTTWEILER

Dogs kept for droving as long ago as Roman times may have been ancestors of the Rottweiler, a breed which originated in Rottweil, southern Germany where it was first known as the Rottweiler Metzgerhund. These dogs were responsible for driving cattle to market and guarding them *en route*. A sharp decline in the numbers of the breed took place in the latter part of the last century due to changes in agriculture.

The Rottweiler and Leonberger Club was founded in 1901, and a standard was established for the breed. When the

Rottweiler was adopted for police work, numbers increased rapidly again. Rottweilers were introduced to Britain in 1936; the year after they were recognized by the AKC. The breed has recently attracted considerable interest in Scandinavia, where its working ability is displayed in competitive trials.

The Rottweiler has proved a stout, courageous dog, and makes a very reliable guard. While the breed had a reputation for being rather temperamental in the past, this trait has been largely overcome. These dogs make devoted and loyal companions.

ROUGH COLLIE

The breed was originally developed in Scotland and northern parts of England, for work with sheep and first came to prominence when Queen Victoria obtained stock for her kennels at Balmoral. The Rough Collie has remained popular ever since. There has been considerable divergence between the working and exhibition Rough Collie. The exhibition dog has a longer head than its working counterpart, and a longer coat. The ears are considered an important feature of a good exhibition dog. They are small and partially erect, with the top third bending forward, back down toward the head. They should also not be set too close together.

Rough-haired Vizsla

Rough Collie

These dogs are strong-willed in some cases. They retain their affinity with open spaces and require plenty of exercise. Their coats need regular attention. Rough Collies have been bred in a wide range of colors, which has helped to ensure their popularity. Tricolored, sable and white, or blue merle are the recognized exhibition colors. In the latter case, one or both eyes are often bluish, or have traces of blue. A pure white form of the breed is also recognized by the AKC.

ROUGH-HAIRED VIZSLA
(Drótszörii Magyar Vizsla)
Rough-coated German Pointers crossed with the traditional form of the Vizsla have given rise to this rough-haired variety, whose development began during the 1930s. The major flaw of the Vizsla as a working dog was considered to be its fine coat, which restricted its performance in the field. The Rough-haired Vizsla has all the attributes of the Vizsla, as well as the ability to work under freezing conditions or in water for long periods. The outer coat can be as long as 2in (5cm), with a thick undercoat, while an extra length of hair around the face is preferred.

RUMANIAN SHEEPDOG
A native breed which has decreased in numbers during recent years, the Rumanian Sheepdog acts both as a herder and guard. It is well adapted to these tasks, as it is powerful and heavy, with a withdrawn, rather suspicious nature. The coat is normally brown, often augmented with white markings. New blood, contributed by other herding breeds such as the German Shepherd Dog, has been introduced and a more recognizable type has resulted.

RUSSIAN HOUND
After the Russian Revolution, many of the older Russian breeds of hound were lost. The Russian Hound resembles the Estonian Hound but is larger, and red or brown with white markings, rather than black. They are not pack hounds, but normally hunt alone; foxes, hares and even badgers are their quarry.

S

SABUESO (Espanol de Monte)
Kept largely in Spain, essentially for hunting, the ancestry of the Sabueso can be traced back to the old Celtic Hound. They are hunted in packs, and also used for tracking. They are often kept as police dogs, although they have a justified reputation for being particularly difficult to train because of their very strong independent streak. The smaller variety is most common and may often been seen exhibited at some of the larger Spanish shows. The Sabueso is a short-coated breed, which is generally black, or orange and white in color.

ST BERNARD

The St Bernard occupies a special place in human affection. Strong, courageous and good at tracking, this breed has been credited with the rescue of many people who have been caught out in snow storms. According to legend, small kegs filled with brandy would be attached to the dogs' collars, for reviving weary travelers. How true these stories are, is difficult to say, but dogs of this type were certainly kept at the Hospice of St Bernard in the Swiss Alps as long ago as the seventeenth century.

The breed was almost lost, however, and only survived with the introduction of new blood in the 1830s, probably from the Newfoundland. This resulted in a long-haired variety. Originally it was thought that such dogs might be better suited to the harsh Swiss winters, but the ice and snow actually froze on their coats and the monks were forced to give long-haired St Bernards away.

When first shown in Britain in 1866, the breed aroused much interest; in 1887, following the International Congress, a set standard was established. Rough and smooth puppies can still occur in the same litter, and both forms are recognized for show purposes.

St Bernards are huge, heavy dogs — certainly not ideal for every household because of the space they require and their large food intake. They have friendly, affable natures, however, and make good companions. Unfortunately, in the quest to increase their size, the soundness of these dogs was compromised to a certain extent, and hindlimb weakness can still be encountered. St Bernards also have a tendency to dribble uncontrollably, which can be a deterrent for house-proud owners.

ST GERMAIN POINTER
(Braque St Germain)

This breed was developed in France at the start of the nineteenth century, and is thought to have arisen from French gundog stock crossed with pointers, which were becoming fashionable at that time. These dogs originated in St Germain en Laye, and this gave rise to their name.

The St Germain Pointer is taller than its English counterpart, but is short-coated, with a combination of orange and white coloring. Kept essentially for work with large game, the breed is both industrious and quiet, and has a rather reserved nature.

ST HUBERT HOUND

The forerunner of many contemporary breeds, the St Hubert hound is very similar in overall appearance to the

St Bernard

St Germain Pointer

Saluki

Bloodhound. It possesses highly developed tracking skills and is very friendly. These hounds were first bred many centuries ago by the abbots of a monastery in Ard and named after a patron saint of hunting, who was supposed to have joined a religious community in the same area.

SALUKI (Gazelle Hound)

Dogs resembling the Saluki were mummified and buried with pharaohs in tombs along the River Nile, and it is claimed that the breed itself may have been domesticated as long ago as 329 BC. Salukis have certainly been kept by the nomadic tribes of the Middle East for centuries, and are still highly esteemed. They can outrun gazelles, which rank among the fastest of the antelopes, and have also been used successfully against hares, foxes and jackals. These sleek hounds hunt predominantly by sight, although they also possess a keen sense of smell. Formerly, it was not unusual for Salukis

to hunt alongside hawks; the birds harassed the quarry so that the dogs could close in on it.

Salukis were first seen in England in 1840, when they were known as Persian Greyhounds, having been introduced from Persia. The breed began to attract serious interest when the Honourable Florence Amherst imported some Arabian Salukis. Since the breed was distributed over such a wide area, slight differences in appearance had resulted, and these particular dogs were smaller, and possessed less feathering on their ears and legs than those dogs of Persian descent.

In the United States, the breed was recognized in 1927, and has since proved a popular show dog in many other countries. Their graceful appearance, and soft, silky hair, makes the Saluki the epitome of elegance. They remain fast, effective hunters, being raced competitively over hurdles in some countries in pursuit of a mechanical lure, like Greyhounds.

Samoyed

SAMOYED

This breed takes its name from the Samoyed Indians, nomads who herded reindeer in northwestern Siberia. Their dogs both guarded and controlled the movements of the flocks, and were used for transport, working in teams and pulling sleighs. The Samoyed resembles other spitz breeds in appearance, and is now widely seen at many shows.

Samoyeds have been sleigh dogs on expeditions to both poles, and accompanied Roald Amundsen on his successful journey to the South Pole in 1911. The luster of their coats is reminiscent of glistening snow, while the two layers form a dense barrier against intense cold. The Samoyed is not a temperamental breed, and is invariably friendly. They are intelligent, active dogs, and are full of fun, making lively pets.

Schapendoes

SCHAPENDOES

These Dutch herding dogs, kept for working with sheep, have shaggy coats like Bearded Collies, and are about the size of Pulis. The numbers of the breed have declined as the pattern of sheep farming has altered, but the breed club has ensured that it will not disappear. Like most working dogs, the Schapendoes is very intelligent and responds well to training. They make good companions.

SCHILLERSTÖVARE

A number of different breeds of hound from Switzerland, Germany and also Austria contributed to the pedigree of the Schillerstövare. It originated in Sweden, where it was developed by a Mr Schiller, whose aim it was to produce a relatively fast dog that would be at home in the open country. As a result, these hounds more closely resemble the coursing breeds, with their long, slender legs, rather than the more ponderous scent hounds, yet they also possess useful tracking skills. The breed is still kept largely for hunting, and, although much older than the Hamiltonstövare, it has not obtained this breed's degree of popularity in the show ring, nor is it kept outside Scandinavia.

SCHIPPERKE

Confusion surrounds the origins of this breed, which appears, at first sight, to resemble a spitz-type dog. Nevertheless, it is thought to be a miniature form of the black sheepdogs which were kept in Flanders and is believed to share a common ancestry with the Groenendael. The Schipperke became a popular barge dog, acting as both a guard and companion; their name means 'little captain' in Flemish. They are very active, inquisitive dogs, alert to the approach of strangers.

The breed became fashionable at the end of the last century, when Queen Marie Henriette obtained a Schipperke at a Brussels show in 1888. Three years

Schipperke

Miniature Schnauzers

later these dogs were introduced to the United States. Today, the Schipperke is less common, although it is relatively popular in South Africa. The preferred color is black; other solid colors are permitted by the Kennel Club, but not by the AKC. The Schipperke is usually born without a tail, but if one is present, it must be docked if the dog is to be exhibited.

SCHNAUZER

The three Schnauzer forms — Giant, Standard and Miniature — have a common ancestry, which dates back to the fifteenth century, but are now recognized as separate breeds. The Standard was first shown in 1879 under the

Minature and Standard Schnauzer

Miniature Schnauzer

description of Wire-haired Pinscher, but has always been regarded as essentially a working breed in its home country of Germany. Indeed, most of the breed clubs still organize trials for these dogs. The winning dog is the one which finds and destroys the largest number of live rats in a set period. Schnauzers can also be trained as retrievers, and make good guards. This latter talent has been encouraged, as the demand for their herding skills has declined.

The careful selection of smaller dogs from various litters has given rise to the Miniature Schnauzer, which is currently more popular than either of its larger relatives. It is quite likely that the Affenpinscher was also used in the development of this breed, and helped to ensure that its terrier instincts were further reinforced rather than lost. In the United States, the breed is classified in the terrier group, but in Britain, the Miniature Schnauzer is known as a utility breed. They are classed as companions by the FCI. These are good-natured, obedient dogs.

SCHWEIZER LAUFHUND
Related to the traditional French breeds, these Swiss hounds are lighter in body and often smaller in size. A short-legged form is also in existence, while coat length can be either short or long. In color, they are a combination of white with reddish markings.

SCOTTISH TERRIER
(Aberdeen Terrier)
There was much dispute at the end of the last century as to which type of dog should be classified as the Scottish Terrier. At many of the early shows, Dandie Dinmonts and Yorkshire Terriers were entered in these classes. Captain Gordon Murray helped to resolve the controversy by describing in detail the appearance of the genuine Scottish Terrier; early in the 1880s a standard was drawn up and breed clubs were founded.

The breed was first introduced to the United States in 1884, when John Naylor imported a pair of these dogs. He then obtained further stock, and did much to popularize the breed. The 'Scottie' has since become one of the most instantly recognizable breeds, possibly as a result of its use in advertising. It is usually black, but other colors are quite permissible in the show ring. Scottish Terriers have the typical temperaments of dogs of this group and, while a few individuals can be rather sharp-tempered, the majority make great companions and prove loyal guard dogs. They are usually wary of strangers.

Scottish Terriers

SEALYHAM TERRIER

Named after the estate in Wales, where it was first developed by Captain John Edwardes over a period of 40 years, the Sealyham Terrier is descended from a number of other terriers. Dandie Dinmonts, for example, were used to introduce shorter limbs. Courage was considered to be an important feature of the breed: the aim was to produce terriers which possessed sufficient character to tackle foxes and badgers underground.

The Sealyham Terrier was first shown at Haverfordwest, in Wales, in 1903, and the breed was then recognized by the Kennel Club and the AKC in 1911. These terriers are not commonly kept as working dogs today, but retain their working instincts nonetheless. As show dogs, Sealyham Terriers have enjoyed much popularity, invariably doing well. Their coats require careful attention, however, since dead hairs tend to remain in place, rather than being shed. Regular brushing and combing is a necessity in order to remove surplus coat and prevent matting. Some trimming may also be required to ensure that the Sealyham looks its best. In temperament, they are lively, amusing and intelligent dogs.

SHAR-PEI

A recent addition to the British show scene, the Shar-Pei was first imported in 1981 and exhibited at Crufts Dog Show in 1983. The breed is an ancient one, however, and has supposedly been kept

Sealyham Terriers

in southern China for over 2,000 years. Initially a hunting breed, it has itself been a source of food!

Shar-Peis are established in Hong Kong, from whence the original stock probably found its way to the United States. The breed has attracted a strong following among breeders, and nearly 1,500 Shar-Peis have now been registered in the United States. British stock was obtained from the United States. Heather Liggett's first Shar-Pei,

Dandelion, mated with a bitch called Honeysuckle, produced the first Shar-Pei litter in Britain in the September of 1982. The Shar-Pei has since been recognized by the Kennel Club, and the breed will probably increase in popularity over the next few years. The breed is already well established in West Germany.

SHETLAND SHEEPDOG

The bleak and forbidding Shetland Islands off the north coast of Scotland were the original home of these sheepdogs, now widely known as 'Shelties'. Shelties still show a close resemblance to the Rough Collie, from which they are descended, but there are recognizable differences, particularly with regard to the features of the head.

The Shetland Sheepdog remained

Shar-Pei

Shetland Sheepdog

isolated for a long period. The breed was first recognized in 1909 as the Shetland Collie and was then classified by the Kennel Club under its present name in 1914. They are currently one of the most popular members within the Working Group, and prove easy to train, since obedience was instilled into the breed early in its development. Shelties also make vigilant watchdogs and, although suspicious of all strangers, they are devoted to members of their immediate circle. They are graceful, agile dogs. Their long, thick coats offer good protection in bad weather and the hardiness of the breed has not been lost since it was introduced to the mainland. The small size of the Sheltie has helped to ensure its popularity.

SHIH TZU

While these small dogs may well have originated in Tibet, they were introduced to China during the seventeenth century. Their leonine appearance ('Shih Tzu' means 'lion'), had a truly sacred significance for Buddhists, and so they were kept in the vicinity of the Chinese court. The care of these dogs was entrusted to eunuchs, who competed to breed specimens that would attract the eye of the emperor. The best dog would be portrayed by an artist and the eunuch rewarded for his efforts. The breed remained popular with the ruling dynasty throughout the period of the Ming era (1368-1628).

Lady Brownrigg, who was in China during the 1930s, sent some Shih Tzus back to England, where they were joined by others acquired by an army officer. These dogs formed the basis of the breed in Europe in the early 1930s, and,

since that time, the Shih Tzu has attracted many admirers.

As might be expected of a dog bred for companionship over the course of generations, the Shih Tzu will settle extremely well in a domestic environment, where its lively, alert nature will also make it the focus of attention. The breed has also done well in the show ring, and is relatively easy to exhibit, not requiring any elaborate preparation. The coat is naturally quite straight, albeit long, and regular grooming, with a bath before a show, will keep it in peak condition.

Siberian Husky

SIBERIAN HUSKY

Another northern sleigh dog, the Siberian Husky was developed by the Chukchi nomads of northeast Asia. The breed, which remained pure throughout the last century, was noted for its ability to pull heavy loads over huge distances, so stamina was a more important factor than speed.

Although the Malmute was already established in Alaska, the Siberian Husky was introduced there shortly after the turn of the century. In 1910 a team driven by John 'Iron Man' Johnson won the All Alaska Sweepstake Race, a demanding 400-mile (644km) course and their success in this race continued in the following years. More serious work won the breed recognition in the United States in 1925 — a team of Siberian Huskies took some supplies of diptheria anti-toxin across the frozen wastelands of Alaska to save the people in the town of Nome.

The Siberian Husky was recognized by the AKC in 1930 after pioneering work by Leonhard Seppala. In Britain, while not grouped as yet by the Kennel Club, these dogs are being bred in increasing numbers, and races have been organized. Siberian Huskies are very well-proportioned and striking in appearance; they are bold, lively and friendly by nature.

SICILIAN HOUND
(Cirneco dell'Etna)
There is a distinct similarity between the Sicilian Hound and the Pharaoh

Shih Tzu

Hound, which suggests a common link, possibly with one of the coursing breeds from the Mediterranean region. The Sicilian Hound has been kept free from any outcrosses in recent times and is mainly in the care of dedicated breeders. The breed is not common, even on Sicily. These are fast dogs, adept at catching rabbits, their preferred quarry. Sicilian Hounds are predominantly red in color, but there may also be some small white patches on their smooth coats.

SKYE TERRIER

The Skye Terrier, unlike most other terriers, has changed little since the time of Elizabeth I (1533-1603). These terriers are named after the island of Skye, to the northwest of Scotland, where the breed originated. Kept very much as a working breed, their short legs enabled the Skye Terrier to pursue quarry underground, while the thick undercoat and long, harsh top coat combined to offer protection against attack or simply dense undergrowth.

The breed has gone into a decline during recent years, but during the late nineteenth century, it was highly valued in the United States, and competition at shows was extremely fierce. Their coats do not require preparation.

SLOUGHI

Confusion exists over the origins of this coursing breed, with some breeders claiming that it is simply a smooth-coated Saluki which has been crossed with similar dogs. The Sloughi originally appeared in northern Africa, although it may well have been introduced here from Saudi Arabia; if so, this would suggest that the Eastern Greyhound was involved in its ancestry.

The name 'Sloughi' was first used during the Middle Ages when it was applied to the Saluki. Several examples of the Sloughi have been introduced to Europe where the breed is now accepted by the FCI, but the specimens seen in Britain to date have largely been of a poorer type. Sloughis are fast enough to pursue both hare and deer successfully.

SLOVAKIAN HOUND
(Slavensky Kopov)

These hounds are the national breed of Czechoslovakia, where they were originally developed. They share a common ancestry with the Polish Hound, although they are smaller in size. Apart from its tracking skills, the Slovakian Hound is still kept for the pursuit of wild boar, and its popularity in the show ring appears to be on the increase. They are short-coated hounds, and are invariably black and tan in color.

Slovakian Hound

SMALANDSSTÖVARE

Bred to hunt in the dense forests of southern Sweden, the Smalandsstövare is the smallest, and the original, member of the Stövare group of hounds. They are relatively stocky — pace is not an important requirement because of the terrain. The Smallandsstövare usually has a short tail, a feature encouraged by Baron von Essen, who helped develop the breed.

The Smalandsstövare was initially recognized by the Swedish Kennel Club in 1921 and makes an impressive show dog. It is predominantly black in color, with white and tan markings on specific areas. Their smooth coat is naturally glossy; regular brushing will ensure it is kept in top condition.

SMALL MÜNSTERLÄNDER
(Kleiner Münsterländer)

The Small Münsterländer still shows signs of its spaniel ancestry. It was bred extensively in the region of Westphalia, West Germany, by combining French spaniel stock with dogs of the Drentse Patrijshond type. It had a reputation for being a very industrious, utilitarian gundog at the turn of the century, but then faded in popularity and nearly disappeared.

Recognized by the German Kennel Club, the Small Münsterländer is again becoming common, especially in West Germany. It is brown and white, the brown replacing the black coloration of its relative, the Large Münsterländer.

Skye Terrier

Smooth Collie

Smooth Collie

SMOOTH COLLIE

These dogs are identical to the Rough Collies, except that their coats are smooth, rather than rough. Both types were bred simultaneously in Scotland, and it seems unlikely that the smooth-haired characteristic was introduced by crossings with other breeds. Rough and Smooth Collies are presently classified separately, although the latter has never achieved any great degree of support. Their development as show dogs took place almost exclusively in England rather than Scotland, perhaps because this breed was not valued as a sheepdog, despite its obvious intelligence. This factor has clearly affected the breed's popularity in Scotland.

SMOOTH FOX TERRIER

A smooth-coated, white terrier, otherwise reminiscent of the contemporary Fox Terrier, is known from paintings to have been in existence as long ago as 1790. It is a British breed, to which the Bull Terrier and the old Black and Tan Terrier, as well as other breeds such as the Beagle, may have contributed. The Smooth Fox Terrier was first shown in the nineteenth century, about 20 years

before the wire-haired form, but they were also crossed together for a period.

Refinement of the breed has produced an elegant show dog, predominantly white in color. It remains a typically lively terrier, with a friendly disposition and alert nature, qualities which make it invaluable as a watchdog. The Smooth Fox Terrier has never really achieved the popularity of its wire-haired relative, although it has always had a strong following.

Smooth Fox Terrier

SMOOTH-HAIRED DACHSHUND

This form of the Dachshund was first seen outside its native Germany during the 1850s, and immediately attracted attention because of its unconventional appearance. Most breeds are relatively square in outline, whereas the Dachshund is decidedly rectangular.

These dogs were an object of ridicule and xenophobia in Britain during the First World War, when they were often called 'sausage dogs', but, by the 1950s, larger numbers were being bred than ever before. Now, the Smooth-haired Dachshund is one of the most popular members of the group. These dogs live happily in either houses or apartments, and their short glossy coats need the minimum of care. They are still tough hounds, although most are now kept as pets. They make great companions for young and old alike.

A miniature form of the Smooth-haired Dachshund has also been bred, but this form differs more than the Smooth-haired one does from the original type, which was a short, heavy dog. To begin with the miniature hounds were classified in Germany on

Smooth-haired Dachshunds

Soft-coated Wheaten Terriers

the basis of chest measurement, rather than weight, which is how they are distinguished now. Like all other Dachshunds, the miniature form is a confident, playful, dog which retains its hunting instinct.

SMOUSHOUND

The Smoushound resembles the Fox Terrier, both in its appearance and temperament, and is kept in Holland primarily as a working breed. These dogs are dedicated vermin-killers on farms, and also make alert guard dogs. A standard for the breed was drawn up in 1905, and helped to ensure its survival. Particular emphasis is placed on the texture of the coat, which should be rough and hard, and on the longer areas of dark hair, which form the apparent eyebrows, moustache and beard.

SOFT-COATED WHEATEN TERRIER

The early history of the breed is now lost, but it has been kept as a working dog on many small farms in Ireland for at least two centuries. Here they were employed as vermin-killers and guards, and occasionally as drovers and gundogs. Being bred at first exclusively for their working qualities, little attention was paid to type or color.

A breed club was founded in 1934, however, and three years later, the Soft-coated Wheaten Terrier was recognized by the Irish Kennel Club. In Britain, the Kennel Club followed suit in 1943, and the breed was first taken to the United States aboard the freighter *Norman J. Colman* in 1946. After AKC recognition in 1973, the breed has continued to grow in popularity. The distinctive color becomes increasingly evident as a dog matures, and by the age of 18 months, the desired shade of wheaten should be apparent. The texture of the coat must be silky and soft to the touch. In show dogs, it has been agreed after considerable discussion that some trimming is permissible, provided it is not excessive.

SPANISH GREYHOUND
(Galgo Espanol)
These greyhounds are smaller than the traditional form, which they otherwise closely resemble in appearance. It is unclear whether the Spanish Greyhound is actually a separate breed, however. Traces of Pharaoh Hound ancestry are apparent, notably the fawn and white coloration. The Spanish Greyhound is still largely seen only in its native country, where it is kept both for coursing and showing. They are intelligent, and possess a considerable amount of speed and stamina.

SPANISH MASTIFF
(Mastin Espanol)
Big and powerful, the Spanish Mastiff makes a tough, determined guard dog, and will hunt big game. They have also been kept for fighting. Although it is related to the ancient Roman breed, the Molossus, the coat of the Spanish Mastiff is longer and the head more refined in shape.

Spanish Mastiff

The breed was first seen in England as long ago as the latter part of the eighteenth century, but has never become popular. At present, these mastiffs are only seen in Spain. They have been crossed with other breeds, especially the Bulldog, and show a deterioration in type as a result. They were known as Spanish Bulldogs for a period, although their legs are much longer than those of the true Bulldog. The Spanish Mastiff is not a difficult breed to train successfully, and is very courageous.

SPANISH POINTER
(Perdiguero Burgalés)
This form of Pointer is a relatively recent development, although dogs of this type have been known in Spain for over 300 years. Two distinct varieties existed early in its history — one the traditional pointer, the other a tracking dog. Both were quite cumbersome dogs, but their appearance was refined by crossings with the English Pointer.

Spanish Pointers make good family dogs, apart from their working abilities as gundogs. They are still quite large, and have a combination of liver and white coloring. The breed is very popular in Spain, and is often well represented at some of the larger shows, but remains unknown elsewhere.

Spanish Pointer

SPINONE
The appearance of these hunting dogs indicates their French ancestry. The Spinone is an old breed, developed from the Barbet and Griffons, among others. Their rough coats, white with chestnut or orange markings, reveal the Griffon influence, while their large heads and longish ears evidence the contribution of Italian hound stock to the breed.

Kept at first for hunting in both wooded and marshy areas, the Spinone has a quiet, calm personality and often does well in the show ring as a result. The breed is easy to train and is normally seen at most championship shows in Italy, but is not significantly represented outside its native country.

Spinone

Stabyhoun

STABYHOUN
One of the smaller breeds of gundog, the Stabyhoun is of Spanish descent, and may well have arisen from crossings of the Drentse Patrijshond with spaniels of French and German origin. Developed in Friedland in The Netherlands, a flat, agriculture district with many drainage ditches, the Stabyhoun has become a good water dog and a highly valued retriever but has never been common.

STAFFORDSHIRE BULL TERRIER
The origins of this breed are far from illustrious. It was developed primarily as a fighting dog during the early nineteenth century from terriers crossed with Bulldogs, a mixture that produced dogs with tenacity, courage and fierceness. The early members of the breed were distinctly aggressive, with very powerful jaws. Their appearance was of no real concern and, indeed, they gained a reputation for being decidedly ugly.

While the English Bull Terrier was soon recognized by the Kennel Club, the Staffordshire was not considered acceptable because of its fighting traits. When dog fights were outlawed, the breed survived and its aggressive nature was bred out, while its intelligence and affectionate disposition were kept and emphasized. Although occasionally quarrelsome towards other dogs, especially

Staffordshire Bull Terrier

a distinct breed from the Cattle Dog. They share a common ancestry with these dogs, however, and are simply a tailless form that has gradually been selectively developed. The Stumpy-tailed Cattle Dog still closely resembles its better-known relative, but has a squarer outline.

STYRIAN MOUNTAIN HOUND (Peintinger)

The Styrian Mountain Hound takes its name from the province of Styria in Austria, where it was developed at the end of the last century. The Austrian hound, as well as the rough-coated form of the Istrian Hound and certain German breeds, all contributed to its development. The Styrian Mountain Hound has evolved into a hunting breed, at home in the rocky, mountainous terrain of its native area.

These dogs have rough coats and range in color from red to wheaten, with white markings often present on the chest. They have a surprisingly loud baying call when they are in pursuit of quarry, which can be heard for miles around. As a rule they possess quiet and affectionate natures.

Staghounds

other Bull Terriers, the Staffordshire makes a great companion. It was finally accepted by the Kennel Club in 1935. The AKC granted the breed recognition in 1974, and it has now become popular in many countries of the world.

STAGHOUND
The Staghound has effectively been lost as a distinct breed. Staghounds were tall, speedy dogs, reputed to be able to track a specific individual in a herd of deer. One pack, kept at the Royal kennels at Windsor Castle, was dispatched to France early on in the nineteenth century and eventually interbred with local breeds, giving rise to some of the taller French hounds.

STEINBRACKE
There are a number of European breeds of hound kept for hunting hares and other quarry, all of which are fairly similar. The Steinbracke itself has characteristics in common with both the Swedish Stövare and various French breeds. It is kept almost exclusively for hunting in West Germany. It is a valued tracker, and has a good nose and an industrious nature. The coat is short and generally tricolored.

STUMPY-TAILED CATTLE DOG
A few of these dogs can still be seen in Australia, where they are recognized as

Sussex Spaniel

Sussex Spaniels

Swedish Vallhund

SUSSEX SPANIEL

It was at Rosehill Park, in Sussex, England, that these spaniels were bred by a Mr Fuller. The rich golden-liver coat, which is such a distinctive feature of the contemporary Sussex Spaniel, was developed over a number of years. The continuance of the stud after Fuller's death was made possible by his gamekeeper, but, by the 1870s, the breed had seriously declined in numbers. A few breeders persevered, however, especially Phineas Bullock. The Sussex Spaniels had a reputation for being difficult to breed successfully, with bitches producing small litters of weak puppies, a result of excessive in-breeding.

The breed was favored for rough shooting, at a time when game was plentiful. It is a relatively slow worker, but never lacks in determination and has plenty of stamina and a keen nose. These spaniels have very placid natures and make loyal companions. Sussex Spaniels are still fairly scarce compared with other spaniel breeds, but have undergone a slight revival in recent years. Although recognized by the AKC, they have never achieved any great measure of support in the United States.

SWEDISH ELKHOUND
(Jämthund)

Various forms of Elkhound have been bred in Scandinavia. This particular breed, while not nearly as popular as the Norwegian Elkhound, is similar in appearance, but larger. The coat is also greyish, but there are cream markings on the face, close to the jaws. The Swedish Elkhound was recognized in Sweden in 1946, and is now being seen at shows more frequently. It is also kept for its more traditional hunting and guarding roles.

SWEDISH VALLHUND
(Väsgötaspets)

The striking resemblance between this breed and the Welsh Corgis has led to considerable discussion as to whether the two breeds were linked at one time, possibly as a result of the Viking invasions of Britain. The Swedish Vallhund has certainly been kept for many years for herding cattle, catching vermin and as a guard dog.

They were only considered seriously as show dogs in Sweden relatively recently, and were officially recognized there in 1943. The breed is now known in England and has attracted considerable interest. Swedish Vallhunds resemble Corgis in temperament, but are a duller color than the Pembroke breed.

T

TAHL-TAN BEAR DOG

The breed owes its name to the Tahl-Tan Indians of Canada, who kept such dogs for centuries. This tribe made an annual hunting trip in search of bears, and their dogs were trained to act as decoys, diverting the attention of the bear from the Indian hunter, who was then able to get close enough to strike a lethal blow. The bears were then skinned and their fur was sold or traded. When the market for bear skins declined, fewer Tahl-Tan Bear Dogs were kept, but the breed survived and was recognized by the Canadian Kennel Club in 1941.

These dogs are small, alert and nimble. They are black and grey in color, with white markings. The tail is usually thick, carried vertically and ending in a white tip. Tahl-Tan Bear Dogs are not seen outside North America at the present time.

TASY (Mid-Asiatic Greyhound)

An old coursing breed that remains confined to Russia, the Tasy resembles the Greyhound in appearance, but is coarser in build. They are used to pursue various creatures, ranging from hares to wolves, and are quick and powerful. The Tasy has been crossed recently with the Chortaj; a related form, known as the Tajgau, exists but is not recognized as a separate breed.

TENERIFE DOG

Dogs of the Bichon group, taken to Tenerife, gave rise to this breed. The actual relationship between the Tenerife Dog and the Bichon Frise is unclear, but they are certainly closely linked.

TIBETAN MASTIFF

While these dogs may bear a superficial resemblance to other mastiffs, they lack the wrinkled brow and large jowls normally associated with dogs of this type. The Tibetan Mastiff was developed around the foothills of the Himalayas, and acted as a herder and guardian of the stock, but it has also been used for hunting.

Tibetan Mastiffs were seen in Britain during the first half of the nineteenth century; King George IV (1762-1830)

Tibetan Mastiff

owned two. Subsequently a Mr Jamrach obtained a relatively large number, and some were exhibited at various shows, including the Crystal Palace show in London in 1906. This might have given a major impetus to start a bloodline in Britain, but the breed attracted little attention, and died out as a result.

TIBETAN SPANIEL

When these dogs were introduced to Britain in about 1900, they bore a close resemblance to the Pekingese. Emphasis was placed on producing specimens with a distinctive muzzle rather than a flat face in order to establish a separate identity from the Peke. These dogs were sacred in Tibet, where they were known as 'prayer dogs'. They worked the prayer wheels on treadmills, a function which was believed to ensure that the prayers were pushed nearer to their destination.

The Tibetan Breeds Association was founded in 1934, and the Tibetan Spaniel is currently the most popular of

Tibetan Spaniels

Tibetan Spaniel

never developed as a working breed, but kept simply as companions and harbingers of good fortune. Tibetan Terriers are loyal and affectionate by nature, quite at home in relatively confined surroundings. The breed is very hardy, developed to survive in an area where temperatures are extreme.

The Tibetan Terrier is bred in a variety of colors. Their coats are no longer left rough for show purposes, but carefully prepared. Their large feet, which allow them to move freely over rough, rocky terrain, remain an important feature of exhibition dogs. The breed was classified by the AKC in 1973.

TOSA FIGHTING DOG
Descended from mastiff stock, dogs of this type were bred in Japan during the latter half of the last century. Various

Tosa Fighting Dog

the breeds originally developed in that part of the world. They have great characters, being forceful and determined, and are relatively strong for their size. The breed has yet to achieve championship status under AKC rules, but there is growing interest in the Tibetan Spaniel in many countries, including South Africa.

TIBETAN TERRIER
It was considered bad luck to sell these dogs in their native Tibet, and they only changed hands as a gesture of thanks or as a mark of respect. During the 1920s, a British physician, called Doctor Greig, received one in return for her services, and started to develop the breed in India, where she was working at the time. On her return to Britain, she founded the Lamleh Kennels, to which the ancestry of many contemporary Tibetan Terriers can be traced. Largely through her endeavors, the breed was recognized by the Kennel Club in 1937, and Lamleh stock, exported in 1956, provided the basis for the United States bloodlines.

These dogs are not terriers in the usual sense, however, since they show no tendency to go to earth; they were

Tibetan Terriers

Weimaraners

fighting breeds contributed to the bloodline, including the Bull Terrier and Bulldog, as well as the Mastiff itself. The Tosa Fighting Dog has loose folds of skin around the neck, which give some protection against attack, while the eyes and ears are relatively small for the same reason. They are big, powerful dogs and probably still retain their aggressive qualities. The breed is scarce outside Japan.

TRAILHOUND

In the Lake District in England, drag-hunting is a popular pastime. A certain course is established by laying an aniseed trail, and hounds race against each other over the rough terrain. The official organizing body of these events monitors the pedigrees of the dogs involved, which resemble Foxhounds; careful outcrosses have increased their pace and height. The Trailhound remains localized, but proves an active family companion, as it is both intelligent and friendly.

TYROLESE HOUND

Various old European breeds of hound have contributed to the development of the Tyrolese Hound, a breed that resembles the Austrian Hound, but is smaller and differs in color. Concentrated initially in the Tyrol region, these hounds make very good trackers and drive game from coverts. They are tricolored and the coat can vary in texture. Rough-coated dogs have a tail resembling a brush, while smooth- and hard-coated forms are also bred.

VOLPINO

The Volpino is clearly related to the larger spitz breeds, but is smaller. The breed is thought to have originated in Italy and may later have been taken to Germany, possibly contributing to the development of the Pomerian. Volpinos are invariably white in color, and have long outer coats, with a thick layer of fur beneath. They tend to make exceptionally good watchdogs.

WEIMARANER

This breed of German gundog is of relatively recent origin — first produced during the nineteenth century from a combination of various native breeds. It was then known as the Weimar Pointer, after the court that sponsored its development. These dogs were used, at first, to take large quarry such as wolves and wild cats, but developed into a more versatile breed when such game became scarce.

Strict rules governed the breeding of the Weimaraner. Matings could only take place with the consent of the official breed club and any puppies with either physical or temperamental defects were ruthlessly culled. The breed was hard to

acquire, even in Germany, and only when a breeder called Howard Knight was admitted to membership of the breed club, did the Weimaraner become well known in the United States. Weimaraners were introduced to Britain during the 1950s, and have since attracted a strong following.

Weimaraners are now highly valued as hunting dogs and can happily spend the rest of their time in domestic surroundings. Their short, sleek coats are easy to keep in good condition with a hound glove, and are a striking shade of grey. The breed has an obedient and friendly temperament.

WELSH CORGI

The two breeds of Corgi, Pembroke and Cardigan, are named after the old counties of Wales where they were first bred. It is believed that the Pembroke is the older breed, and may date back as far as the twelfth century. The original function of the Corgi was to drive cattle. They were able to move even stubborn animals by darting in quickly and nipping a leg, but were small enough to escape injury.

Corgis remained largely unnoticed

outside Wales until the formation of the Welsh Corgi Club in 1926. At first, no distinction was drawn between the two breeds but, in 1934, the Kennel Club offered separate Challenge Certificates for each variety. While both breeds were often, in the past, haphazardly mated together, there are now several clear, distinguishing features; the Pembroke possesses a shorter body, and straighter, lighter legs. The most obvious differences are seen though, in the ears and tail. The Cardigan has rounded ears and a long tail, whereas the Pembroke has pointed, erect ears and a short tail. In temperament, the Pembroke is generally more excitable and active.

The Pembroke has become the most popular of the two, almost certainly as a result of interest shown in them by the British Royal Family. These Corgis, often seen accompanying The Queen, have achieved a widespread following in countries such as Australia.

Corgis have many attributes, and still possess the tough, hardy natures of their working ancestors. Intelligent, obedient and naturally responsive to training, as well as friendly, they are also very good watchdogs.

Pembroke Corgis

Cardigan Corgi

WELSH SPRINGER SPANIEL

The close relationship between the Welsh Springer and its English relative is immediately obvious when the two breeds are seen together, but the Welsh dog is smaller, with correspondingly shorter ears, and is always a rich red and white in color. The actual development of the breed is a subject of controversy, with some suggesting that it is of recent origin, being bred from the English Springers crossed with Clumber Spaniels. The Welsh Springer was nevertheless recognized as a distinct breed in 1902 and, while still well represented in its native country, its popularity has spread to many countries of the world. The Welsh Springer is a versatile breed, well able to adjust to an extensive climate range, and proves a good water dog, as well as being a reliable retriever on land.

These spaniels have stamina and are used to working hard, but can prove difficult to train for this reason. The breed is being seen with increasing frequency in the show ring, and has become less nervous than it was previously. Welsh Springers are quite easy to prepare for showing. Their coats are relatively soft and any sign of curling is considered a distinct fault.

WELSH TERRIER

These terriers are descended from the Old Black and Tan Wire-haired Terrier, once common in many parts of Britain, and they are the same color. They became established in north Wales during the latter part of the eighteenth century, where they were kept for hunting a variety of game, including otters. Welsh Terriers were shown at Caernarvon in the mid-1880s, sometimes staged as Old English Terriers. A club was founded for the breed in 1885, with Kennel Club recognition following a year later.

Welsh Terriers were then introduced to the United States in 1888, but remained scarce for some number of years. Although never one of the most popular breeds, the Welsh Terrier has achieved a dedicated following. They are obedient dogs, at home in country or town surroundings, and make good pets as well as working dogs. They are less independent than similar breeds. They do not require regular washing prior to shows, unlike some of their paler-colored relatives.

WEST HIGHLAND WHITE TERRIER

Most Scotch terriers originally had localized distributions, and the West Highland White Terrier is no exception.

Welsh Springer Spaniels

Welsh Terrier

West Highland White Terriers

It originated at Poltalloch, in Scotland, where it had been bred for as much as a century by the Malcolm family. Shown initially as Poltalloch Terriers, these agile and courageous dogs were well adapted to battling with foxes in their stony lairs.

'Westies' today have shorter legs than their ancestors but their character has not changed. These terriers are still hardy; they are very alert guards and good house dogs, but must be trained from an early age because they have rather independent natures. They are invariably white in color. The coat has two layers; with an outer layer that is quite long and hard and shows no trace of curling. The appearance of this terrier is best maintained by grooming

WESTPHALIAN DACHSBRACKE

Kept for hunting in a pack, the Westphalian Dachsbracke arose from crossings between Dachshunds and German hounds. The aim was to produce a hunting dog with speed. The Westphalian Dachsbracke is of intermediate height and has a smooth coat. An obedient dog with considerable stamina, the breed is rare outside Germany.

WETTERHOUN

An old breed from Friesland in The Netherlands, the Wetterhoun is undoubtedly related to the old Water Dog, having a curly coat and similar markings. These hounds have a powerful build, and used to be kept for hunting otters, a task which called for a muscular, courageous dog.

Since its traditional role is no longer significant, the Wetterhoun has been adapted into a gundog breed, working in or near water. It is often also kept as a watchdog on farms. These hounds have a reputation for being difficult to train successfully, because of their strong, independent natures. At present, they are

Wetterhoun

largely seen in The Netherlands and Germany, and have decreased in numbers.

WHIPPET

During the first half of the nineteenth century, dog racing became a popular pastime in the industrial cities of northeast England. The Whippet, known colloquially as the 'poor man's racehorse', raced over a straight course of 200yd (183m). Dogs were thrown into the start by their owners. Times of 11½ seconds over this distance were considered exceptional, with bitches often proving to be faster than male dogs. The Whippet is still the fastest breed of dog, able to outpace the Greyhound over a short distance.

The Whippet may have been used for hare coursing, after bull-baiting and similar pursuits were outlawed. The breed was first developed from small Greyhounds and terriers, and both rough- and smooth-coated forms were originally bred. Later, when Italian Greyhound blood was introduced, the breed acquired its elegant appearance.

Whippets were introduced to the United States by emigrant workers from England, and early racing was concentrated around Lowell and Lawrence,

Whippets

breed in the peak of condition. The Wire Fox Terrier cannot be recommended as a breed for the novice, for this reason, but experienced exhibitors often win top awards with these dogs. They are alert, and friendly with their immediate circle, but wary of strangers.

WIRE-HAIRED DACHSHUND

The wire-haired form of the Dachshund was first bred in Germany at the end of the last century, and arose probably from crossings of the short-coated variety with a wire-haired breed such as the Schnauzer. Other breeds, including the Cesky Terrier, were used to reduce the length of the breed's legs without affecting the texture of the coat. These particular Dachshunds were valued for hunting in undergrowth, and their wiry coats afforded a degree of protection against thick scrub.

Wire-haired Dachshund

in Massachusetts, gradually transferring to Baltimore, Maryland. The breed was not recognized by the AKC until 1976, but it has been classified by the Kennel Club since 1891. Whippets are often represented at many shows today, and prove an ideal breed for accustoming young exhibitors to the atmosphere of the show ring. They are extremely good with children, being friendly and clean. Like the Greyhound, Whippets need relatively little exercise, providing they are allowed to gallop around in an open space.

WIRE FOX TERRIER

Although the Wire Fox Terrier shares a common ancestry with the Smooth variety, it is believed that the Black and Tan Wire-haired Terrier played a more significant part in its development. In the early days, it was commonplace for both Wire and Smooth forms to be paired together, in an attempt to improve their respective qualities. In the case of the Wire Fox Terrier, it was hoped to introduce the more distinctive outline and the white coloring of its smooth-coated relative. Now, the two forms are classified separately.

Unfortunately, the coat needs a great deal of skilled attention to keep this

Wire Fox Terrier

Wire-haired Dachshunds

Wire-haired Pointing Griffon

Today, wire-haired Dachshunds have become quite popular, but are still not as common as related breeds on the show scene. The breed has retained its hunting instincts, and has an obstinate side to its character as a result, but generally proves obedient and makes a good pet. A miniature form has been developed, which was recognized by the Kennel Club in 1959. The distinction is made on the basis of weight, rather than the height of a dog.

WIRE-HAIRED POINTING GRIFFON

A Dutch breeder, E. K. Korthals of Haarlem, set out to produce a distinctive breed of dog in 1874, beginning with a grey and brown Griffon bitch called 'Mouche'. A number of other breeds of various coat types were subsequently utilized and, by 1907, the Wire-haired Pointing Griffon had gained recognition as a breed but otherwise did not differ significantly from other hounds in this group. Korthals lived in France for a considerabl period, before he moved to Germany and spread the popularity of the breed on his travels.

The Wire-haired Griffon is a slow but dedicated worker, with a good nose. It is a tough breed, with its hard coat offering good protection in marshy surroundings, and it can also swim if necessary. The breed was exhibited in Britain soon after it was developed, and classes were established by 1888, but it has since died out here. It is still recognized by both the AKC and the FCI.

WORKING SHEEPDOG

These dogs are not a breed in the usual sense, but are grouped by the International Sheepdog Society solely on the basis of their working abilities. They are usually of Collie stock and prove their skills at sheepdog trials, which have become increasingly popular in recent years, possibly as a result of television coverage. The most famous meeting is the Longshaw trials in Britain, which first took place in 1894. Working dogs of this type are not suitable as pets.

Yorkshire Terrier

YORKSHIRE TERRIER

These terriers were bred in Yorkshire, England, during the latter part of the nineteenth century. Much of the early pioneering work was undertaken by local weavers. The breed was shown, initially, as the Broken-haired Scotch Terrier, in 1861, but nine years later it became known as the Yorkshire Terrier. It traces its ancestry back to the old Waterside Terrier, which was common in the area. These terriers were crossed with the Black and Tar Terrier; when Scottish weavers moved to Yorkshire they brought their Clydesdale and Paisley Terriers, which also contributed to the breed's development. Other terriers, such as the Skye, may also have contributed.

By the turn of the century, there was a growing inclination towards smaller Yorkshire Terriers, with long coats. Larger bitches are still preferred for breeding and are mated with smaller dogs in an attempt to overcome their obstetrical difficulties. Puppies can vary greatly in size, however, and the bigger dogs are often sold cheaply as pets.

The Yorkshire Terrier was initially shown in separate classes in the United States in 1878. At first, they were distinguished by their weight. The picturesque custom of tying bows in the Yorkshire Terrier's hair has become an essential part of the management of exhibition dogs since the fine, silky coat can be damaged unless protected in this way. Before a show, the coat is brushed straight, and trails down to the ground. Coloration is also a distinctive feature of the bred. Steely blue hair extends from the occiput (the back of the head), right along to the base of the tail. The remainder of the coat is tan. Puppies are always black and tan, and develop their characteristic coloring in time. While Yorkshire Terriers are often highly pampered, the breed retains its terrier instincts and can hunt vermin, if the opportunity arises.

YUGOSLAVIAN HERDER (Jugoslovenski Ovcarski Pas-Sarplaninas)

Descended from the mastiff stock, the Yugoslavian Herder is a large dog with a longish grey and white coat. Size is considered such an important feature that only specimens over 25in (62.5cm) high can be kept on for breeding purposes. Apart from working as herding dogs, they are also considered to be particularly suitable as guard dogs.

The breed was originally developed in southeast Yugoslavia, but has since spread to other regions of the country. It was first recognized as a breed by the FCI in 1939.

YUGOSLAVIAN HOUND (Paninski Gonic)

These hounds are a traditional, Yugoslavian breed, kept for hunting foxes, hares and similar quarry by scent. They are medium-sized, with a shortish, thick coat, which is predominantly black and tan in color. A small area of white on the chest is permitted. The Yugoslavian Tricolor Hound is almost identical in appearance, and is only distinguishable on the grounds of its coloration. Both types are extremely powerful and fast; they are also very affectionate, and calm when they are not pursuing quarry.

Points of the dog *The diagram* (below) *clearly illustrates the anatomical parts of the dog. For showing purposes it is particularly important that each individual point is up to the 'standard' of the breed. This is basically achieved through good breeding and then care and presentation.*

Posture *A dog must have presence in the show ring. Stance should be corrected and practiced when the dog is young* (right) *so that it becomes comfortable and natural. It is vital that the show dog looks relaxed and happy.*

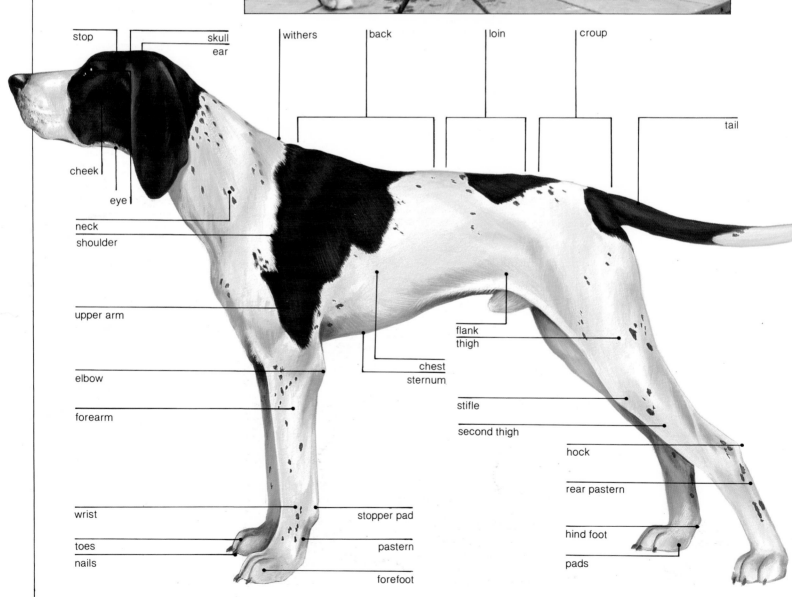

stop

skull

ear

withers

back

loin

croup

tail

cheek

eye

neck

shoulder

upper arm

flank

thigh

chest

sternum

elbow

forearm

stifle

second thigh

hock

rear pastern

wrist

stopper pad

hind foot

toes

pastern

pads

nails

forefoot

SHOWING

There are no short-cuts to successful showing for the intending exhibitor. The first step is to become as familiar as possible with the breed requirements, both in terms of the official standard, and show preparation. Special classes are organized for novice exhibitors; it is also important to practice the training routine as much as possible, so that both dog and handler know what is expected when they enter the show ring for the first time. It is also a good idea to attend a few shows to observe the procedures, and talk to other exhibitors.

Rules of shows can vary considerably from country to country: puppies, for example, are only shown from the age of six months in Britain, three months later than is allowed under Australian regulations. The routine of showing, however, is broadly similar. A schedule listing the various classes and an entry form must be obtained first from the show secretary. After the form is completed with details of the dog's registration, it should be returned with

the necessary payment well in advance of the closing date given in the schedule. Prior details of shows are listed in the various trade papers.

The experienced exhibitor plans well in advance for a show. The amount of preparation — such as grooming and clipping — required depends to some extent on the breed of dog. At pedigree shows, good preparation is no substitute for physical qualities, however, but merely serves to emphasize the finer points of the dog.

Larger shows are often termed 'benched'; the bench is usually wooden staging, with vertical partitions. Dogs are allotted individual cubicles where they are confined when not actually in the show ring. At unbenched events, dogs can be left tied up in cars. Always remember, however, to leave windows open in warm weather. To prevent escapes, it is best not to leave a dog unattended.

It is advisable to take a blanket, a drinking bowl and a clean container of drinking water to the show. While water is always available at shows, it is often more convenient to have one's own supply. On long

Pre-show grooming
Naturally, the amount of preparation for a show depends on the breed of dog. A short-haired dog such as a Beagle will just require brushing, perhaps using a chamois leather to bring out a glossy sheen. Many of the terrier breeds, however, should be trimmed regularly to improve the quality of their coat. The Scottish Terrier (left) *should be groomed daily and have its beard trimmed periodically. Other finishing touches include nail-clipping and tidying up around the ears and tail. It is not always advisable to wash a dog immediately before a show, particularly wire-haired breeds, as this may make the coat soft and fluffy. Grooming and trimming are often sufficient.*

trips, a feeding container and food will also be necessary. Grooming equipment, such as brushes, spray and similar items are also important, while a coat and possibly leg protectors may be needed to prevent the dog's appearance being spoiled by bad weather. At the bigger shows, a benching chain will be required; a nylon show lead will be necessary for any show.

Allow plenty of time for the journey, so that the dog is able to settle down on arrival, rather than having to go straight into the show ring. If a dog detects an atmosphere of anxiety, it may prove difficult to handle. At the show ground, the first step is to acquire the catalog, which gives the times of classes and numbers of entries. Judging takes place in rings, with several operating at once at larger events. Locate the bench space alloted to the dog, and its show ring. The benching chain is used to tie the dog to the metal loop on the staging. Once the

dog is settled, it can be left safely while you locate the show ring. This is generally close to the benching area for the breed concerned.

The ring number card that identifies each entry must be clearly worn by the exhibitor in the ring. The class will be organized by a steward, who will call the exhibitors into line. The judge then decides how the dogs are to be walked; be sure to follow the judge's wishes.

The dogs will be judged to the official breed standard, devised by the national kennel club or council. At American conformation shows, a maximum of five points are awarded for each winner, depending on the number present in the class and other factors. Dogs which score three or more points at a single event have achieved a 'major'. These points are accumulated, and once 15 have been scored, the dog is then awarded the title of Champion. In Britain, the system differs in that Challenge Certificates rather

Cruft's dog show *The most famous event of its kind in the world, the first Cruft's dog show took place in 1886; in its early days it enjoyed the royal patronage of Queen Victoria. Run by the Kennel Club, it has been held at Olympia in London since 1948 (above). This huge exhibition hall is only just large enough to accommodate* *the vast number of entries the event attracts each year. Competition is stiff as dogs are required to have won prizes at other shows, but prestige is high if a medal (right) is won. Dogs are allocated benches during the three-day event and then can be transported in cages (above right).*

than points are awarded, and when a dog achieves three of these certificates, under different judges, it becomes a Champion. The FCI to which many kennel clubs are affiliated, awards its own certificates, the CACIB, to outstanding dogs; these, in turn, can compete for the title of International Champion.

Judges are usually willing to advise novice exhibitors after the official judging is over. Their verdict may not always be encouraging; in which case, it may be necessary to retire the dog from the ring.

Apart from breed shows, the governing canine authority may also organize other events, such as field and obedience trials. These events test the working abilities of various breeds, rather than their physical type, and are judged accordingly.

In the heat of the moment, winning may seem of vital importance, but shows are really about meeting people with similar interests. A class can only have one winner, but everyone should enjoy it.

Top *The Yorkshire Terrier has a very fine, silky coat, which requires a great deal of attention for show purposes. Much shampooing and combing is needed; to prevent the dog's coat from spoiling during the journey to a show, it is often tied up in curl papers or 'crackers'.*
Above *Preparing a setter for a professional show is a lengthy business. Regular grooming with a steel comb and brush is required and a good wash and trim before the big day.*
Left *A local country show is entered and enjoyed with as much enthusiasm as a more professional event. These two terriers, a Border on the left and Lakeland on the right, require very different preparation, however, and it is often worth considering how much time you are prepared to dedicate to grooming.*

OBTAINING A DOG

Dogs are among the most demanding animals to keep in a domestic environment, a fact that is sadly illustrated by the thousands of dogs abandoned by their owners every year. Before undertaking the responsibility of caring for a dog — a commitment that may well last for 15 years — it is essential to consider your own resources and preferences very carefully.

Taking care of any dog is relatively expensive and time-consuming, but breeds vary so widely in size, appearance and temperament that it is possible to select one which will fit your own circumstances. Age and gender are other factors to bear in mind: puppies settle easily and females may be more manageable. Whatever disruption or inconvenience they may cause in the household, however, dogs truly become part of the family.

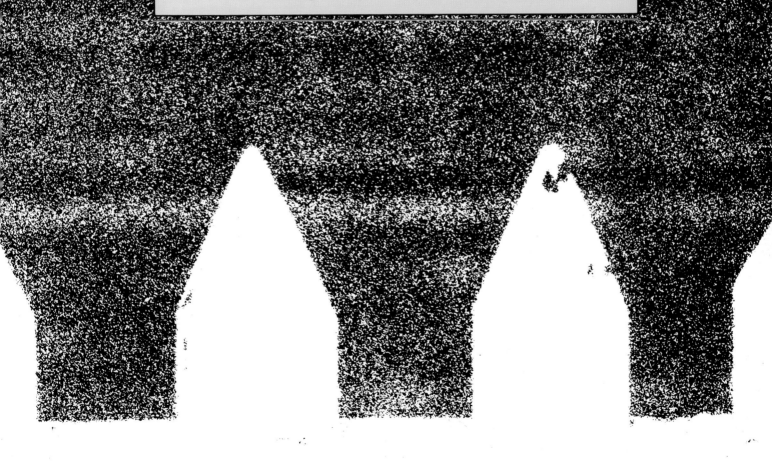

AGE

BASIC CONSIDERATIONS

Age

In the long term, puppies are easier to manage than most older dogs, which may have had a number of different owners. Puppies demand a great deal of patience until they are fully trained, but settle more quickly in new surroundings than adult dogs. The temperament of a puppy is likely to be trustworthy, but an older dog may be nervous, even aggressive. Adult dogs that have spent most of their lives in kennels will not be house-trained, and it often proves extremely difficult to correct this fault, even if they are otherwise obedient. It will also take time for an older dog to respond to a new name or to trust a new owner.

Breed

Breeds of dog vary considerably in appearance, size and even, to a certain extent, in temperament. The choice of breed involves consideration of a number of factors, ranging from issues of personal taste to more practical questions. In general, dogs with long coats or hair which requires constant trimming will need more care than the short-haired breeds, and may create more mess around the home during periods of molting. Larger dogs need more space, more food and usually more exercise; dogs that have been bred for their working characteristics, whatever their size, are less easy to manage in a domestic environment. Some working breeds, such as working sheepdogs, should never be kept as pets. Certain breeds are naturally quieter than others, which can be an important consideration if there are neighbors close by. Chihuahuas, despite their size, can bark quite persistently, often for no apparent reason. But once all these factors have been taken into account, certain breeds will undoubtedly appeal more than others and on this basis the final choice will probably be made.

Because individual breeds have been developed to conform as closely as possible to prescribed standards, specified by the governing canine authority of the country concerned, certain features are actively encouraged, or altered artificially. The tails of certain breeds such as the Boxer are docked shortly after birth and the double dew claws on the hindlegs of others, such as the Briard, are retained.

Unfortunately, although particular features have been emphasized, weaknesses have also been in-

Right Basenjis are unusual dogs in several respects, not least because they do not bark in the normal way. For this reason, they make an unsuitable choice for those who are looking for a guard dog. Their short coats do not need a great deal of grooming, however, and they have lively, affectionate natures.

troduced. Dachshunds, for example, which have relatively elongated bodies, often suffer from intervertebral disk problems. Some of these defects are actually encouraged by the breed standard. The folds of skin on the face of the Bloodhound, for example, can become a site of infection and interfere with vision. The huge head of the Bulldog means that bitches can encounter difficulties giving birth and puppies often have to be removed by Cesarian section. Much effort is currently being expended to modify the breed standards, in cases where these are responsible for such faults.

A significant proportion of abnormalities associated with particular breeds are inherited, however, and are not directly related to show points. One disorder of this type is collie eye anomaly, which causes impaired vision and even blindness in severe cases. The British Veterinary Association and the Kennel Club have initiated a joint scheme to check breeding stock for such defects. Certificates are issued if the dogs show no signs of the condition.

Certain disorders are more commonly encountered in particular breeds. Great Danes can suffer from a narrowing of the vertebral canal in the neck region, causing pressure on the spinal cord and affecting movement. Such dogs become unsteady on their feet and are described as 'wobblers'. Surgery may help, but the treatment is complex and expensive.

Although many individuals will never suffer from such difficulties, potential breed weaknesses must be thoroughly considered before a final choice is made. Even relatively minor flaws can be distressing. The noisy, snuffling breathing of the brachycephalic dogs, such as the Pekingese, which is due to their compressed faces and nasal passages, is one such example. Deafness, typically associated with white Bull Terriers, also requires understanding from the owner.

Many mongrel dogs are also chosen as pets; some people prefer them to pedigrees. It is untrue, however, that mongrels will not succumb to the same illnesses as pedigree dogs, although mongrels are certainly less likely to suffer from some hereditary disorders. Mongrels still need as much care and attention as other dogs. They are much cheaper to acquire than pedigree dogs, but their temperaments are generally less easy to predict unless their ancestry is known. It is important to visit the litter if at all possible.

Choosing a breed *The choice of a breed should be influenced by other factors aside from personal preference. Big dogs, such as Irish Wolfhounds* (far left) *are relatively expensive to feed and require spacious surroundings and plenty of exercise. Toy breeds, such as the Skye Terrier* (above), *by contrast, are cheaper and easier to care for and may even be content with living in an apartment. Certain breeds, such as the Bloodhound* (left), *whose skin folds may encourage infections, have inherited weaknesses.*

Size

Size is a crucial factor when selecting a dog. Although big dogs may deter intruders, they are more expensive to keep and require larger surroundings. It is easier to choose a pedigree breed for size than a mongrel whose parentage may be unknown. While is is usually hard to predict how big a mongrel puppy will grow, the size of the feet should give some guidance. Puppies with large feet are almost certain to grow into biggish dogs. By four months, a dog should be about two-thirds its final height. The size of the bark is not always an adequate reflection of a dog's size, since some small breeds, such as the Beagle, have a powerful voice.

It is particularly important to train large dogs, since they are invariably strong. If they are not controllable, they can prove a liability for older people and children, and a nuisance in the home. The sight hounds, such as the Afghan, can be very difficult to train to return once they are off the lead. Large breeds kept as guard dogs, such as the Doberman, need firm handling from an early age, since they possess determined, sometimes aggressive natures. They are not suitable for a home with young children. The smaller toy dogs are often ideal companions where space is limited, but must be watched with children who can physically hurt or injure them, albeit unintentionally, by rough handling. This in turn can cause the dog to become distrustful, making it liable to bite. As a general rule, the life expectancy of a small breed is longer than that of one of the giant breeds.

Gender

The sex of the dog is another factor which must be considered prior to deciding on a particular individual. Male dogs are supposed to be less demanding than bitches, but this is not always the case. They are certainly more prone to wandering, particularly if there is a bitch on heat in the neighborhood, and may prove harder to train since they possess more dominant natures than bitches. Bitches are preferred as guide dogs for these reasons.

The major drawback of owning a female dog is the two periods of heat which are likely to occur every year through to old age, and the accompanying risk of unwanted puppies. At these times bitches may themselves wander away to look for a mate and are more highly strung. The accompanying discharge from the vagina can cause problems around the home, and the bitch must be closely supervised to prevent uncontrolled mating.

After a period of heat, an additional problem may arise in certain bitches, especially those of the toy breeds, and is known as false or pseudo pregnancy. This state, as its name suggests, resembles a genuine pregnancy to the extent that milk can be produced, although the bitch was never mated during the preceding heat. Pseudo pregnancies can become a persistent complaint in some cases, and affected bitches prove rather temperamental, and

Size *Puppies are very appealing, whichever breed they are, but it should be remembered that even small puppies may grow into big dogs. To assess the future size of a mongrel puppy, look at its feet: if they are relatively big, the dog will probably grow to a fairly large size. In the case of pedigrees, a much more accurate assessment can be made from studying the breed standards. Those puppies will grow into dogs of very different sizes: from the small Jack Russell* (far left) *and the medium-sized Staffordshire Bull Terrier* (below left), *to the huge Great Dane* (left).

possibly even aggressive at such times. Neutering is one option which can be considered under these circumstances, but the cost of this surgery in a bitch is likely to be twice as much as for a dog. There are various ways of controlling the sexual behavior of dogs of both sexes. If, however, the dog is required for showing, a bitch, which could later be used for breeding, should be chosen, rather than a male dog.

SOURCES

Puppies are available from a variety of sources but not all are suitable. Certain pet stores stock mongrel and even pedigree puppies and there are also large suppliers, who advertise a range of breeds in newspapers. Since in neither case are the puppies likely to have been bred on the premises, such sources are usually best avoided. The puppies will almost certainly be stressed, after having been moved from a breeding unit and mixed with other dogs in an environment which may not be ideal. Stress has been shown to be a major predisposing factor to parvovirus infection.

Many people prefer to acquire mongrels from animal welfare organizations. Addresses of these societies can be found in telephone directories, or obtained from a veterinarian. Litters of mongrel puppies are frequently given to these organizations, and make delightful pets. If new homes are not found for these puppies, they often have to be destroyed.

Obtaining an adult dog from this source is more risky, however, especially if the temperament and background of the dog are unknown. No organization will knowingly try to find a home for a vicious dog, but an individual may prove relatively withdrawn and nervous after maltreatment by previous owners. Due allowance must be made for such behavior, especially at first, but, despite being warned beforehand, people still take on such dogs, only to return them a few days later. Ill-treated dogs require considerable patience and may never completely regain their trust in humans. Those closest to them will probably be accepted eventually. Homes with small children are not ideal environments for dogs of this type, because any teasing, particularly with food, can have serious consequences.

Increasing numbers of pedigree dogs are also passing into the care of welfare organizations, often because their owners can no longer afford to keep them as pets. Before allowing pedigree dogs to go to new homes, many societies will want to be assured that the dog will not be used for breeding, and will often retain the dog's pedigree for this reason when a new home is found. Some insist on neutering, and the new owners will probably be interviewed to establish whether they will provide a good permanent home for the dog. Enquiries of this type and even home visits are not unusual, and should not be taken as a personal slight. The society is trying to ensure that the dog has a stable future.

Sources *Direct contact with a reputable breeder is always the best way to obtain a pedigree dog. Most breeders want to find good homes for their puppies and take considerable care to ensure that they are healthy prior to sale* (right). *Dogs that have spent much of their lives outside in kennels rarely adapt very well to domestic environment* (far right). *They will not be housetrained and may be shy and withdrawn.*

Animal welfare organizations are rarely wealthy. Feeding and other expenses mean that costs often run alarmingly high, with no guarantee of income. Whenever accepting a dog from an organization of this type, a donation should always be made to their funds, to help their work to continue.

Greyhounds which have been retired from the track, certainly by the age of five years and often younger if they have not proved fast enough, are sometimes offered as pets. Since these dogs have been kept in kennels for their entire lives, it is not easy to adapt them to a domestic environment. Such dogs will not be housetrained, and other pets such as cats may be at risk until they have settled down satisfactorily. Nevertheless, it can be possible for them to adapt, and various specialist greyhound homing groups now exist to train them for this purpose. Contact with an organization of this type can be made through the nearest track.

When seeking a particular breed of dog, it is strongly recommended to contact a breeder directly and explain one's requirements. The vast majority of breeders are genuine enthusiasts and, although they cannot keep all the dogs they breed, they will have an interest in ensuring their subsequent welfare. There are various means of discovering the addresses of such people, depending partly on the breed required and the purpose for which the dog is intended.

Local newspapers often run advertisements from breeders in the immediate vicinity, but for more unusual breeds, traveling further afield will probably be necessary. Directories listing breeders under breed headings are published in many countries, and revised annually. These may be available in libraries. Specialist papers and periodicals will also provide details of breeders and reports of shows, revealing which bloodlines are winning consistently. Visiting shows is also recommended for those seeking a potential show dog. Veterinarians may also be prepared to pass on addresses of breeders known to them. If these sources prove of no value, then direct contact with the canine governing authority of the country concerned may yield results.

Breeders, if requested, will notify a prospective owner when a litter becomes available. The price paid for a pedigree dog depends to some extent on the breed, the bloodline, and the qualities of the individual dog. Rarity value can often be significant; Shar-Pei puppies, for example, currently fetch about £800 each in Britain, $2,000 in the United States. Although breeding dogs on a small scale is rarely a profitable enterprise, a recognized winning stud will charge high prices for stock. Pedigree and type will be important factors for the intending exhibitor but are unlikely to concern someone seeking a pet dog.

If one of the puppies in a litter has an insignificant fault, such as incorrect coloration or markings, which renders it of little value for show purposes, the breeder will probably be pleased to find a good

Choosing an individual *Aside from health considerations, visiting a litter before choosing a puppy can be very useful for assessing behavioral characteristics. While the breeder will probably be more interested in specific show points — color, type and other physical characteristics — the pet owner will be more concerned about general temperament. Observing the litter at first-hand gives an ideal opportunity to pick an individual that suits your particular requirements. However, while some differences may be noted between different members of a litter, there is more likely to be variation from litter to litter than from puppy to puppy. In general, it is best to avoid the most submissive or nervous puppy and the most aggressive: in later life, these may be unpredictable and difficult to manage. Although a puppy displaying a lively, outgoing temperament may merely reflect the fact that is has been given more attention, it is likely to settle better in a new home, prove more acceptable and more responsive to training.*

home for it, usually at a reduced price. Bargains of this nature must be approached with slight scepticism, however, if the dog has a real deformity, since this could prove a costly source of trouble later. It is well worth enquiring about any examination which the breeding stock may have undergone, for hip dysplasia for example, with a view to minimizing the risk of hereditary or congenital diseases in the puppies. Most breeders will readily volunteer such information.

SELECTING AN INDIVIDUAL

Puppies will not be fully independent and able to go to a new home until they are at least eight weeks old, but breeders are generally happy for litters to be seen beforehand, often around five weeks after birth. The environment where the puppies are being kept is significant. Their surroundings should be relatively clean, and any motions in the pen must be firm, not loose or runny in consistency, which indicates a digestive disturbance. A litter which has been reared close to people, rather than being kept isolated in a kennel, is likely to prove more amenable to human company, and the puppies will settle more quickly in a new home.

Puppies at this age naturally sleep for long periods, and then become very active for short spells. Bearing this in mind, dominant individuals can most easily be spotted at feeding time. These more pugnacious puppies, as well as the most submissive and the smallest, are best avoided, in case these traits become emphasized in later life. The puppies should show no signs of lameness or any deformities of the limbs. The bitch herself may appear slightly thin at this stage, having nourished her offspring for over a month, but this should not be a cause for concern.

Being able to recognize a healthy puppy is particularly important if it is obtained in a pet show where the staff are unlikely to be as knowledgeable as a breeder in this respect. A puppy which appears thin, with its ribs in evidence, is likely to have been undernourished and if it also has a pot belly, it probably has worms. In any case, a closer examination of a puppy should always be carried out, with the owner's permission. The coat is an important indicator of good health and should be shiny and full, unless it is wiry. Signs of fleas, or lice (more common in puppies than adult dogs), indicate a general lack of care.

The skin of a puppy is quite pliable, and should be loose to the touch. It is worth feeling the skin underneath the puppy, in the midline, to see if there is a swelling under the skin, which could indicate an umbilical hernia. This is not usually a serious complaint, although it may require surgical correction later. Herniation elsewhere on the abdomen is less common. The eyes must be clear and bright, while the ears should not show any signs of discharge or smell unpleasant. There should be no hint of lameness when the puppy walks.

Signs of health *Ask the owner's permission to carry out a routine health check before making your final choice* (far left). *Specific points to look for include* (left)*: any discharge or dullness in the eyes (1); an abdominal swelling which might indicate a hernia (2); unpleasant-smelling ears (3). In general, the coat should be clean, shiny and full (unless it is wiry) and there should be no signs of fleas or lice. The puppy should be sleek and well-nourished, without a pot belly, which could be a sign of worms. The puppy should have an easy gait, without any hint of lameness.*

It is best to acquire a puppy when the weather is mild enough for training outside. Dogs should never be obtained before the new owner goes away on holiday. Apart from the disturbing effect on the animal, most kennels will not take puppies, as often they do not settle well away from home. Dogs should never be obtained at Christmas either when the household will probably be in temporary chaos.

A conscientious breeder may well ask prospective owners various questions, to ensure that they appreciate the responsibility of owning a puppy, and will be able to care for it. There is now a trend toward waiting until the puppy is about nine weeks old before moving it to a new environment. The actual phase of social development in puppies is concentrated largely in the 4- to 12-week period after birth. Individuals are at their most impressionable at this time and start to relate to their littermates and other creatures, including humans. Puppies begin to learn the sensation of fear at about eight weeks of age and so moving a puppy at this stage will serve to emphasize the traumatic experience of isolation from its dam and littermates. Research has revealed that if puppies have not experienced human attention by the age of three months, they are likely to be withdrawn, and subsequently prove unresponsive to training. Individuals isolated too soon from other puppies show the reverse effect, being disadvantaged in later life when meeting other dogs, and bitches may even refuse to mate for this reason.

SETTLING IN

Essential equipment

It will be necessary to obtain various items for the dog prior to its arrival. A vast range of pet equipment is now available, but only certain items will be essential at the outset. Feeding and drinking bowls are obviously necessary, and various types are stocked by most pet stores. Plastic generally is not to be recommended, since most bowls made of this material are easily chewed or scratched, and prove difficult to clean thoroughly as a result. Stainless steel containers are relatively expensive, but are much more hygienic, although they can be tipped over quite easily. The traditional glazed earthenware bowl is easy to clean and stable.

A bed is a very important part of the puppy's world and the puppy must be taught to recognize its bed as its own particular territory. In the beginning, the bed need not be expensive or elaborate. A puppy will be quite content with a clean cardboard box, with the front cut away for easy access. The bottom of the box should be lined with newspaper, and a blanket provided on top. As the puppy grows, the box can be simply replaced with another of a larger size. Once the deciduous teeth are lost, and the accompanying chewing phase is passed, a permanent basket can be obtained. A large number of types are currently produced, but it is important to select one for its functional rather than its decorative value. The main criterion must be to ensure that the basket can be easily and thoroughly washed, to prevent fleas.

During recent years, bean bags manufactured for dogs have gained greatly in popularity. Available in a variety of sizes, these are filled with polystyrene beads and, apart from providing somewhere to

Below *Essential equipment for a new dog includes: a cardboard box (1) or dog basket (2); rubber balls (3); a hide chew (4); feeding dishes (5); and drinking dishes (6).*

Above *An outdoor kennel can be a useful investment for dogs that will be spending much of their time outside. It should be constructed on a concrete base, for ease of cleaning, and located in a cool spot. Blankets make suitable bedding material.*
Right *Feeding and drinking bowls are essential equipment. They are marketed in a variety of materials — stainless steel is among the most hygienic.*

1

5

6   2

3   4

sleep, they can also serve as a play area. The outer covering should be removable and washable, and must also be tough enough to withstand any chewing or scratching. The dog can select the most comfortable sleeping position by snuggling down and displacing the beads in the bag. Some designs have fire-retardant properties.

A special pen can also be acquired to restrict the puppy's domain. These come in the form of wire mesh panels, which clip together as required and will store flat when not in use; they can be fitted into the back of a car to make a traveling cage.

A thin collar should be obtained, so that the puppy can get used to wearing one around the home, although it should not be taken out on a lead until after its course of vaccinations is completed. Most collars are still made of leather. Nylon collars are also popular and are easily washed, and strong without causing damage to the fur. Plastic collars are not as durable as nylon or leather. Some collars cannot be altered in size, whereas others are adjustable and prove most useful for a growing dog. Broader collars are recommended for bigger dogs.

An identity medallion of some kind is a legal requirement in various countries, including Britain and the United States. These should give the dog's home address, and a telephone number if possible. Depending on the country concerned, other information, such as a license number and details of rabies vaccination, may also be necessary. Plastic capsules, containing this information written on a piece of paper in indelible ink, are an alternative. Some dogs, such as racing greyhounds, are tattooed with a number on the inside of the ear but this is not a usual method of identification.

Many dog toys are now available, but the least elaborate are generally preferable. Care must always be taken to avoid those which could be chewed into sharp fragments or inadvertently swallowed. Small balls are included in the latter category, and may even prove lethal. A large, lightweight plastic football is better. Various hide chews also provide good, safe exercise.

The new puppy

It is always better to collect the puppy during the morning if possible, so that it will have time to settle in its new surroundings before nightfall. If you are driving, take a secure container to put the puppy in; otherwise, the puppy can be allowed to travel on a passenger's lap, which should be protected with an old blanket. The unfamiliar sensations of the journey may make a young dog sick, and paper toweling may be needed for clearing up.

If the puppy is pure-bred, it will be necessary to obtain its pedigree from the vendor. This document gives details of all direct ancestors extending back over at least four generations. The prefix 'Ch.' indicates that a particular dog was recognized as a champion, and suggests that the puppy itself may do well in the show ring eventually. Registration papers or the correct form which must be sent to the registration body to show transfer of ownership, will also be needed.

A vaccination certificate, giving details of past vaccinations is an important document for future reference, and this applies to any dog, not just a pedigree puppy. A two-month-old dog will probably have received its first set of vaccinations; another set will be required about a month later to complete the protection and enable the dog to be taken out safely. A diet sheet must also be obtained from the breeder, to show what the puppy has been eating and the frequency of feeding. For the first week, it is

Left *Puppies, particularly at teething time, will investigate their immediate surroundings by chewing and licking. Since some household items can prove toxic and others may be dangerous if gnawed into pieces, this practice should be discouraged. Toys should be sufficiently big and sturdy not to be accidentally swallowed.*

Settling in *The critical period for socialization is between five and 12 weeks of age; after this time puppies will have difficulty in accepting human company. To accustom a puppy to being around people it is a good idea to visit and play with it while it is still with the rest of the litter* (far left). *A single pupppy will pine for a while after it has been moved to a new home* (left); *two puppies are less likely to* (below).

While contact with other animals must not be forced by the owner, some surprising alliances can be formed if circumstances are right (left). *Without a period of adjustment, however, the traditional enmities may break out, resulting in real clashes* (above).

sensible to follow this closely, to minimize the risk of digestive disturbances. Changes in feeding should only be introduced gradually, over a period of time.

After the journey, the puppy will want to relieve itself, and should be encouraged, right from the start, to do this outside, supervised so that it cannot run away. If the weather is bad, the puppy should be taught to use a dirt box filled with cat litter, placed on newspaper in the house, or in a suitable adjoining outbuilding.

The puppy will take time to adjust to its new environment and may not eat heartily at first. When food is offered, the puppy should be left alone with its bowl for about a quarter of an hour. Any food remaining after this period should be removed, but a fresh supply of water must always be available. After a brief period of play, the young dog can be placed in its bed and will probably go to sleep.

It is likely that the puppy will be restless on its first night, after being separated from its fellows and finding itself in strange surroundings. Some owners put the basket in their bedrooms, with a pen around it, for perhaps a fortnight until the puppy feels more secure. Left on its own, the young dog is almost certain to cry and howl for a while, but must not be punished, particularly as every effort should be made to forge a strong bond between puppy and owner during these early days.

Above *The new puppy should be transported home in some type of carrier, preferably a special carrying cage designed for the purpose* (right). *If this is not available, a sturdy box will do.*

The older dog
How well an older dog settles in the household will depend very much on its previous history. If it has been trained, and is used to living in a home, then it will probably adapt quite quickly, unlike one that has spent its life in kennels. If its vaccinations are up to date, there will be not need to restrict an adult dog to the garden, and it can be taken out on a lead for exercise. This is particularly useful if two dogs have to be introduced, since their first meeting can take place on neutral territory, such as a park.

Introductions to other pets
Two puppies of similar age kept together are often less of a problem than a single individual, since they will provide company for each other and will play together. Dogs, being pack animals, are very social creatures and for this reason, should not be left on their own for long periods every day. Under certain circumstances, however, a dog already established in the household may well resent a newcomer, unless the introduction is carefully controlled.

Trouble is particularly likely to arise if the new dog is younger and receives much more attention. The older individual, who would normally be the

dominant member of the pair, is likely to feel that its position is being challenged. It is important to ensure that the established dog receives equal, and preferably more attention than the puppy, to reinforce its dominance. The situation may subtly alter over a period of years, however, as the younger dog assumes the dominant role from its aging companion. Two bitches normally live most contentedly together, particularly if they have been brought up together. Feeding times are always especially likely to lead to disagreements, and the dogs should be fed separately, well out of reach of each other, and preferably in separate rooms.

In the case of older dogs, careful supervision will be required to prevent them fighting to decide an order of dominance. Once again, the established dog must receive adequate attention from the owner, to emphasize its dominant position and lessen the risk of subsequent disputes.

With other pets, like cats, a similar method of introduction should prevent difficulties arising, although the cat may resent the puppy for a few days and disappear for longer periods than usual. It will take several weeks for dog and cat to accept each other fully but they may then become devoted companions.

Left *When there is already an established dog at home, the introduction of a new puppy must be carefully controlled, particularly once the younger dog has grown more assertive. Fighting is particularly likely to break out over food. Dogs should always be given their food in separate rooms, out of each other's way. Introduce two adult dogs on neutral territory, such as a local park, rather than on home ground, where the newcomer is more likely to be viewed as a challenger.*

DAILY CARE

Pets are not able to look after themselves and dogs are no exception; they are considerably more dependent on their owners than cats. A balanced diet and regular exercise are really the essence of daily care. Although breeds vary in the amount of exercise they require, all dogs need supervised walks or runs outside every day; similarly, all dogs appreciate an organized feeding routine.

For dogs to adapt fully to domestic conditions, training is very important. Every dog must be housetrained, obedient and easy to manage on a lead. Regular grooming is also essential and will help to keep both the dog and the home presentable.

FEEDING

Nutritional requirements

Dogs, because of their dentition and relatively big stomachs, can consume large amounts of food in a short space of time. They are essentially carnivorous in their feeding habits, yet they are not obligate carnivores like cats. They show a preference for meat, but will also eat a wide variety of other foods. While dogs are easier to feed for this reason, they are also more like to suffer from obesity than cats. In the wild, the dog's food intake would consist largely of proteins and fats from the muscles and viscera of its prey. Carbohydrates such as starch and sugar are not present in any significant amounts in body tissues.

Proteins, composed of amino acid residues, are necessary both for growth and for healing damaged tissue, and can also be converted to energy if necessary. Fats protect vital organs such as the kidneys and provide a concentrated source of energy. Both fats and proteins are vital to cells, forming an integral part of cell membranes, as well as being necessary for many cellular functions. On the other hand, excess carbohydrate, surplus to the body's immediate energy needs, can only be converted to fat. A relatively small amount is stored, mainly as glycogen in the liver, to be used as a quick source of energy if required. Maintaining the correct balance of these three basic classes of foodstuffs is of considerable importance in keeping a dog both healthy and well nourished.

Vitamins and minerals must also be present in the diet, in relatively minute quantities. Vitamin D is especially important, since it is ultimately responsible for sound bone development; the minerals calcium and phosphorus are also significant in this respect. Vitamin A is one of the fat-soluble group of vitamins that are stored in the liver. It helps to ensure good eyesight and prevent infections. Vitamin C, important for preventing infections, is less vital in a dog's diet, since most can manufacture this vitamin in their bodies. About one dog in every 1,000 is unable to carry out this process, however, and will require dietary supplementation: 100mg of ascorbic acid for every 55lb (25kg) of body weight. Vitamin C is a relatively unstable compound, and can deteriorate quite rapidly: it should not be stored for long periods before use.

A small amount of roughage, such as bran, is also beneficial. Although indigestible, and thus not of nutritional value, it provides bulk and assists the movement of food through the intestinal tract. To provide themselves with roughage might be why dogs consume grass. Grass may also act as an emetic; young puppies suffering from roundworms often eat grass and then vomit both grass and worms in an apparent attempt to purge themselves. In view of such behavior, it is unwise to treat areas of rough grass with chemicals: these areas, rather than lawns, are favored for this purpose.

RECOMMENDED NUTRIENT CONTENT OF DOG FOODS

NUTRIENT	CANNED %	SEMI-MOIST %	DRY %
Dry matter	25.00	75.00	90.0
Water	75.00	25.00	10.0
Protein	12.00	19.95	24.0
Fat	9.725	6.75	8.0
Linoleic Acid	0.275	0.825	1.0
Fiber	1.00	3.00	3.6

Types of food

Prepared food The manufacture of dog food is a major industry today and much study and research has been carried out to ensure that such products conform to dogs' nutritional requirements. Canned foods are still the most widespread and palatable of all the commercial dog foods, and most of these offer a complete, balanced diet. The label should always be checked nonetheless — a few brands contain only meat, with no added vitamins or minerals.

Canned foods contain a high level of water, sometimes more than 80 percent. If water content is high, the dog will need to eat more to satisfy its nutritional requirements. The price of canned dog foods can vary widely from brand to brand, usually reflecting differences in the amount of cereal included. Cheaper brands contain more carbohydrate in this form, whereas more expensive canned foods contain actual chunks of meat in a runny gravy. Manufacturers often suggest supplementing canned food with a biscuit meal, especially if the brand contains a relatively high proportion of meat. This helps to reduce the overall cost, as the biscuit is used to provide the energy content of the diet, while the meat contributes protein. It is important to feed the biscuit meal according to the instructions on the pack, since an excessive intake will lead to obesity.

Manufacturers have recently started to produce more specialized foods. Many ranges now include canned foods designed for puppies, which contain a relatively high level of protein to assist growth. Small cans are also marked for fussy eaters or delicate dogs, notably some toy breeds. Canned cat food can be fed to dogs (but not vice-versa, since cats require the amino acid taurine in their food) and is generally higher in protein, which may tempt fastidious eaters.

All canned foods can be kept, unopened, for over a year. Once opened, however, even if stored in a refrigerator as recommended, they will not stay fresh for more than a few days.

Semi-moist dog foods are often prepared to resemble raw chunks of meat but in fact contain relatively little meat. Soya bean meal is a common ingredient, providing part of the protein value of the foodstuff. The water content of semi-moist foods may be as little as 25 percent; various chemicals are added to prevent the food from drying out or spoiling. Sucrose is often added for these reasons, and to improve the palatability of the food. These products are sold in sealed foil packets and, unlike canned foods, do not need to be refrigerated, but must be used within three months or so.

Dried dog foods are marketed in various forms, such as pellets, flakes, meal and expanded chunks. Heat is used in the manufacturing process, and serves to make the starch component more digestible, but also destroys certain vitamins, particularly Vitamin A and members of the Vitamin B group. To compensate for this loss, vitamins are added in proportionately larger amounts at the start of the process, or included in the fat that is sprayed onto the foodstuff after the water has been removed to improve its palatability. Dried dog foods do contain some water, normally about 10 percent, and can be stored without refrigeration. They can also be kept for long periods without losing their vitamin content, but most manufacturers specify an expiry date on the packaging.

There are certain advantages in feeding dry food. Relatively little in terms of weight is required, and dry food is also supposed to reduce the risk of accumulations of tartar on the teeth. Manufacturers usually recommend soaking dry food when first introducing it to the diet, and there is no reason for not continuing this preparation, apart from the fact that any remaining uneaten at the end of the day must be discarded, or it will turn moldy, particularly in damp weather. If dried food is not soaked, the dog will need to drink more water to compensate.

Various meat products are also available, sold in blocks or tubes in many pet stores. Most need to be kept refrigerated, especially once opened, and contain no additional vitamins or minerals, or even cereal in some cases. These foods do not provide a balanced diet on their own and must be mixed with biscuit meal to ensure that vital nutrients will not be deficient.

Fresh foods Although there is no need to keep changing the diet if commercially prepared foods are given, variety is important if the diet consists of fresh food. It is not adequate to feed just meat on its own, since this is deficient in various vitamins such as A, D and E, as well as minerals such as iodine. In addition, the ratio between calcium and phosphorus, which should be of the order of 1.2 to 1, is seriously imbalanced in meat, with the tissues containing excessive amounts of phosphorus. This will cause skeletal abnormalities, particularly in young dogs. In severe cases, bones may fracture easily, and the dog will be reluctant to walk.

Apart from meat from body tissues, internal organs or offal, can also be fed. Heart, kidneys, 'melts' (spleens), 'lights' (lungs), and tripe, which comes from the stomachs of herbivores, are all sold cheaply by butchers for pet food. In kennels, tripe is sometimes fed raw, not dressed as it would be for human consumption, and although favored by many dogs, it smells extremely unpleasant in this state.

While there is certainly no truth in the story that raw meat makes dogs aggressive, various parasites and infections can be transmitted by this means; to kill these, it is always advisable to cook meat before feeding it to the dog. The meat should be cooked for about 20 minutes; any longer and excessive loss of vitamins will occur. Allow the meat to cool to prevent burning the dog's mouth, but slightly warm food is more palatable than cold, and may tempt a dog with a poor appetite to start eating again. It is often easier to cook a relatively large quantity of fresh food at one time — perhaps a week's supply — and then freeze some for later use. All frozen food must be completely thawed before feeding to the dog to prevent digestive disturbances.

Fresh food must be mixed with a biscuit meal supplemented by vitamins and minerals. Approximately equal quantities of fresh food and biscuit should provide an adequate balance. Some dogs are allergic to gluten, which is a component of protein present in flour, and cannot be fed biscuits or meal. Potatoes which have been well boiled, or boiled rice, can be given as alternatives, with a vitamin and mineral supplement.

Vegetables are of no direct benefit to dogs, since they are relatively indigestible; some, such as boiled cabbage, tend to precipitate flatulence. Their only value lies in the fact that they add bulk to the diet without significantly increasing the calorific value of the meal, and thus help satisfy the appetite without causing weight gain. Some dogs like raw carrot, which provides carotene, converted in the body to Vitamin A.

Bread can sometimes be harmful to dogs. Flour used to contain a bleaching agent to emphasize the color of white bread and the chemical used for this purpose, nitrogen trichloride, caused fits in dogs until its effects were realized. The use of this chemical has now been banned in most countries. Both brown and white bread are safe in Britain and the United States.

A practical diet How much you feed a dog and how often will depend on the type, size and age of the dog and on its state of health. Young, pregnant or lactating dogs require more food than normal adults and will probably need to be fed more frequently. Active, working dogs, especially those which spend much of their time outside, such as hunting hounds, need more food than pets. Overweight individuals must be given a modified diet, as will those suffering from specific ailments.

The recommendations given by manufacturers on the labels of canned and prepared foods can be followed with confidence. Most of these guidelines are in the form of a weight or volume of food to weight of dog ratio, specifying, for example that a 15oz (430g) can daily will be adequate for dogs weighing about 30lb (3.6kg). If your dog is a particular breed, it will be easy to establish how much it should weigh by consulting either the breed standard or a reference book. If there is uncertainty

Puppies generally learn fairly quickly to eat from a plate or bowl (top), typically picking up this skill from their mothers (above). If they are reluctant to do so at first, hand-feeding — by offering food on a finger — may help. In any case, supervision at mealtimes will help to ensure that each puppy has enough to eat and is not bullied out of its ration by boisterous littermates (right).

Far right All dogs enjoy bones and it is thought that chewing helps to keep their teeth free from tartar deposits. Great care must be taken, however, that no bones which could splinter or lodge in the throat, particularly chicken bones, are within a dog's reach. Big marrow bones are the best type to offer.

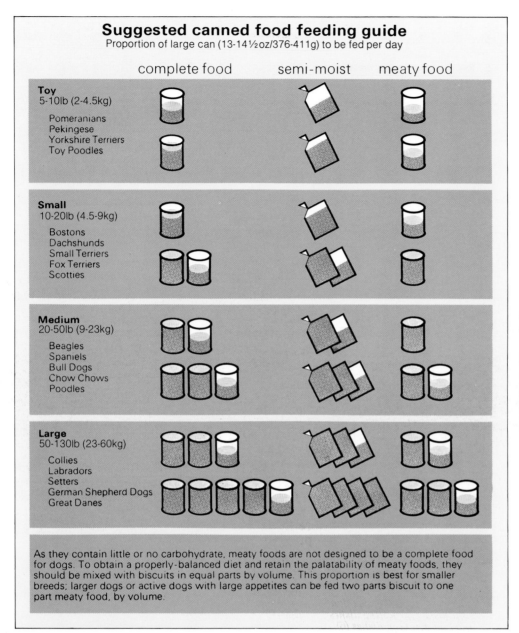

Suggested canned food feeding guide
Proportion of large can (13-14½oz/376-411g) to be fed per day

	complete food	semi-moist	meaty food
Toy 5-10lb (2-4.5kg) Pomeranians Pekingese Yorkshire Terriers Toy Poodles			
Small 10-20lb (4.5-9kg) Bostons Dachshunds Small Terriers Fox Terriers Scotties			
Medium 20-50lb (9-23kg) Beagles Spaniels Bull Dogs Chow Chows Poodles			
Large 50-130lb (23-60kg) Collies Labradors Setters German Shepherd Dogs Great Danes			

As they contain little or no carbohydrate, meaty foods are not designed to be a complete food for dogs. To obtain a properly-balanced diet and retain the palatability of meaty foods, they should be mixed with biscuits in equal parts by volume. This proportion is best for smaller breeds; larger dogs or active dogs with large appetites can be fed two parts biscuit to one part meaty food, by volume.

Above *Bad habits are often encouraged by the dog's owner. Feeding scraps from the table will only lead to persistent begging and pestering for food.*
Above right *Wherever they are — this Rottweiler is at a show — dogs must always have access to fresh drinking water. How much they need will depend partly on their diet; those fed dried food will need more water. Thirst also increases in hot weather.*

or if the dog is a mongrel, weighing is a simple procedure. Most dogs can be weighed by subtracting your weight from the weight shown on the scales when you are holding them.

Most dogs are fed once a day, or in half-rations morning and evening. Recent studies suggest that either is satisfactory. It is best, however, to feed a dog immediately before the rest of the household, so that it is less likely to become a nuisance at the table. Dogs should never be fed late at night either, because they will probably want to relieve themselves afterward, since food in the stomach stimulates intestinal movement.

Only dry food can be left in the feeding bowl during the day. Any left over the following day can be placed on top of the new supply, or simply discarded. This method of feeding is not recommended for young dogs, however. Other types of food will at-tract flies and spoil if left for long in warm weather. In any case, dogs usually bolt their food within minutes. After the dog has finished, its bowl should be washed using detergent, separately from the utensils used for humans, and then rinsed.

Dogs appreciate a routine and, once a feeding pattern is established, it is best not to alter it. Dogs do not seem to get bored with the same food every day, but some owners still offer fresh food once or twice a week.

Water
The volume of water consumed will depend partly on the diet, as dogs fed on canned rations drink less than those given dried foods. More water will be drunk during warm weather and after a period of exercise. Various medical conditions can give rise to an abnormal thirst; if a disorder of this type is

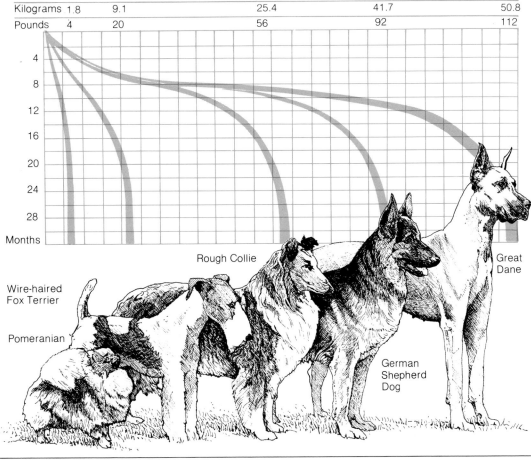

Kilograms	1.8	9.1			25.4		41.7			50.8
Pounds	4	20			56		92			112

Left *This chart illustrates the age to weight relationship of different breeds — their growth curves. While these are broadly similar, certain breeds take longer to reach their optimum weight.*

Months
4
8
12
16
20
24
28

Wire-haired Fox Terrier

Pomeranian

Rough Collie

German Shepherd Dog

Great Dane

suspected, the amount of water drunk each day should be recorded to help the veterinarian make a diagnosis. It is always dangerous to withhold or restrict the water available, even if the dog is proving incontinent.

Many dogs prefer to drink from puddles rather than a bowl and this should be discouraged because of the danger of disease. They must also be prevented from drinking from toilet bowls, not only for reasons of hygiene, but also because of the risk of ingesting harmful substances such as bleach. This behavior can be avoided by ensuring that the lid of the toilet is always kept down.

Treats

Chocolate drops manufactured especially for dogs can be particularly valuable for use as rewards in training, but must never be fed above the recommended level. Other candies are of no value and will probably lead to tooth decay; excessive sugar may well result in diarrhea. Yeast-based tablets of various kinds are highly palatable, and act as a valuable source of B vitamins. Dogs are very much creatures of habit, however, and feeding treats between meals will cause repeated pestering — it is best to set a time, such as late evening.

Bones are again not essential from a nutritional viewpoint, but dogs undoubtedly appreciate being able to gnaw on a bone. This may also lessen the risk of furniture and carpeting being chewed and helps to prevent a build-up of tartar on the teeth. Great care must be taken, however, not to give bones that can splinter, or be swallowed and become lodged in the mouth or throat. Big marrow bones, obtainable

Smaller breeds suffer from loss of appetite more often than larger dogs, and the condition can be the result of a variety of factors. Feeding titbits between meals can be responsible. Human treats — such as ice-cream — are best avoided (bottom). *Natural foods, such as apples or carrots, can be given occasionally and will not lead to tooth decay* (below).

from butchers, are most suitable, providing the cut ends show no signs of flaking. Bones from poultry and rabbits are among the most dangerous, and should never be given; make sure none are left lying around where dogs could steal them.

Milk is not essential either, and is indigestible for many dogs, including greyhounds, which lack the enzyme, lactase, necessary to break down the sugar present. The sugar is then converted by bacteria in the gut into lactic acid, which causes diarrhea. Other beverages are not recommended, although dogs will often drink cold tea, especially if it contains sugar, but they do not like saccharin.

Loss of appetite

Some dogs can be fussy eaters — easily put off their food by the presence of strangers or alterations in their surroundings. This applies particularly to the smaller breeds, although the problem is rare. Since loss of appetite can be a symptom of various diseases, some of which are serious, it is always best to check with a veterinarian if such behaviour does occur. If there is a bitch in heat nearby, a male dog may also be distracted from its food; dogs may also lose their appetites if they are scavenging elsewhere.

Feeding titbits between meals is likely to spoil the dog's appetite, and, on a regular basis, will lead to obesity and other harmful effects. If a dog is genuinely fastidious about food, it is possible to improve palatability by smearing margarine or some other type of fat over the surface. Canned or fresh foods are generally more acceptable than dried diets.

Left Dogs should not be allowed to eat from dishes used for human food because of the risk of transmitting disease. Scavenging should also be firmly discouraged, since it can lead to a variety of problems, such as digestive disturbances, loss of appetite and obesity.

TRAINING

Training is a vital part of dog ownership, and will ensure that the dog lives its life with a greater degree of safety, apart from increasing the owner's bond with their pet. An untrained adult dog is a liability in every sense. Because it has never had to adopt a submissive role, and it may regard itself as dominant to its owner and prove aggressive. Basic training is not difficult to accomplish, but must be carried out regularly to a fixed routine. Much can be achieved by varying the tone of the voice, to express displeasure for example, and physical punishment should only be used in the very last resort: a sharp tap from a rolled-up newspaper is more than adequate. Praise and affection greatly stimulate good behavior.

Housetraining

A small area of garden should be set aside for the dog's use. Scent plays an important part in the selection of a site for urination and defecation. Dogs are naturally clean animals and, once shown the correct routine, will normally attempt to follow it after a short period of time. After meals, and last thing at night, the puppy should be placed on the designated spot; repeated use of a phrase such as 'Clean dog' will help to ensure that it learns to associate this sound with the required response. Best results are likely if the puppy is monitored during this activity, rather than being allowed to wander off, or follow its owner back to the door. Once it has performed, it should be praised. Good training relies on repetition of words or actions.

A dirt box, low-sided to permit easy access, should be provided for young puppies if the weather is bad. A large plastic tray, filled with cat litter, is ideal for this purpose. The tray should be lined with newspaper, and sheets spread around the floor nearby, in case of accidents. The underlying surface should also be easy to wash off and disinfect if required.

If an accident does occur, there is no point punishing the puppy unless it is caught in the act. Dogs are not capable of associating harsh treatment with a past transgression and rubbing a dog's nose in its excrement is both useless and unpleasant. Once the area is cleaned up, it should be washed thoroughly with one of the commercially available descenting preparations or vinegar, which will remove the puppy's scent from the spot. Certain pine disinfectants are now believed to reinforce scents. If any trace is left, the puppy will be attracted back to the site for the same purpose. There are also chemicals which can attract a puppy to a certain spot, and these can be useful if the puppy cannot be let out for any reason, especially if it is still unvaccinated.

Especially where young children are present, it is very important to ensure that dog feces are removed as soon as possible, because of the accompanying health risks. One means of disposal now available is a bucket-type container with slits in the side which can be buried in a corner of the garden and covered with a lid. The feces are deposited inside with a shovel and chemicals break down the excrement. This will not guarantee to destroy parasitic worm eggs, such as those of *Toxocara canis* which can present a serious danger to human health, but will provide some protection for children.

It will take about three months to train a puppy to ask to go out when it needs to and slightly longer before it performs on demand. In unfamiliar surroundings, such as a veterinarian's surgery when a urine sample is required, the latter command may be ignored, particularly by bitches. Whereas a puppy might relieve itself as much as six times during the course of a day, an adult dog will only defecate once or twice and has much better control of its bladder. Letting the dog out last thing at night and early in the morning should ensure that there is no soiling indoors. When the dog is asleep, urine production falls naturally in any case.

Male dogs urinate much more frequently than bitches, because their urine also acts partly as a territorial scent marker. When out, dogs often sniff at lampposts and trees, before lifting their legs and urinating to leave their scent. Bitches invariably squat when urinating, as do young males before puberty. In public places such as parks, specific areas are sometimes set aside for dogs, and these should be used whenever posssible. Much of the unpopularity of dogs in city areas stems from the soiling of walkways; if an accident does occur the owner should clear up the resulting mess. Under no circumstances whatsoever should dogs be allowed to use children's sandpits or play areas because of the risk of transmitting disease from their excrement.

A breakdown in toilet training may occur in elderly or sick dogs and the introduction of a new dog to the household may cause an established male to lose its sense of housetraining. The dog is only emphasizing that it is already settled in the territory and should return to its old habits once it has accepted the presence of the intruder.

Obedience training

Various commands must be taught to ensure obedience. A combination of patience and firmness achieves the best results; it is counter-productive to punish a puppy harshly if it fails to respond correctly every time, especially at the beginning.

At mealtimes dogs will be more receptive to teaching. A young dog will soon learn to come if its name is called when food is offered. It can be taught to sit before being given its dinner, but must never be teased with food as this is likely to lead to serious problems later. Sitting is a normal posture for a dog and this command is often easily mastered. At first, it may be necessary to exert gentle pressure over the hindquarters to encourage the puppy to adopt the required posture.

It is important to teach a puppy to 'stay' on command, to enable it to be controlled off the lead and in city areas. After play, the puppy can be placed in its bed, and told to 'stay'. It might remain there if it is tired, but if not, it should be put back and the command repeated.

Training reinforces the bond between dog and owner. A successful training routine depends on repetition of words and actions over a period of time, and on praise. Simple commands, such as 'Come' (far left) and 'Stay' (left), used together with clear gestures, will gradually be understood; subsequently, more complex lessons can be taught. Praise is an important part of the process; repeated punishment for wrong-doing will only serve to bewilder the dog and make it over-submissive and fearful.

Teaching a dog to sit *Sitting is a natural posture for a dog and most do not need much encouragement to sit on command. The command 'Sit' should be given first (1), and then gentle pressure applied to the dog's hindquarters (2). When the dog has adopted the required posture, it should be praised warmly (3).*

1

2

3

After the commands of 'sit' and 'stay' have been learned, the puppy can be taught to 'lie down'. This is more difficult because young dogs are normally active and will not stay in this position for long. Once again, they may have to be put in the required posture initially, praising them when they obey.

Another important command is 'drop'. This command is vital for retrievers. In the home, a dog which has not been taught to give up an item readily is likely to be both very possessive and possibly aggressive in later life. Care must be taken when trying to train older dogs of uncertain temperament, since they may bite if someone attempts to take what they believe is their property away from them. Gently prize the jaws apart to retrieve an item from a puppy, while repeating the command. This also accustoms the dog to having its mouth opened, useful for veterinary examinations.

Lead training

The first step is to accustom the puppy to wearing its collar — at first, it may well attempt to pull it off. The collar should fit comfortably, neither excessively tight, causing it to rub on the neck, nor so loose that it slides forward towards the head. The size needs to be adjusted as the puppy grows.

There are various types of lead or leash, some of which are only used in certain situations, such as the show ring. For general purposes, the most impor-

Choke chains *Choke or check chains are not universally popular among dog trainers, but they certainly do deter a dog from persistent pulling. It is vital that the chain is the right size and that it is fitted correctly (top). If the chain is fitted incorrectly, it will not slacken when pressure on the lead is relaxed and the dog may suffer injury or discomfort (above).*

Many dogs, notably retrievers, have a natural enthusiasm for fetching (above right). To encourage good posture, some breeders feed their puppies from a raised bowl (right).

tant feature of a lead is a secure means of attachment to the collar. Leather leads are more traditional and easier on the hand if the dog is untrained, but nylon is also increasingly available. Harnesses are used for guide dogs, and recommended for breeds such as Dachshunds, which can often suffer from disc problems in the neck region. A harness also makes it easier to pick up a small dog, since the straps will support its weight.

The puppy should be accustomed to a lead before it is actually taken outside the garden. Walk the puppy along a fence or similar barrier so that it cannot pull away in all directions. The puppy will try to go ahead and this should be gently, yet firmly, corrected using the word 'heel'. Short periods of exercise, lasting a maximum of 10 minutes, are sufficient at this stage, and greatest benefit will be gained if they are repeated once or twice daily.

For older dogs, choke or check chains are often employed to facilitate lead training but these are not necessary and a lead and collar can be used in a similar way. It is vital, however, to ensure that the correct size of chain is chosen and that it fits properly; otherwise, a variety of injuries can be inflicted on the unfortunate trainee. The size required can be calculated by taking the measurement around the base of the throat and up over the ears, and adding an extra 2in (5cm). Chains with large links are less likely to cause physical injury. When pressure from the lead is lessened, the chain should slacken, rather than remaining tight. The dog should be walked on the handler's left side, with the lead held in the handler's right hand. If the dog starts to pull ahead, the command 'heel' should be given; if ignored the command should be followed by a quick, sharp jerk on the lead, and the instruction repeated. The chain will grip tightly around the throat, causing an unpleasant feeling. When the dog learns to walk at the right pace, it should be praised.

Dogs should not be allowed off the lead in towns for their own safety; byelaws often prohibit this in any case. If the dog is going to be allowed off the lead, choose a spot well away from traffic, people and other dogs. By this stage, the dog must be trained to respond to its name, stay reliably and come when called. Whistles can be useful if the dog disappears off into the distance. A number of blasts on a high-frequency whistle, which will be almost inaudible to the human ear, will help the dog to locate its owner from a long way away.

Professional training

Dog obedience classes are held in many areas, under the guidance of an experienced dog handler, and can be valuable for overcoming specific problems with an individual dog. Advanced classes are also often available, once basic training has been mastered. Details of such courses can be obtained from a veterinarian or a local library or information bureau; the cost is usually nominal. It is also possible to send a dog to a professional trainer, at much greater expense. The outcome is less likely to be satisfactory because, although the dog may respond to the trainer, it will not subsequently take commands from its owner as readily. Personal involvement is a prerequisite for successful training.

One method of training, which is sometimes advised for difficult cases but which should not be attempted, is the use of a shock collar. There are various types on the market; some are notoriously unreliable and potentially very dangerous. The electric shock, triggered by the trainer when the dog fails to respond, may cause physical injury if water is present on the coat. Certain models which are activated by barking can be set off by other dogs, and simply serve to confuse the dog who is wearing the collar.

Common behavioral problems

When puppies reach the age of six months they will be teething and, to relieve the irritation, are likely to chew anything within reach. This is a natural tendency, the effects of which can be made less devastating by providing hide chews and by ensuring that shoes and similar items are not left lying around. In older dogs, destructive chewing often occurs when the owner is out for long periods. It may indicate a lack of security or inadequate exercise. The remedy lies essentially with the owner, who must compensate for the deficiency and give the dog more attention. A pregnant bitch may also chew or scratch in an attempt to make a nest. This is normal breeding behavior, and even may occur in pseudo pregnancies. The phase will pass, although treatment of the pseudo pregnancy may be required.

Jumping up at people is an annoying habit, and stems from inadequate training. It is a sign of exuberance, but must be treated firmly nevertheless. The dog's front legs should be put back on the floor, with the command 'No'. The dog should then be ignored for a few minutes.

Dogs often bark at the approach of strangers or at sudden, unexpected noises, but prolonged periods of barking must be discouraged, if only for the neighbors' sakes. Such behavior again often stems from excitement and is generally encountered in small breeds such as the Chihuahua rather than bigger dogs. Barking can also be

Special training
Dogs are capable of performing quite complex tasks. They can be trained for a variety of police and military work, such as attacking and chasing suspects, crowd control, detection of narcotics and explosives, and tracking.

Other specialized working dogs include guide dogs for the blind and 'hearing' dogs for the deaf. Certain breeds are more suitable for this high level of training than others, notably German Shepherds and Labradors.

unintentionally encouraged by an owner: for example, if a dog barks when it wants to come inside and the door is opened at once, the dog will associate barking with the door being opened, and carry on until it is let in the house. Leaving a dog alone for a long period may also cause it to bark. If a dog barks persistently when people are present, spraying a jet of water at its head, avoiding the eyes, may discourage it. A muting operation (ventriculocordectomy) is not advisable, although in special circumstances, such as wartime, dogs have been muted so that they could not betray their position.

Wandering is more common in some breeds than others; Beagles, for example, are particularly bad in this respect. Prevention is the easiest solution. Ensure that all gates are kept closed and fences around the property are well maintained. An urge to wander can result from lack of exercise or from sexual instincts, especially in the case of male dogs when there is a bitch in heat nearby. Neutering has been shown to prevent most males from wandering. If a dog does escape and causes a road accident, its owner may be sued for damages. Insurance against this eventuality is strongly recommended, and is available at very moderate cost, often as part of a health insurance scheme.

One of the most unpleasant behavioral problems is coprophagia, when dogs eat their motions. It has been suggested that a Vitamin B deficiency may predispose to such behavior, but there is often no obvious explanation. Coprophagia is a relatively common vice of dogs which have been kenneled in unsanitary surroundings for much of their life. Breaking the habit can be difficult, but if temptation is removed as soon as possible, this will help to overcome the problem.

Chihuahua
Average daily walk: ½ mile (0.8km)

West Highland White Terrier
Average daily walk: 1 mile (1.6km)

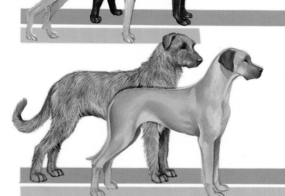

Greyhound
Average daily walk: 3 miles (4.8km)

Labrador Retriever
Average daily walk: 8 miles (12.9km)

Irish Wolfhound
Average daily walk: 9 miles (14.5km)

Great Dane
Average daily walk: 6 miles (9.6km)

Above *Exercise requirements do vary considerably from dog to dog, even between those of similar heights. A 'Westie' for example, enjoys a good walk, whereas a Chihuahua is more than happy with a short stroll each day. Surprisingly, the Greyhound does not require nearly as long a walk as the Labrador, a working dog which needs good, solid exercise every day. The bigger dogs should have a substantial daily outing, although puppies must avoid lengthy walks as these can affect bone and muscle development. Remember that the mileage required by each of these dogs does not mean that the owner also has to walk this distance, as a dog will run to and fro, covering at least twice as much ground.*

EXERCISE

The amount of exercise required depends partly on the breed. Toy breeds are often quite content with a walk of about half a mile (1 km) every day, but larger dogs, especially those with a working ancestry, need up to 8 miles (13 km). Size can be deceptive, however, when assessing a dog's exercise requirements.

Regular daily exercise is important, rather than marathon sessions at the weekend. If the dog does not settle down when it returns from its walk, the walk was probably not long enough. Where the dog can be let off the lead, encourage it to run back and forth chasing a ball or toy; in this way, it will cover two or three times as much ground. Under no circumstances should dogs be allowed to run free close to livestock, especially sheep. Dogs can inflict hideous injuries on sheep, especially at lambing time and farmers are legally entitled to shoot to protect their flocks or their herds. For the dog's own safety, running free off the lead should also be curtailed in urban areas. In some cities, this is banned by law, in any case.

In certain cases, exercise must be restricted. Young puppies of giant breeds, such as Wolfhounds, must not be exercised excessively before they are skeletally mature, since this can cause problems later with their joints. Old dogs,

The gallop *The Greyhound has a gait that is distinct from any other dog. Movement at the gallop consists of a series of bounding leaps, leaving the dog airborne for considerable periods of time. This means the dog uses up more energy.* Leads *A wide range of leads is available and it is important to choose carefully. A 'check chain' or a plaited leather lead is best for strong dogs; a longer training lead and puppy collar with elasticized inset are suitable for young dogs; and a short town lead is useful for controlling tall dogs.*

especially those with heart complaints, and pregnant bitches will also need less exercise. Dogs should not be taken out during the hottest part of the day in summer; during warm weather, Pekingese, Boxers and similar flat-faced breeds may become distressed and start to breathe very noisily.

Dogs can also be exercised in the garden, on a running chain attached to a stake fixed firmly in the ground. This enables the dog to cover quite a large area without actually being free. Shelter must be available from the sun and the elements, and water must be within easy reach. Dogs do seem to resent being tethered for any length of time, however, and may try to escape. Tethering can also encourange aggressive tendencies.

GROOMING

It is best to accustom a dog to grooming at an early age, even if it is a short-haired breed. Aside from improving the dog's appearance, grooming provides an opportunity to look for fleas and other parasites which may have attached themselves to the body. Frequent short periods of grooming are preferable; if carried out regularly, there is little risk of mats forming in the coats of long-haired breeds. These, aside from being unsightly, can be difficult and even painful to remove.

If matting does occur, it may just be possible to

tease the hairs apart. In bad cases, the hair will have to be cut off and allowed to regrow. Special de-matting combs are available but can cause considerable pain, and it is often kinder to take the dog to a veterinarian or a grooming parlor; some degree of sedation may be required.

Brushing and combing

For normal brushing, a brush comprised of pig bristles is best; nylon brushes create static electricity and may damage the hair. Wire brushes can also be harmful if used excessively, but can remove dead hair from breeds do not molt in the conventional sense, such as poodles. A rubber brush with a strap which fits over the hand is ideal for grooming a smooth-coated dog. A studded hound glove will also help to give the coat a good luster. Soft brushes are best for puppies.

Plastic combs can be used for fine-coated breeds, but steel combs, with rounded teeth to prevent damage to the skin, are best for long-haired dogs since the teeth will not break off easily. A comb mounted on a handle is preferable, and a relatively broad gap between the individual teeth is recommended for general purposes. A fine-toothed comb can be used on the head and for finishing touches. Certain breeds may require specific grooming tools — Afghans, for example, are prepared with a pig-bristle brush and a plastic comb.

To brush or comb a dog, stand it on a flat surface, such as an old table. Brushing should begin on the head and run in the direction of the fur. Particular parts of the body require more attention in some breeds, such as the ears of spaniels, and the so-called 'feathers' or fine hair at the back of legs of dogs such as Irish Setters; in general, these need careful combing. A thorough combing is recommended in most cases after brushing, which will have removed most of the loose hair. The amount lost will increase noticeably at certain times of the year when the dog is molting. The undercoat is largely shed in spring in some cases.

Clipping

Most dogs molt naturally and their coats do not need clipping. In certain conditions, however, such as very hot weather, breeds with profuse coats, like the Old English Sheepdog, may be more comfortable if they are trimmed. Medical disorders can also be a reason for clipping. In elderly dogs, especially long-haired breeds, the coat around the anus may become soiled. Clipping will help to keep this area clean and decrease the likelihood of fly strike. The inside of the spaniels' ears may need to be trimmed to reduce the risk of ear infections, or to facilitate treatment of such conditions. The long hair between the toes of dogs such as Golden Retrievers should be cut if an infestation occurs.

Certain breeds are more demanding as far as grooming is concerned. Spaniels and setters need to have the hair on their ears trimmed to prevent infections (right). *Long-haired dogs need frequent brushing* (below right). *Young dogs may need their nails clipped* (center right). *Bathing is best carried out in the garden to prevent mess* (far right).

Essential grooming equipment (below) *includes: a soft brush (1), scissors (2), nail clippers (3), wire brush (4), comb (5) and fine comb (6).*

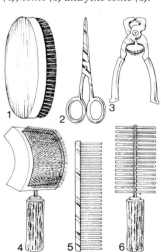

Those breeds which do not shed their coats must be clipped at intervals of six weeks. Various types of trim are recognized for exhibition dogs; for show poodles, the clip recognized by the country concerned must be adopted. Since poodles have very sensitive skins, scissors are more often used than mechanical clippers, which can cause a rash.

'Stripping' — removing dead hair, usually in the spring and autumn — is often necessary for wire-coated terriers. For show dogs, stripping is carried out by hand, which takes considerable time as well as skill. The coats of pet dogs are usually stripped with mechanical clippers, and thinned with special scissors.

Many people prefer to have their dogs trimmed at a grooming parlor; some of these operate a home visiting service. For the serious exhibitor, there are courses where such skills can be learned. For maximum efficiency and minimum discomfort for the dog, the clippers must be well maintained. The cutterheads of electric clippers, which should be interchangeable, should be oiled regularly. Magnetic-type clippers are probably best for the home groomer, however, as they are simple to operate.

Bathing
Bathing is not as essential as brushing and general grooming, although it is an important part of show preparation for certain breeds, notably the York-

shire Terrier. Try to accustom the dog to bathing from an early age; if suddenly introduced to this treatment later on, it may resent it. Pets will need to be bathed if their coats become soiled, but otherwise a bath every two or three months should be adequate, and will prevent them from smelling. Shampoo will remove some of the coat's natural grease, which normally acts as a waterproofing agent, but this is soon replaced. Excessive bathing, however, will make the coat dull and less attractive.

Wash the dog outside if the weather permits, using a tub or even an inflatable paddling pool for a big dog, although this may be punctured by its claws. Never use the family bathtub. The water should be lukewarm; which shampoo you use will depend on the state of the coat. Some dog shampoos are suitable for all breeds; others are recommended for long-haired dogs, and help to prevent tangles. Shampoos that highlight particular colors are often used on poodles, while others are formulated for puppies and dogs with delicate skins. Baby shampoo is also suitable as an alternative. Medicated shampoos should only be used under veterinary advice; any insecticidal preparations, for controlling fleas for example, must be mixed and used strictly in accordance with the manufacturer's instructions.

Half-fill the bath and put on some type of protective clothing. The dog may need to be lifted into the water and then, using a jug or even a milk bottle, wet the back and hindquarters first, moving up the body gradually. The shampoo should be applied and rubbed into a lather. Make sure to shampoo between the toes where the eccrine sweat glands are. Rinse the coat with clean water; certain medicated shampoos, however, may have to be left on the coat for a while before rinsing.

The head should be washed last. Great care must be taken to ensure that shampoo does not enter the eyes. Once the head is wet, the dog will probably shake itself, spraying water everywhere, and it should then be lifted out of the bath as soon as possible. It can be rubbed down with an old towel and dried off with either an electric hair-dryer or one of the dryers used in grooming parlors. The dryer must be moved back and forth over the body to prevent the hair and skin from being scorched by the heat. Separating the wet fur with a brush will also help it to dry more quickly, and, with a towel, may be the only way of drying the fur of a dog that is disturbed by the noise of a hair-dryer.

After the dog has been bathed, make sure it does not immediately run away to roll in earth or manure. Such behavior is thought to result from the dog's desire to improve its social status by increasing its body scent, which will have been removed to a large extent by washing.

Dry shampoo is sometimes used as an alternative to ordinary shampoo, especially for a show, and will not degrease the coat like wet washing. It is useful in cases where wet shampooing is inadvisable, for example, if the dog is elderly. The powder is rubbed in, left for a period, and then brushed out again. Dry shampoo will not clean a very dirty coat, and traces will show up on dark fur. Considerable brushing may be required to remove the shampoo, which, in turn, may cause a build-up of static electricity and prevent the coat from settling down properly. Powders can also lead to runny eyes and sneezing if they are applied indiscriminately around the head. Talcum powder is one of the main ingredients of dry shampoo, and is also used to improve the appearance of white breeds such as the Bichon Frise.

Various commercial preparations, designed to improve the appearance of the coat, are also available. Some come in the form of aerosols, and are sprayed onto the coat to make it shiny, while others are quick-drying liquids and must be rubbed in. Since rubbing in must be done evenly, aerosols are often easier to use. The value of such products is debatable, although they may be useful for giving finishing touches before a show.

BOARDING KENNELS

It is not always possible to take the dog with you on vacation, particularly if you are going abroad. If kenneling is necessary, then the arrangements should be made as far as possible before the date of departure. Satisfied clients will take their dogs to the same kennels every year, and it is often difficult to find a vacancy at peak holiday times, especially in a well-run establishment. A kennel should be chosen on recommendation, either from a breeder or veterinarian; if not, then a visit to the kennels under consideration should be arranged, as this will afford an opportunity to inspect the premises. Much can be gathered from simply seeing the surroundings and meeting the people who care for the dogs. The kennels and outside runs ought to be clean, with no signs of overcrowding. The occupants should look alert and well. The interiors of the kennels should be dry and snug, and the water bowls should be filled and clean.

In most countries, reputable kennels ask for certificates of vaccination against leptospirosis, canine infectious hepatitis, distemper and also parvovirus. For additional protection, vaccination against *Bordetella bronchoseptica*, a bacterium which is partly responsible for the kennel cough syndrome, is now available. This disease is normally relatively minor, but spreads rapidly among dogs in kennels at holiday time. It is important to inform the kennel staff of any significant medical condition, such as a heart complaint, and to supply the correct treatment, together with the name, address and number of the dog's veterinarian. A vet may be prepared to take a chronically sick dog, such as a diabetic, for a holiday period.

Although a few do not adapt readily to kennel life, particularly if it is their first time, most dogs settle well. Older dogs are more likely to pine.

Although most dogs settle well in kennels, it may be unwise to board an old or chronically sick dog, even for a relatively short time (above). It is important to make all kenneling arrangements well ahead of time, since the best kennels in any area are usually booked well before the peak holiday season (right). Most will want to see evidence that the dog is fully vaccinated against major infectious diseases, such as distemper.

TRAVELING

At some point, the dog will have to be transported by car and will probably adapt fairly quickly to the experience. During the journey, the dog must be properly restrained so that it will not distract the driver, or damage the upholstery. If a dog is allowed to travel free in the car, it should be accompanied by a passenger who can restrain it if necessary in the back seat. Traveling cages which fit into the back of an estate car or station wagon are one solution but another option is to install a dog guard. These can be acquired from motor accessory stores and, depending on the model of car, either may need to be fitted to the body shell or may be held in place by suction pads attaching to the roof or floor. With fine-nosed breeds such as greyhounds, square or rectangular meshes are essential, as it is possible for the dog to push its head through horizontal bars and get stuck.

A dog must never be allowed to ride with its head out of a window. Apart from the obvious and fatal risk of colliding with another object at speed, the velocity of the air is likely to lead to conjunctivitis, and small particles of gravel may also enter the eyes. In warm weather the interior of a car heats up very quickly and, without ventilation, a dog can be killed in a frighteningly short space of time. Always ensure that windows are left partially open if the dog has to be left in a car for any length of time.

All dogs should be kept on a lead when you are traveling on public transport. Small dogs can be held on the lap; large dogs should be kept under close control, well out of the way of other passengers. If the dog has to be transported by air, special shippers can be contacted to organize both the necessary paperwork and the crating. Various health tests will also be required for dogs being sent abroad.

Above While farm dogs ride happily in the back of open vehicles, this type of transport cannot be recommended for most dogs, which are liable to be distracted by a scent or another animal.
Left It can be dangerous to allow a dog to ride in a car with its head out of the window. Most breeders transport their dogs in special carrying pens or behind fitted dog guards.

HEALTH CARE

Great advances in the field of canine health care in recent years mean that most dogs today have a much longer life expectancy than did previous generations. The major killer diseases of the past, notably distemper, can now be prevented by regular vaccination. Even parvovirus, a serious illness widespread in the late 1970s and early 1980s, is now controllable by vaccination. Unfortunately, many dogs still die from these diseases every year because their owners forgot, or did not choose, to give their pets this protection.

The owner can do much to ensure that their dog remains healthy, lively and alert. A sensible diet and regular exercise will help to prevent obesity, together with the related complications such as heart disease, which may arise later in life. Frequent and careful grooming will help to keep parasites at bay. At the first sign of illness, the dog should be taken to a veterinarian for a check-up: early treatment aids speedy recovery.

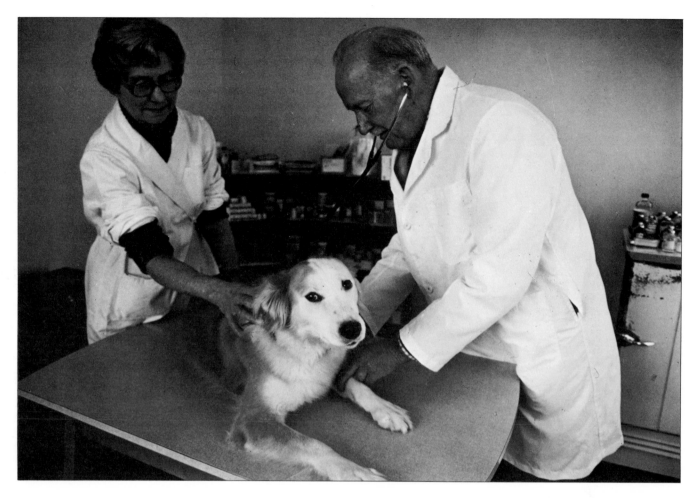

CONSULTING A VETERINARIAN

Choosing a veterinarian is the first step to be taken after acquiring a puppy. While a personal recommendation from a breeder or friend may be followed up, all veterinarians have undergone several years of rigorous training and will prove reliable. In rural areas, veterinarians may concentrate more on farm animals than pets, but they will nevertheless be quite competent to treat dogs. Most 'small animal' practices are based in towns; occasionally, cases requiring specialist equipment may be referred from country practices.

It is a good idea to take a new dog for a check-up and vaccinations soon after obtaining it. Serious diseases that are preventable by vaccination are distemper, infectious canine hepatitis, leptospirosis and parvovirus, all of which can be fatal. The veterinarian will be able to advise on the scheduling of vaccinations; until the dog has had a full set of vaccinations, it should be kept away from direct contact with other dogs. When taking a puppy to a veterinarian, it should be confined to a traveling box, or otherwise isolated. Even after one set of vaccinations, the puppy will not be adequately protected against the killer diseases.

For a close examination, the dog will need to be lifted up onto the veterinarian's table. This is most easily accomplished by placing the right arm around the dog's rear quarters, with the left arm extending around the chest and shoulders in a horizontal direction. Once on the table, the dog should be restrained by its collar, and this should never be removed unless requested by the veterinarian. If a procedure which may cause pain is required, it should not be taken as a slight if a muzzle of some kind is placed over the dog's jaws to make it safer for everyone.

Health insurance

While health insurance schemes do not cover the cost of vaccinations or neutering operations, they can help defray the cost of unforeseen accidents or injuries. Orthopedic surgery, for example, after an accident, can be very expensive. Since there are a number of different policies on the market, it is important to compare what each offers, paying particular attention to the exclusion clauses, which often concern congenital defects. The minimum amount which the owner must meet in the event of a claim should also be noted, and whether certain benefits, such as costs of advertising, are available if the dog disappears. Combined health and third-party liability policies are available, or both can be taken out separately if preferred. Veterinary surgeries often carry details of such schemes, as do the trade papers.

Far left *A routine examination is likely to entail listening to the dog's chest with a stethoscope. Since most veterinarians are assisted by a nurse, it is not essential for the dog's owner to remain in the consulting room while the dog is being examined or given vaccinations.*
Left *Persistent scratching can be symptomatic of a variety of skin disorders. Fleas are a common cause of irritation and their presence can be detected by a careful examination of the coat. Treatment is essential to prevent the dog from injuring itself. Scratching around the ears may be a sign of ear infection.*

PARASITES

External parasites

Fleas Fleas are probably the most widespread external parasite and, although often present in a dog's coat, they may be hard to spot. The first, obvious sign is persisent scratching and biting, especially along the back and at the base of the tail.

Fleas are most easily detected by grooming, and special fine-toothed metal combs are available for this purpose. It is preferable to groom the dog outside, so that if any fleas escape they are less likely to find another host. When a flea is caught, it can be squashed with a thumbnail, or dropped in a pot of water, and flushed down a toilet. Their presence is often betrayed by flea dirt removed by the comb. These tiny black specks will turn red if dampened on blotting paper, as they contain partially undigested blood taken from the host.

Flea infections are worse in summer; the flea's lifecycle is controlled by humidity. These parasites will not hesitate to bite humans. This is one reason for keeping dogs out of bedrooms as fleas do not actually breed on the dog itself, but in the immediate surroundings. Control of fleas will not be accomplished simply by treating the dog, although obviously this is important. Aerosol sprays can be used, but are relatively expensive, whereas powder may be more effective as it is rubbed into the coat. Since dogs can ingest such chemicals by licking their coats, care should be taken; not all preparations are safe for puppies.

Insecticidal shampoos and soaps are valuable in severe cases and the effects often last for several days. Flea collars, impregnated with an insecticidal compound. are also long-acting, but some dogs may be sensitive to them. Such collars must be applied as directed and may not be suitable for young dogs. Flea medallions are also available in certain countries.

The dog's bed should be washed about every three weeks — the lifecycle of the flea is an average of four to five weeks long. Bedding must also be washed, preferably with a shampoo, or discarded. Regular vacuuming around the home will do much to remove flea eggs except for those close to the walls. It may be necessary to spray such areas. In a really severe outbreak, a pest control agency can be contacted to treat the house; some local agencies also offer a service of this nature. In professional hands, this job is straightforward, although other pets such as fish will have to be removed or covered, as the spray may be toxic to them.

Since cats can transfer fleas to dogs and viceversa, both must be treated at the same time. Certain preparations are not safe for use with cats,

Right *Insecticidal shampoos developed especially for dogs are a valuable means of controlling external parasites such as lice and fleas. They may also have a residual effect, preventing against reinfection for several days. All such shampoos must be used as directed; subsequent rinsing may not be advised in all cases.*

however. Fleas also act as intermediate hosts of the tapeworm *Dipylidium caninum*, which can affect both dogs and cats, and elimination of fleas is significant in controlling this parasite as well.

Mites Mites can occur in a variety of localities; some have a fairly specialized distribution. The larvae of the harvest mite *(Trombicula autumnalis)* attach to the skin between the toes, causing intense irritation. The dog will lick and nibble its feet and will suffer considerable discomfort. When the foot is examined, minute clusters of these larvae, which look like tiny dots, may be visible. Infections of this type are prevalent in late summer, before the larvae turn into the adult form. Adults resemble tiny red spiders. Treatment with an insecticidal shampoo will overcome the problem, although infections often recur.

Dogs can also contract mite infections from other animals. In hounds especially, *Cheyletiella parasitivorox* may be a problem, often causing a scurf along the back, as well as irritating the skin. It also occurs in rabbits, which can transmit the infection to dogs.

The ear mite *Otodectes cynotis* is a common inhabitant of the ear canal, where it can cause severe irritation and long-standing infections. These ear mites look like tiny, greyish-white dots. They feed by penetrating the skin, taking lymph for their nourishment. An accumulation of dark brown wax in the ear canal is usually evidence of their presence.

Veterinary advice should be sought for ear infections; for the best chance of recovery, the correct therapy must be started as soon as possible. There is always a danger that infection will spread from the ear canal into the tympanic cavity, causing not only deafness, but also damage to the vestibular apparatus, which will affect the sense of balance.

Mange is a skin infection caused by mites. *Sarcoptes scabiei* lives and reproduces in the skin, causing considerable irritation and thickening of the affected area. The incidence of infection is highest in young dogs, and often starts as red patches around the inside of the thighs, and the neighboring region. Loss of hair may also occur around the eyes, and scabs, with an odor reminiscent of mouse urine, appear on the body. This is a highly contagious disease and can cause scabies in children. Infection is normally confirmed by a veterinarian taking a scraping from the skin, which is then examined microscopically to confirm the presence of mites. An infected dog should be isolated and a disposable bed is recommended for the duration of treatment. This is likely to be prolonged to ensure the eradication of these parasites.

The other form of mange which is of particular importance in dogs, especially short-haired breeds such as the Dachshund, is caused by *Demodex canis*. Infections of this type are referred to as follicular mange, since the parasites actually live in the hair follicles, causing loss of hair and inflammation. Over a period of time, the skin will thicken and pustules form as the follicles become infected with bacteria, often staphylococci. The bacterial infection may in turn lead to a generalized illness.

Demodex mites are acquired early in life, transmitted from the dam to her puppies, but actual symptoms may not become evident until much later. The infection can be confirmed by means of skin scrapings, but the mites are often harder to detect, since they invade deeper into the skin. Treatment is both difficult and prolonged, while antibiotics will be necessary to overcome any bacterial infection that might arise. Bitches suffering from *Demodex* should not be used for breeding.

Ticks These insects only spend part of their lifecycles on a host. They are common in rural areas, especially where sheep are present. They feed by sucking blood, swelling to become as large as ½in (1.25cm) in length. Ticks are most easily removed by dabbing at the site of attachment to the dog's skin with cottonwool soaked in methylated spirit; a few minutes later, after they have loosened their grip, they can be pulled off with tweezers. In some cases, the mouthparts of the tick will break off, and may still be lodged in the skin. The site can be dabbed with a non-toxic antiseptic cream, to decrease the slight risk of infection.

Ticks do cause a dog some irritation, but the major threat they pose to canine health stems from the fact that they can transmit serous protozoal diseases like babesiosis. This is caused by a protozoal infection, spread by the brown dog tick, *Rhipicephalus sanguineus*, which is widespread in both tropical and temperate areas. The protozoan responsible for the disease, *Babesia canis*, causes a very sudden and severe anemia which results in the urine turning brownish red; hence the illness is also known as 'redwater'. Both drugs and blood transfusions may be necessary to save the lives of affected dogs. Animals brought into an area where such infections frequently occur are most at risk, since they are unlikely to have much, if any, resistance. Dogs taken to tropical areas from temperate countries must be watched accordingly. The protozoa themselves can be identified by means of blood smears, which are stained and viewed under a microscope.

Lice Lice found on dogs can be divided into two categories. Members of the Sub-Order Anoplura, such as *Linognathus setosus*, actually suck blood like fleas, whereas the Mallophaga group, including *Trichodectes canis*, feed on skin debris. These parasites spend the whole of their lifecycle on the dog, and are usually spread by close contact with other dogs or transferred by grooming tools. Lice often congregate around the head; egg cases attached to individual hairs can be seen on close examination. Infections of this type are relatively common in puppies, and treatment is best carried out by a veterinarian. Treatment will probably have to be repeated at least once, after about a fortnight, in order to break the lifecycle of these parasites.

Flystrike In elderly or sick dogs, especially those with long coats, fecal soiling is likely to provide a site for fly strike, particularly during warm weather. Flies will be attracted to such areas to lay their eggs and these rapidly hatch into maggots. The maggots bore into the tissue and release toxins; they may lead to bacterial infections. The hair will need to be cut away from the affected region and the maggots removed with forceps, while the area may have to be treated with an antibiotic powder. If the illness is more severe, antibiotic therapy may be required.

Internal parasites

Tapeworms A significant proportion of dogs are affected with tapeworms. Tapeworms (cestodes) are so-named because of their appearance, which is flat and ribbon-like. Their heads remain attached to the gut wall, while mature segments, known as proglottids, are passed out with the feces, or may actually migrate out of the anus. These segments often adhere around the anus, resembling rice grains or cucumber seeds in appearance. The lifecycle of tapeworms is indirect, since their eggs must be consumed by an intermediate host before they can infect a dog. The most common tapeworm is *Dipylidium caninum*, especially in greyhounds, which uses fleas or lice as its intermediate host; a dog contracts the infection if it ingests one of these parasites.

Other tapeworms adopt vertebrates, usually herbivores such as rabbits and sheep, as sources of infection for dogs. When a dog then eats raw meat containing the tapeworm cysts, the lifecycle is completed. While many tapeworms have specific intermediate hosts, *Echinococcus granulosus* is an exception. This poses a danger to human health, especially in sheep farming areas. Sheep are the usual intermediate host, but humans can also be infected by the intermediate stage of the lifecycle. Much progress has been made towards the elimination of *Echinococcus* from New Zealand, where worming of dogs is required by law.

In spite of its small size *Echinococcus* can produce relatively large cysts in the body of its intermediate host. In human infections, the cyst can reach a size in excess of 6in (15cm) in diameter before rupturing to form other cysts. Depending on the location of such cysts in the body, they may have serious if not fatal consequences. The adult worms in the dog cause very little adverse effects, and rarely grow to more than 1/5in (5mm) in length, but large numbers may be present in the gut of an infected dog.

Roundworms Roundworms (nematodes) are different in shape from tapeworms, as their name suggests. They usually have a direct lifecycle and can be spread without the need for an intermediate host.

Ascarid worms are the most important members of this group, and two forms are significant to the dog, *Toxascaris leonina* and *Toxocara canis*. The two species can be distinguished by examining fecal samples for eggs. *Toxocara* eggs are spherical and pitted; *Toxascaris* eggs are smooth and oval. *Toxascaris leonina* also does not have a dormant phase, like *Toxocara canis*.

After being excreted, the eggs require a period of time outside the body before they become infectious. Young dogs are most at risk; they can become infected *in utero* by *Toxocara canis*. In these cases, some of the larval worms that invaded the dam's body originally will have localized in various tissues and become dormant. Their development is triggered by pregnancy and they then migrate, crossing the placental barrier to settle in the developing puppies' lungs and livers. A week after the puppies are born, the larvae move to the intestines and mature into adult worms. The bitch may also contract another infection by licking her puppies and ingesting larvae. Signs of infection in puppies are pot bellies, diarrhea and vomiting. Before the larvae have left the tissues of the gut, coughing and lung damage may occur.

A variety of treatments are effective against these parasites. Breeding bitches should always be wormed approximately four weeks before the puppies are due to be born, although this does not destroy larvae dormant in the tissues. The pups themselves must be dosed regularly from the age of three weeks until they are weaned. It is always preferable to obtain worming tablets from a veterinarian, since modern, more potent and effective anthelmintics are only available on veterinary prescription. As similar symptoms may be caused by other diseases, complications may occur if the dog is dosed indiscriminately with anthelmintics.

The infective eggs of *Toxocara canis* are extremely persistent in the environment and present a danger to human health if they are ingested. Children are most at risk. The larvae that hatch from the eggs migrate from the intestine to various organs such as the brain, liver and eyes. The life-cycle cannot be completed in humans, but fits and blindness may result from this migration, known as 'visceral larval migrans'. *Toxascaris leonina* does not act in this way, but treatment for *Toxocara* will also eradicate this nematode. Frequent worming, as directed by a veterinarian, will help to prevent reinfection, which is especially likely in terriers and other dogs which catch rodents. Adult dogs should always be wormed when first acquired.

Other nematodes There are a number of other nematodes, some of which are more likely to be encountered in dogs such as racing greyhounds which live in kennels. Lungworms *(Filaroides osleri)* form nodules close to where the trachea divides to enter the lungs. The swellings are likely to result in a partial blockage of the airways, and a dry cough during exercise is a common symptom. The tracheal worm *(Capillaria plica)* produces similar symptoms.

The heartworm *(Dirofilaria immitis)* is transmitted by biting insects, typically mosquitoes that have fed on infected blood containing immature larvae

Right *A fiber-optic endoscope can be used to examine a dog's throat and airways. This instrument is used to detect the presence of parasites such as lungworms and to diagnose other disorders. This type of equipment is expensive and not very durable.*

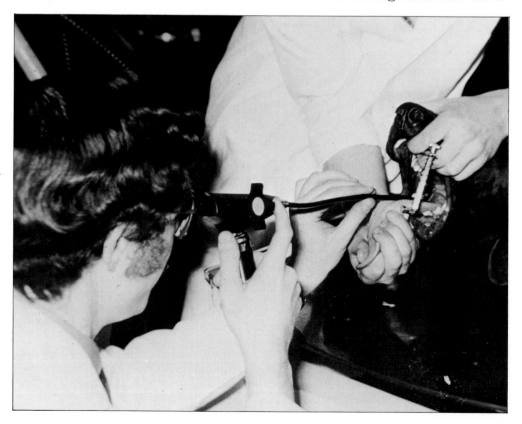

known as *microfilariae*. These then develop in the new host, causing blockages in the vicinity of the heart and pulmonary artery. Actual treatment of heartworms *in situ* is dangerous; regular preventative dosing of dogs in countries where the parasite occurs, such as Australia, is therefore recommended as a means of control.

A significant proportion of racing greyhounds will be affected with whipworms *(Trichuris vulpis)*. These worms live in the cecum in the intestine and cause few symptoms, apart from sporadic diarrhea cases. Hookworms are potentially much more serious in their effects. Larvae can enter the body by mouth or through the feet. In cases of *Uncinaria* species, they localize in the feet and cause severe irritation, but the *Ancylostoma* hookworms actually migrate to their host's intestine where, feeding on blood, they can cause both anemia and severe debility which may prove fatal if left untreated. Affected dogs may even need blood transfusions before they can be wormed safely. The effects of *Uncinaria* in the gut are less severe, but large numbers may cause diarrhea.

The most notorious nematode affecting dogs is undoubtedly the giant kidney worm *(Dioctophyma renale)* which does not occur in Britain or Australia, but is seen occasionally in many other parts of the world. Females may be 40in (100cm) long and ½in (1.25cm) in diameter. Dogs can be infected by eating raw fish or shellfish, also a source of other illnesses, such as salmon poisoning disease. The giant kidney worm localizes almost exclusively in the right kidney, which it gradually destroys over a period of time, and the only treatment is surgical removal of the kidney.

Protozoa These unicellular organisms are widely distributed, but cause disease more frequently in warmer areas of the world. Leishmaniasis, for example, is a disorder carried in the blood, like babesiosis, which occurs particularly in countries of the Mediterranean and may be transmitted from dogs to humans by insect bites. Other protozoa can affect the intestinal tract predominantly, causing diarrhea, especially in puppies. Such diseases are often referred to as coccidosis. Another common protozoal illness, toxoplasmosis, can give rise to a much wider range of symptoms, and will have to be confirmed by laboratory tests. The dog only acts as an intermediate host for this parasite; the final host is the cat. The dog cannot transfer the infection to humans, who can be another intermediate host; cats can only become infected if they consume an infected dog. The majority of cases of *Toxoplasma* in dogs can be traced back to the consumption of infected raw meat containing the toxoplasmosis cysts. A large number of dogs possess antibodies to *Toxoplasma*, which show they have been infected, but have never exhibited clinical signs. There is a danger in pregnant bitches that this protozoan will cross the placenta, and cause defects in the puppies.

ACCIDENTAL INJURY

Road accidents

A dog which has been hit by a vehicle may seem relatively unhurt at first, but could have suffered severe internal injuries, such as a ruptured spleen. Great care must always be taken when approaching a dog after it has been involved in an accident, particularly if it has been left standing, because it will probably be in a state of shock and may not hesitate to bite. If possible, the dog should be caught without direct handling; use a lead to form a collar by looping the lead through its handle, making a noose which can then be tightened around the dog's neck. Rather than attempting to examine the dog, which may be in pain, take it to a veterinary surgeon. If it cannot be caught immediately, then patience and a soft voice will help to gain its confidence.

In some cases, the injured dog will be unable to walk, and will have to be carried from the scene of the accident. A blanket is most suitable for this purpose. The dog should be transferred carefully to the

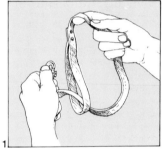

Handling an injured dog *If a dog has been injured, for example in a traffic accident, it will be necessary to restrain it in some way so that it cannot bite or cause itself further harm. A simple noose can be made by looping the end of the lead through its handle and slipping it over the neck of the dog* (1). *If the dog has been knocked over, a blanket makes an ideal stretcher* (2). *Under no circumstances lift the forequarters of the dog above the rest of the body; the diaphragm may be ruptured and such an action may force the organs in the thoracic cavity into the abdomen.*

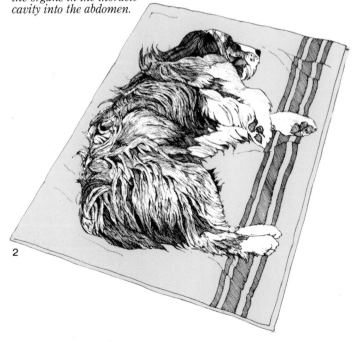

Bandaging *Any bandage must be securely tied to prevent the dog from removing it. In an emergency, such as a cut pad — which will bleed quite profusely — binding a bandage tightly around the foot is the best means of stemming the blood loss. Bandages will also be necessary for other injuries such as broken limbs. At first, the owner may need to carry the dog to prevent weight being placed on the affected leg (below).*

Ear *Cover affected ear with bandage, leaving other ear free as anchor.*

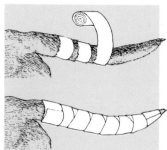

Abdomen *Bandages may be secured along the spine or at the tail.*

Tail *Prevent slippage by including hair; anchor with adhesive tape.*

Leg or foot *Wrap the bandage down the back and up the front of the paw, then*

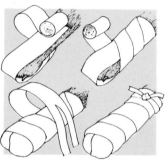

across the leg. Tie ends securely or finish with adhesive tape.

Tourniquet *Use a handkerchief twisted above injury. Loosen often.*

Splint *Two flat pieces of wood secured with tape can support a fracture.*

center of the blanket and carried to safety by two people holding opposite corners. If there is bleeding, pressure at the external site of blood loss may help to stem the flow. Bleeding is often profuse if the pads are cut, and the foot should be bandaged quite tightly before the dog is taken to a veterinarian. The veterinarian may need to sedate the dog to inspect the foot and repair any damage, to tendons for example.

There are various types of fractures. A simple fracture is a clean break in the bone. A compound fracture is where the bone is forced through the skin, and is more serious since there is a higher risk of infection developing at the site of the injury. X-rays will be needed to assess the damage before repair can be undertaken. There are various means of repairing broken bones, depending on the site and type of fracture. External fixation, using splints and casts, is often chosen in less serious cases, while internal fixation, with pins, wires or plates or a combination of these, means that an operation will be necessary.

Foreign bodies

A variety of foreign bodies can penetrate a dog's skin, but grass seeds rank among the most common. The sharp, protruding end of a grass haulm can get between a dog's toes and be driven in further as the dog continues walking. The first signs of such an injury are that the dog starts licking the area after exercise and may be reluctant to put any weight on the foot. This is an acutely painful condition, and the

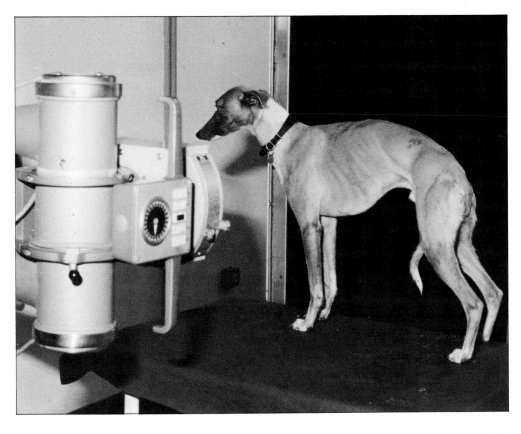

Left *This Whippet is undergoing an X-ray examination, a procedure that can be useful for detecting foreign bodies or broken bones. In some cases, it may be necessary to anesthetize the dog beforehand. To X-ray the intestinal tract, a radio-opaque substance such as barium is usually given to highlight the site of obstruction.*

dog may well try to bite if it is examined without being muzzled. Unless the seed is clearly obvious, the dog will have to be taken to a veterinarian.

If the grass seed is not visible, the dog will probably have to be injected with a sedative before it can be examined. The drug will make the dog drowsy in a few minutes and can stimulate defecation. The seed may have formed an abnormal hole, or sinus; if so, special forceps can be used to remove the source of the problem. If the haulm has tracked up the leg, further complications may result, but once it is discovered, recovery is usually uneventful.

Dogs living in areas close to water sometimes get fish hooks stuck in their mouths. These must always be removed by a veterinarian to prevent the injury from bleeding profusely once the hook has been removed. Similar injuries can result if a dog comes into contact with a porcupine, an animal which sheds its quills as a defense mechanism. The quills usually lodge around the head and chest and are painful to remove; sedation is recommended. Before the quills are removed, vinegar can be applied to the skin where the quills have penetrated to soften them.

Some dogs accidentally swallow small stones or pebbles, which may lodge in the intestinal tract, causing a total or partial blockage. Repeated vomiting is often a sign of an obstruction of this type although symptoms will depend to some extent on the part of the gut where the object is stuck. Small balls accidentally swallowed will give rise to similar symptoms. A veterinarian can detect the presence of a foreign body in the intestinal tract by means of contrast media X-rays. A radio-opaque substance such as barium which causes a white outline on the X-ray, is given by mouth, and sequential exposures, as the barium passes down the tract, will identify and outline the precise position of the blockage. It is not always necessary to operate to remove this kind of foreign body; some pass through the gut if their passage is assisted.

Burns

Puppies are most at risk from burns and scalding, because of their inquisitive natures. As an immediate first-aid measure, the affected area should be soothed with cold water to decrease the pain. Veterinary help will usually be needed. The extent of the injury may only become evident several days after the accident. Healing is usually a very slow process, and the risk of infection is high. Hair may never regrow if the skin has been badly burned. Owners sometimes cause burns by applying chemicals such as turpentine to the dog's coat to remove tar or paint, or by holding a hair-dryer too close to the dog's skin.

Young dogs, especially those that are teething, may electrocute themselves by gnawing through a live electric wire; no appliances should be left connected to the mains in a room where the puppy will remain unsupervised for any length of time. If an accident of this kind does occur, it is vital to switch off and disconnect the plug *before* the dog is touched. If the dog has stopped breathing, it will have to be

Artificial respiration Serious injuries, such as severe burns, may cause the dog to stop breathing. In such an emergency, artificial respiration may be the only way of saving the dog's life. First check that the tongue is free, and not blocking the airway at the back of the mouth (1). The dog should be lying on its right side. Gentle pressure should be exerted on the rib-cage at five-second intervals (2). Check that the heart is still beating by feeling either the femoral artery at the inside top of the hindleg (3) or the left side of the chest near the elbow.

given artificial respiration. This is usually carried out with the dog lying on its right side, while gentle, even pressure is exerted over the rib cage, by pressing down at about five-second intervals. Check that the tongue is free, pulling it forward if necessary to clear the airway. The dog should revive if the heart is still beating. The heartbeat can be felt on the left-hand side of the chest between the ribs, approximately at the point which the elbow reaches when this joint is flexed. Flat-nosed breeds such as Boxers, are more likely to need artificial respiration, especially since the soft palate in such dogs can obscure the windpipe and trachea.

If there is damage to the chest wall, close the dog's jaws tightly and exhale up the nose for a few seconds, pausing briefly between each breath. This will maintain the oxygen supply to the lungs if the normal pressure differential between the chest and the outside world has been lost.

Heatstroke
Any dog confined where it is exposed to direct sunlight or shut in a car during warm weather can rapidly succumb to heatstroke. Excessive panting and drooling are early signs; eventually the dog collapses. The treatment is to lower the animal's body temperature immediately and douse the skin with cold water. Signs of recovery ought to be evident within five minutes or so, and the dog will then need to be dried carefully and given water to drink.

Poisoning
Research indicates that one in every 2,500 dogs consumes a potentially toxic chemical, more often early in its life. Certain poisons actually attract dogs. Metaldehyde, which is used as slug bait, and ethylene glycol, a component of antifreeze which is converted in the body to toxic oxalic acid, are two

such chemicals which are common in many homes. Ethylene glycol is favored because it has a sweet taste, and as little as 1oz (30ml) can kill a 15lb (7kg) dog.

All chemicals should be kept out of the reach of dogs. Rodent baits, such as Warfarin, are another potentially fatal group of compounds, especially if ingested in small quantities over a period of time, as they lead to internal hemorrhaging. The symptoms of poisoning depend very much on the chemical concerned. In all cases veterinary advice should be sought immmediately, and details of the poison given if known. A suitable emetic can then be prescribed where appropriate.

It is possible to poison a dog unintentionally, through carelessness. Lead-based paints should never be used on kennels, nor should such woodwork be treated with preservative unless the chemical is known to be safe for dogs. Failure to follow instructions can prove fatal. If a bitch's mammary glands are washed with a prescribed antiseptic, they must be thoroughly rinsed afterwards to avoid poisoning the puppies. DDT and similar compounds should never be used on dogs or other animals. When a dog is trapped in a fire with poisonous fumes, it must be brought out into fresh air as soon as possible and, if it has stopped breathing, artificial respiration will need to be given. When no heartbeat is present, cardiac massage can be attempted to start the heart contracting again.

Snake and insect bites
If a dog is bitten by a snake it is important to be able to identify or even just describe the species responsible, so that correct treatment can be given. In Britain, there is only one poisonous species, the adder *(Vipera berus)*, but in other countries many more

potentially lethal snakes occur. After being bitten, the dog should be taken to a veterinarian with minimum delay, so that the appropriate anti-venom may be administered. Whenever practical, the dog should be carried or transported in a car so that the venom does not become widely dissipated in the body. A handkerchief should also be tied quite tightly above the site of the bite, if a limb is affected. The snake's fangs will leave two small holes, and a noticeable swelling if the bite was poisonous. If there is any ice available, an ice pack can be prepared by placing cubes in a sock or the sleeve of a shirt, tying the ends if necessary and applying this directly to the bite.

Puppies quite often get stung by wasps and bees, until they learn better. Most insect bites are relatively harmless but a bite on the tongue can be serious since it may swell up and block the airway. In such cases, urgent veterinary attention must be sought. Bees normally leave their stings behind, which look like splinters lodged in the surface of the skin. The sting should be removed at once, and the affected area can be soothed by application of an insect pain reliever. Certain dogs are allergic to stings, and collapse shortly afterwards; these cases also need prompt veterinary treatment.

SERIOUS CONTAGIOUS DISEASES

Distemper
Distemper is also known as 'hardpad' because it sometimes causes the pads on the feet to thicken. Its other effects are much more serious and, although it usually affects young unvaccinated dogs, it can also strike older individuals with little or no immunity, often with fatal consequences. Distemper is a virus transmitted by close contact with an infected dog, spreading from body secretions such as urine and saliva. The virus localizes first in the tonsils and neighboring lymph nodes. At this stage, the body may produce defensive antibodies to overcome the infection and symptoms will be relatively mild — an affected dog may lost its appetite for a short time and then recover without further trouble.

In certain cases, however, the infection spreads to other parts of the body, and about a fortnight or three weeks later from the first attack, the dog will become very ill. Symptoms include vomiting, bouts of diarrhea and a high temperature. More significantly, the eyes and nose will be runny and derangement of the nervous system may become evident, leading to fits and even paralysis. The neurological symptoms can occur years after the original infection, with the virus surviving in the brain until it is triggered in some way. This form of distemper is commonly seen in older dogs, and is sometimes known as 'old dog encephalitis'. A characteristic sign of a dog which has had distemper and recovered, is damage to the enamel covering of the teeth which results in the teeth being brownish in color, with pitted surfaces.

Distemper is a very unpleasant disease, for which there is no real treatment, although antibiotics can decrease the risk of secondary infections, which may otherwise lead to pneumonia. Euthanasia will almost certainly be required once nervous symptoms are evident.

The distemper virus is similar to the virus that causes measles in humans, although it is not a zoonosis. Despite this, however, measles vaccine provides some protection against distemper, and is particularly useful in situations where young unvaccinated puppies may have been exposed to distemper. Adminstering distemper vaccine in these cases is unlikely to provide immunity, since any maternal antibody which the puppies receive from their mother's milk will neutralize it. The first distemper vaccination is normally given at the age of about eight weeks, when the level of maternal antibody is declining and the next vaccination is given about a month later, when there is no maternal protection left. Since the measles vaccine is not affected by maternal antibodies the puppy develops its own immunity to distemper earlier than usual. Measles vaccine should only be given to young puppies when recommended by a veterinarian.

Infectious canine hepatitis (Rubarth's Disease)
Infectious canine hepatitis (ICH) is another viral disease which, as its name suggests, affects the liver, causing severe inflammation. There are two forms of canine adenovirus, CAV-1 and CAV-2, and CAV-1 is responsible for this illness. As with distemper, some unprotected dogs that encounter the infection develop few, if any, clinical signs. The route by which this virus gains access to the body is significant. Hepatitis, rather than respiratory disease, occurs if it enters via the mouth. As a result of the inflammation of the liver, the dog will show signs of abdominal pain and jaundice, which turns the mucous membranes, such as those on the inside of the mouth, a yellowish color. The blood clotting system is also disturbed and hemorrhages may be evident.

Once the dog starts to recover, its appetite returns, but the accompanying weight loss is only made up slowly. In about a quarter of cases, a dog will develop the characteristic 'blue eye' after about a week, which is a bluish opacity visible across the surface of one or both eyes. This normally resolves itself spontaneously, but the virus may remain in the body, localizing in the kidney and will be excreted in the urine for a period of months, spreading the disease to other dogs. 'Blue eye' is especially prevalent in Afghan Hounds, and can even result from administering a live vaccine to this breed.

Leptospirosis
Leptospirosis is caused by bacteria, normally either *Leptospira canicola* or *L. icterohaemorrhagiae*. Terriers and other 'ratters' are particularly at risk from

the former strain, since this bacterium is commonly associated with rats and excreted in their urine. The disease can strike dogs at any age, but is more prevalent in male dogs, possibly because of the importance of urine as a scent marker. Infection can spread simply by sniffing at urine, or from close contact with the genital area of a recovered individual which is still excreting the causal organisms. This group of bacteria can also survive for long periods in water and may enter the body directly through the skin, particularly through a cut or wound.

The symptoms in both forms of infection are similar, and again can range from mild to fatal. Vomiting, diarrhea and a high temperature are often the early signs, followed by a sharp fall in temperature, with increased thirst and labored breathing. Antibiotics can help to overcome the infection. Jaundice occurs more commonly in cases of *L. icterohaemorrhagiae* infection, whereas permanent kidney damage may result from *L. canicola*, with ulcers often on the tongue and in the mouth.

There is a risk of leptospirosis being transmitted to humans, and so dogs which may be affected need to be handled carefully, preferably with gloves so that no discharges come into contact with the skin. When exporting dogs to certain countries, it is necessary to have them tested for leptospirosis, since *L. canicola* is not currently present in much of Scandinavia, as well as Australia and New Zealand. The risk of introducing the disease comes from dogs which have had a mild, virtually symptomless infection yet are still carriers of the disease.

Parvovirus

Parvovirus infection in dogs attracted great attention when it first appeared in the late 1970s; the disease assumed epidemic proportions. Early outbreaks occurred in Australia and the United States, and the virus soon spread to Europe. Its origins are still unknown, but it seems likely that it arose as a mutant form of the feline panleucopenia virus. Indeed, in the early days of outbreaks, vaccines intended for cats were used to protect dogs from the disease. Now specific vaccines for dogs have been produced, and may be combined with vaccines for other diseases.

The disease can take two forms and the course of the illness depends largely on the age of the dog affected. In puppies, younger than five weeks, the virus attacks the heart muscle, causing sudden death. Any puppies which do survive are almost certain to have permanently damaged hearts, and later exhibit the usual signs of heart failure.

In older dogs, parvovirus leads to a severe enteritis, which is often hemorrhagic, and, with the vomiting, leads to rapid dehydration. It is sometimes possible to keep such dogs alive using an intravenous drip, but recovery will be slow. The damage to the intestinal lining may permanently impair the absorption of foodstuffs, and persistent outbreaks of diarrhea are not unusual.

The virus is named after its size — 'parvo' means 'small'. After being shed from the body it can remain in the environment for a year or longer and will survive exposure to most common disinfectants, apart from sodium hypochlorite (bleach) and those of the aldehyde group. As a result, infection is easily spread, especially where dogs congregate, at kennels and shows. It can be transferred both on footwear and feeding bowls. Vaccination is highly recommended.

HEART DISEASE

The heart is comprised of four chambers, separated by valves. In older dogs, valvular thickening is not uncommon, and causes blood to leak back into the previous chamber, rather than being pushed forward. Several types of cardiac failure are recognized, and the symptoms depend on which part of the heart is actually failing. If the left side is affected, the dog will not want much exercise, will tire rapidly and have difficulty in breathing. Prolonged bouts of coughing, especially at night, and restlessness, are other typical symptoms. When failure is centered on the right side of the heart, then edema, or build-up of fluid in the tissues, occurs, with an accumulation in the abdomen as well, known as ascites. Closer examination by a veterinarian will also reveal a swollen liver and spleen. In generalized heart failure, a combination of signs with be noticed.

Treatment entails modification of the dog's diet and lifestyle. It will need more rest to decrease the burden on the heart, and a diet low in salt is also recommended. Two types of drugs are usually employed to treat congestive cardiac failure. Diuretics, which increase sodium and water loss via the kidneys, and cardiac glycosides, responsible for slowing the rate of the heart while increasing its contractility, making it more efficient, are usually prescribed together. The actual treatment regimen depends on the severity of the condition. Once the condition is stabilized, treatment will need to continue for the rest of the dog's life. If the dog starts to vomit after being given the drugs, the veterinarian should be informed, since this can be a sign of a toxic reaction to glycosides such as digitalis, and it may be necessary to alter the dose accordingly.

Various congenital heart diseases can occur in puppies. Signs of congestive heart failure may show up before the dog is mature. It may be possible to correct the defect successfully by surgery, but the dog might have to be treated in a veterinary hospital, where more elaborate equipment will be available. In severe cases, however, puppies die shortly after birth.

RESPIRATORY DISEASE

There are a variety of causes of respiratory disease. A common ailment, affecting the trachea and bronchi of the lungs, is infectious tracheobronchitis, also

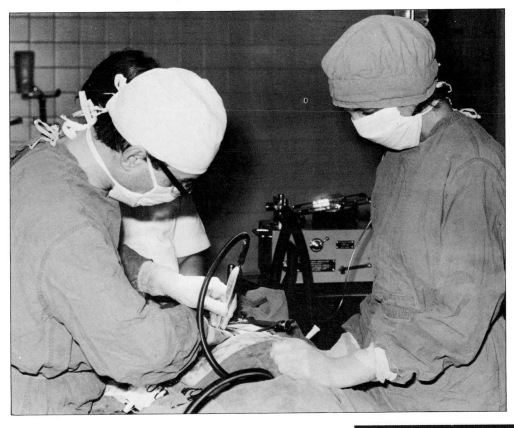

Left *Thoracic surgery poses particular problems for the anesthetist. A ventilator, to keep the dog breathing while the chest wall is open, is shown here in the background. Successful surgical treatment of many heart conditions is now possible.*

known as kennel cough. In this instance, a range of infectious organisms can be responsible for the condition, commonly canine adenovirus type 2 (CAV-2), parainfluenza virus and the bacterium, *Bordetella bronchoseptica*.

Kennel cough usually occurs where a number of dogs are kept together, such as boarding kennels. The incubation period can be as long as 10 days, and the most common sign is a dry cough which can become paroxysmal. This response can be easily elicited by touching the throat area over the trachea. There may also be an accompanying nasal discharge. Kennel cough rarely proves serious and normally resolves itself, but antibiotics can prevent secondary infections developing. A vaccination is available for kennel cough, protecting against the most likely causes, and it is worth considering if a dog is going into kennels, or mixes with other dogs frequently, at shows for example.

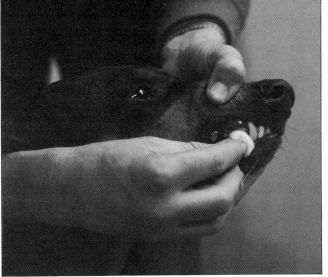

TOOTH DECAY

The teeth of some dogs, poodles in particular, rapidly accumulate tartar. This brownish deposit is usually seen initally at the base of the tooth, on the outer surface, extending onto the gum where accumulations will not be wiped off naturally. The debris hardens and bacteria develops, causing the gum to be inflamed, turning bright red. The bacteria can then gain access to the root of the tooth, causing a painful abscess and loosening the tooth, so that it will have to be removed. The first sign of

Cleaning the teeth *A dog's teeth should be cleaned regularly to prevent a build-up of tartar, which will otherwise lead to tooth decay and gum inflammation. A piece of dampened cottonwool and canine toothpaste is ideal for the purpose* (above). *Puppies should be trained to become accustomed to having their mouths opened. One hand should be placed around the muzzle and the other used to prize the jaws apart* (left).

periodontal disease is often bad breath, although this can be a symptom of other problems, notably kidney disease. The dog may dribble, and will have difficulty eating. In severe cases, the only means of removing the build-up of plaque is for the dog to be anesthetized first. Any seriously damaged teeth will be pulled out at the same time. Further accumulations may be prevented by brushing the teeth weekly, using a canine toothpaste applied on a soft toothbrush. Care should be taken to ensure that brushing does not make the gums bleed and, unless the dog has been accustomed to having its mouth opened regularly from an early age, it is very likely to resent having its teeth brushed at all.

DIARRHEA

Diarrhea is not a disease in itself, but is a symptom of various disorders. Under normal circumstances, passage through the dog's digestive tract will take at least five hours, but it can fall to as little as 20 minutes, and there are many possible causes of the resulting diarrhea, some of which are non-infectious, such as gluten and milk sensitivities. Diseases caused by a number of bacteria, such as *Salmonella*, and viruses can also result in diarrhea certain parasites, including the protozoa *Coccidia*, responsible for the disease coccidosis, also produce these symptoms.

Diarrhea is often self-limiting if food is withheld for a day or so, but it is likely to be serious in puppies, since they can easily become dehydrated, especially when vomiting as well. Veterinary advice must then be sought without delay, particularly if the feces contain traces of blood; excreted blood is usually brown-red in color if it entered the gut in the small intestine. Breakdown and absorption of food takes place in the small intestine, whereas lower down the tract, in the colon, water rather than foodstuffs is absorbed. Straining to pass feces which have a jelly-like consistency and traces of blood, is indicative of colitis, a condition which is seen especially in collies.

A serious problem, usually encountered in big, deep-chested dogs, is acute gastric dilatation, often linked with torsion. It can be caused by feeding the dog a heavy meal immediately before prolonged exercise. Gas builds up in the stomach, causing it to dilate, and then the organ can twist, leading to torsion. The dog becomes restless and tries to vomit, with no effect. Its abdomen rapidly swells and signs of shock, such as profuse salivation and difficulty in breathing, are apparent. Immediate veterinary assistance is required for this condition, which otherwise will rapidly be fatal.

ANAL GLANDS IMPACTION

When a dog defecates, secretions from a pair of anal sacs are deposited on the feces, acting as a scent marker for other dogs in the vicinity. Unfor-

tunately, in many dogs, these sacs, also referred to as 'glands', do not empty properly, and the resulting blockage causes considerable discomfort. The dog may attempt to relieve this by 'scooting', dragging its hindquarters along the ground, and by biting the anal region. If left untreated, defecation will become painful and local infections can develop, causing abscesses.

These sacs will need to be emptied by a veterinarian. Repeated blockages are quite common and if not cleared, actual fistula open up on the external anal skin. It may be necessary to wash the sacs out with a salt solution to prevent further blockage, and give antibiotic treatment to reduce the risk of infection. In severe cases, surgical removal of the sacs may be advisable. Increasing the roughage content in the diet of dogs prone to anal sac obstructions, by adding bran, may help to prevent a recurrence of the problem.

URINARY DISORDERS

Incontinence can be essentially behavioral in origin, but certain developmental defects can also be responsible. The ureters normally run from each kidney, conveying urine for storage in the bladder. If one or both ureters link directly with the urethra, which leads from the bladder, or with the vagina, then urine will be voided as soon as it is produced, since it cannot enter the bladder for storage. Such 'ectopic' ureters can be corrected by surgery. The condition is most common in female dogs and usually becomes evident from the age of three months on.

Infections of the urinary tract are also common in bitches since the female urethra is shorter than that of the male, making it easier for bacteria to enter the body. Antibiotic treatment will then be necessary. If the bladder is affected the disorder is known as cystitis.

Infections can also predispose to the formation of stones or calculi in the tract. These calculi can vary in consistency, with certain breeds such as the Dalmatian being genetically predisposed to formation of particular types. Pain and difficulty in urination are typical signs to watch for. In male dogs, enlargement of the prostate gland can also produce similar symptoms. Treatment of calculi will depend very much on the extent and severity of the blockage. Blockage of urine flow is obviously serious, since the bladder only has a finite capacity, and can rupture if it becomes overfull. Calculi can occur throughout the urinary tract, even in the kidneys. In this site, it may be possible to flush them through, without recourse to surgery. Recurrences are common, however, and antibiotic therapy may help to prevent repeated episodes, if a low-grade infection is present. Calculi in the tract can be located by the use of contrast media X-rays. Catheters may also be used to break down blockages of this kind affecting the urethra.

The dog's kidneys are likely to decrease in efficiency as it gets older. Increased thirst and urine output, with intermittent vomiting, decreased appetite and weight loss are the symptoms of chronic renal failure. Bad breath, as a result of the uremia can also be indicative of a renal problem. The changes occurring in the kidney tissue leading to renal failure cannot be reversed, but the symptoms can be treated and the condition alleviated to a great extent.

Dietary changes are important. The level of protein in the diet needs to be reduced and only protein of high biological value, such as that derived from eggs, given. It is advisable to feed the canned foods prepared specifically for dogs suffering from this condition. These are usually available only from veterinarians. Water must be constantly available, and vitamins of the B group will need to be supplemented since these are not stored in the body, and will be lost in increasing amounts via the urine. Anemia may occur since the hormone responsible for stimulating bone marrow development is normally produced in the kidneys; 1,25 DHCC, a chemical that controls calcium absorption from the gut and its storage in the body, is also produced by the kidneys so skeletal problems can arise.

NERVOUS DISORDERS

Rabies

The most serious disease affecting the nervous system is rabies, which can be easily transmitted to humans by an infected dog, and is invariably fatal. Rabies is not currently present in Britain or other countries such as Australia, and great efforts are made to keep the infection out. If the virus responsible establishes itself in the wildlife of a region, it proves virtually impossible to eliminate. In mainland Europe, the fox is an important natural host species, while in North America, skunks fulfill a similar role. Dogs usually contract the disease by being bitten by one of these creatures, or another dog or cat. The incubation period can be very variable, depending largely on the site where the virus entered the body. It tracks along the peripheral nerves, before passing to the central nervous system. At this stage, usually about one or two months after the bite, symptoms become evident.

The first sign of rabies is often a change in temperament. The dog becomes aggressive or withdrawn and changes in its voice may be noticed. The eyes often take on a strange appearance. Swallowing becomes increasingly difficult as the throat muscles become paralyzed, and saliva drools from the mouth. Death can occur in the accompanying convulsions or during a coma. Dogs do not show hydrophobia (fear of water), unlike the majority of humans who fall victim to the disease.

Humans are most at risk of being infected by dog bites, and the virus can live in saliva a day before clinical signs become apparent. As an emergency first-aid measure, any wound caused by an animal

Below *Rabies is caused by a virus and usually transmitted by saliva. It is not necessary for a human to be bitten to succumb to the infection, since the virus can enter the body via a cut. In dogs, aggressive behavior and a change in the voice, are often the first signs of the disease.*

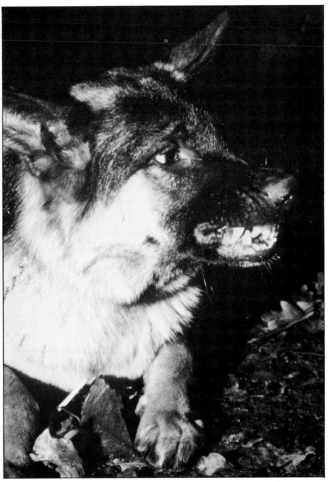

suspected of having the disease should be washed out, preferably with ethanol, or rinsed under a running tap, and iodine applied afterward. Medical advice should be sought without delay. Since the saliva is infective, it is not necessary for a bite to introduce the virus to the body. It can enter through existing cuts or breaks in the skin, and so any animals which may be suffering from rabies should never be handled — even after death they can pose a threat to human health.

In view of the lethal nature of this disease, strict quarantine measures are enforced for animals entering countries where the virus is not already endemic; a six-month quarantine in approved kennels is required in Britain. Vaccination against the disease is a legal requirement in much of the United States and parts of France, whereas elsewhere in Europe, such as Germany, this is a voluntary procedure. The use of rabies vaccines is not permitted in Britain, however, except for dogs which are going abroad to areas where it is required. Advice can be obtained either from a veterinarian or the Department of Agriculture of the country concerned.

One illness that can produce similar symptoms to rabies is Aujeszky's Disease, also known as pseudo rabies. The infection is most common in pigs, and dogs kept on pig farms, or those which may have eaten contaminated uncooked pork, are most at risk. The virus produces nervous symptoms; an affected dog often scratches and paws repeatedly at its face, which has led to the disease being termed 'mad itch'. Aggression towards humans and other creatures is not a feature of Aujeszky's Disease. There is no cure.

Epilepsy
This is a distressing and frightening condition. Without warning or previous symptoms, a dog will suddenly collapse on its side and its legs will start to move, as if it were running. Defecation and urination may occur. After a minute or so, the dog will regain its feet, albeit often unsteadily, and will appear unharmed. The cause of such convulsions is unknown, although the condition has been shown to be inheritable, and is sometimes described as idiopathic epilepsy. It is most common in the Cocker Spaniel, with seizures often beginning during the second year of life, yet they can also occur beforehand. Various drugs are available to control seizures.

GLANDULAR AND HORMONAL DISORDERS

Adrenal disorders
The adrenal glands lie close to the kidneys. The outer layer, known as the adrenal cortex, produces two major hormones, aldosterone and cortisol. There are two associated disorders, which resulting from under- or overproduction of these hormones. Addison's Disease, more common in female dogs, is caused by an abnormally low rate of hormone synthesis, and its effects are most likely to be seen when the dog is stressed, for example after a period of prolonged exercise. Lack of cortisol will cause decreased appetite and possibly vomiting, while an aldosterone deficiency leads to excessive dehydration, often worsened by vomiting. Confirmation of the disease is by bloodtest. Once an acute case has been stabilized, synthetic forms of these hormones will have to be given for the rest of the dog's life.

The hormonal output of the adrenal glands is controlled by the brain. If the area of the brain concerned is affected by a tumor, output will be excessive; this will also happen if the gland itself becomes diseased in a similar way. Under certain circumstances, the actual zone in the glands responsible for the production of the hormones may increase in size, and this will lead to an increase in synthesis. Symptoms are likely to include an increase in appetite and thirst, with a corresponding increase in urine production. In addition, there will be hair loss on both sides of the body. The abdomen will swell into a pot belly and the underlying muscles will

weaken. Tests will be necessary to discover the precise cause of the condition, which is known as Cushing's Syndrome. If a brain tumor is responsible, the prognosis is very poor, but drugs can be given to prevent the gland over-producing.

Diabetes
Two forms of diabetes are recognized. Diabetes mellitus results from a decrease or total lack of the hormone insulin, which is produced by cells in the pancreas. This hormone normally lowers the glucose level in the blood, by stimulating individual cells to take it up. A lack of insulin causes a glucose deficiency in the cells, and an abnormally high concentration in the blood. This sugar is passed in the urine, giving it a characteristically sweet smell. There will be an increased volume of urine, leading to a greater thirst than normal. Since the cells are unable to obtain glucose, body tissues are broken down to meet energy demands, resulting in weakness and weight loss over a period of time.

This disease, sometimes referred to as 'sugar diabetes' is at least five times more common in bitches than dogs, and usually occurs after the age of five years. One of the more unexpected symptoms may be the formation of cataracts in the eyes. Blood-tests will confirm the disorder. In very mild cases, manipulation of the diet by eliminating carbohydrate (which will be converted to glucose) as much as possible, and feeding a relatively high level of protein, may be adequate. Otherwise insulin will probably have to be given. Regular check-ups will be necessary to make sure that all is progressing well.

The other form of diabetes, diabetes insipidus, is much rarer. It is marked by an excessive thirst, and a high urine output. This disease results from a deficiency of the hormone known as ADH (anti-diuretic hormone) which acts on the kidney, controlling urine output. The most likely cause is a brain tumor. A urine sample, as for diabetes mellitus, collected in a clean, sugar-free container, will help to distinguish this condition from other diseases where urine output is increased, such as chronic nephritis. A synthetic form of ADH can be administered, even if the primary cause of the illness cannot be treated.

Pancreatic insufficiency
The pancreas, apart from producing hormones, also synthesizes enzymes, which are vital for the digestion of food in the small intestine. If there is a shortage of these, food will pass through the tract in a relatively undigested state, resulting in pale, often quite liquid feces which smell unpleasant and contain high levels of fats and proteins which have not been broken down. This disorder is easily confirmed by laboratory tests on a series of fecal samples.

The lack of enzymes can be corrected by means of tablets or capsules, while the addition of ox sweetbreads (pancreas) to the diet can also help. Altering the diet by increasing protein and decreasing the levels of fat and carbohydrate is recommended. Dried diets are also produced for this condition, and may serve to obviate the need for further supplementation. Pancreatic insufficiency seems to occur more commonly in breeds such as the German Shepherd, and, although the condition itself will respond to treatment, the desired weight gain does not occur in about half of all cases.

Thyroid imbalance

The thyroid glands, located in the neck, produce the hormones thyroxine and triiodothyronine, which are important in controlling the level of body activity. If output is depressed, dogs become sluggish, obese and very sensitive to cold surroundings. Other signs may include hair loss and a greasy skin. Supplementation of hormones will reverse these effects, but has to be given over a long period of time, although tablets are not expensive. A deficiency of dietary iodine can also lead to hypothyroidism; the Basenji appears to need relatively high levels of this mineral. Over-activity of the thyroid is a rarer condition in dogs, and generally results from a tumor of the thyroid glands.

DISORDERS OF THE SENSES

Eye problems

There are, in fact, various hereditary problems that affect the eyes of certain breeds and may need surgical correction. When the eyelids are turned in toward the eye, the condition is described as entropion. This is encountered most often in Chows, Golden and Labrador Retrievers, setters and St Bernards. Ectropion is the reverse of entropion: the lower lids are turned out away from the eye. As with entropion, physical injuries can also give rise to the condition. Spaniels and Bloodhounds commonly suffer from ectropion.

In certain breeds such as the Pekingese, the tear fluids, which keep the surface of the eye moist, do not drain away properly, and run down the face, causing stains which are especially obvious against a pale coat. Preparations to remove such marks are available in pet stores. An anatomical defect of the tear ducts is usually responsible; severe cases may be corrected by surgery.

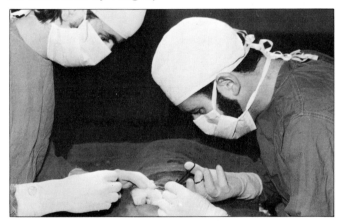

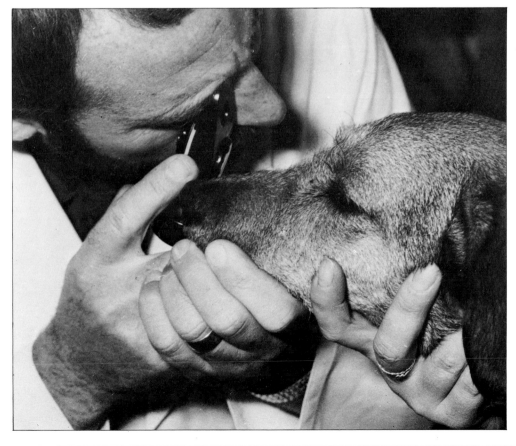

Above *Significant advances have been made in the field of eye surgery in recent years. Apart from correcting deformities of the eyelids, surgery on the eye itself, to treat such conditions as cataracts, may also be performed.*
Left *Examination of a dog's eyes is carried out in a darkened room using an opthalmascope. This instrument enables the veterinarian to inspect the posterior chamber of the eye, including the retina.*

Symptoms of eye disorders often include watering and reddening of the eyes, with frequent blinking. When the eye is suffering from an irritation, such as the inturned eyelashes associated with entropion, then the dog will paw at the eye in an attempt to relieve the irritation. Eye preparations prescribed for infections need to be applied frequently, several times daily, since the tear fluids will rapidly wash the treatment out of the eye.

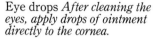

Cleaning eyes *Use cottonwool moistened with warm water and wipe gently.*

Eye drops *After cleaning the eyes, apply drops of ointment directly to the cornea.*

Damage to the surface of the eye, causing corneal ulceration, is especially common in dogs with prominent eyes, such as Pugs or Pekingese. These dogs can also suffer from prolapsed eyeballs, in which the eyes are forced out of their shallow sockets by fighting or rough handling around the neck. Although highly unpleasant, it is quite possible to correct this injury. Immediate veterinary assistance should be sought, and the eye kept on a damp, clean pad of lint or cloth while the dog is adequately restrained.

Other eye complaints can be encountered more often in older dogs, notably cataracts, which cause opacity of the lens, giving the eye a whitish appearance. Increasing clumsiness is often the first sign of a deterioration in vision, and if there is any reason to suspect that a dog is losing its sight, then a veterinarian should be consulted without delay. When a dog becomes blind, it can often adapt quite well, particularly in familiar surroundings. The sense of sight is not as important to dogs as humans, since they possess a more highly developed sense of smell. Some eye conditions, such as progressive retinal atropy (PRA) are inherited, and breeding stock should be checked to minimize the risk of transferring the defect to the next generation.

Ear problems

Congenital deafness is usually associated with white-haired dogs such as Bull Terriers and Dalmatians. Although all puppies are deaf for the first three weeks after birth, a problem of this type will be evident before the dog matures. It can be difficult to assess the extent of the disability, as the deafness may be partial rather than total. No treatment is possible; this type of deafness is inherited, caused by abnormality in the formation of the cochlea, where the sound waves are received.

Apart from the connection with coat color, deafness can also be genetically linked with blindness. For this reason, Merle Collies are not paired together, nor are Harlequin Great Danes. Dogs possessing the gene responsible for this condition have irides which are both white and blue and are described as 'wall-eyed'. Although normal themselves, the offspring of two such dogs will be severely handicapped.

Ear infections are common in breeds such as spaniels, whose long, heavy ears obscure the ear canals. Regular, gentle cleaning is recommended to decrease the risk of infection, using a little olive oil applied on cottonwool. The ears are very sensitive structures, however, and should not be probed. Signs of infection include repeated head shaking and rubbing of the ears; infected ears usually smell unpleasant as well. If the ear flaps become very traumatized, hematomoas may form, resulting in noticeable swellings. These are caused by the accumulation of blood in the tissue, and may have to be corrected surgically.

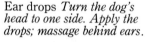

Cleaning ears *Use moist cotton buds to remove wax or dirt but do not probe deeply.*

Ear drops *Turn the dog's head to one side. Apply the drops; massage behind ears.*

Most ear infections are mixed in origin, with bacteria, fungi and even parasitic mites being implicated. Examination of the ears by an auroscope will help a veterinarian to decide on the best course of treatment. Most types of treatment must be given for a fairly longish period; recurrences are not uncommon. In persistent, severe cases, an operation to open up the vertical part of the ear canal, known as aural resection, may be advised. Dogs which suddenly develop an acute irritation of the ear may have a grass seed lodged inside, and a veterinary examination will again be necessary.

SKIN DISEASE

Skin disease in dogs is often linked to other disorders, such as Cushing's Syndrome, but an important cause, because it can be transmitted to humans, is ringworm. In spite of its name, this infection is causing by a fungus, usually *Microsporum canis*, and any part of the body surface, even the bases of the nails, can be affected. The fungus develops on the skin, causing circular, scabby patches with accompanying hair loss over the region. The hairs become brittle, and break off easily. The

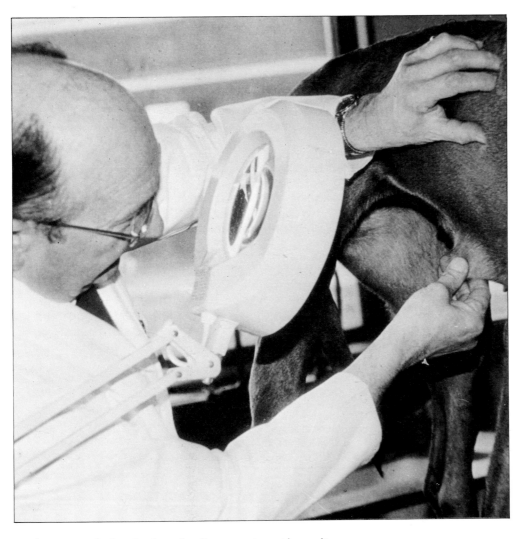

Left *Here a veterinary dermatologist is examining a Great Dane using an illuminated magnifying glass for a closer view of the skin and hair. Skin scrapings are also valuable for diagnostic purposes.*

perimeter of the lesion is the most active site. Humans can be infected by contact. Reddening and irritation of the skin are often the first signs of ringworm in humans; the forearm is a likely site of infection if the dog is picked up regularly.

In many cases, the fungus responsible will glow fluorescent green when the lesion is examined with a special light, known as a Wood's lamp. Microscopic study of affected hairs and cultures may also be necessary and, since fungal growth on culture media is notoriously slow, it may be a fortnight or so before the results come through. Treatment is likely to entail the use of the antibiotic griseofulvin, although this cannot be given safely to either humans or animals during pregnancy. A course of treatment will last at least a month. Once ringworm has been confirmed, other animals in the household should be examined, especially cats, as they may also be suffering from the disease. The effects of ringworm are likely to be much less apparent in cats. The fungal spores may persist in the environment for a year or more, and will be present on grooming tools and bedding. Washing items in iodophor-type disinfectants and alcohol can destroy any spores which may be present.

AGEING

The problems of age in dogs are usually insidious in onset. Coat color fades and the dog becomes less active. A range of diseases occur more often in older dogs, and are generally of a degenerative nature. Cardiac disease and chronic renal failure are two such examples. Inter-vertebral disk weakness is also seen more frequently. The disks between the vertebrae of the spinal column normally act as shock absorbers, but with time their outer casing may rupture, causing the softer, inner core to impinge on the spinal cord itself, and giving rise to a degree of paralysis and considerable pain. Complete rest and keeping the dog confined in a small pen, may lead to some improvement. Running up stairs, or jumping onto a chair frequently precedes injuries of this type, the vast majority of which occur in Dachshunds, although other breeds such as Pekingese can also be affected. There is a form of paralysis, however, which is progressive by nature, and causes death within a week of the original signs, by preventing the muscles responsible for breathing from operating normally.

Osteoarthrosis, a degenerative change occurring

in the cartilage lining the joints, typically affecting the hip and stifle, is more often encountered in larger breeds. It results in stiffness, which will be particularly evident when the dog gets up after a period of rest, yet disappears to some extent following movement. The condition will be made much worse if the dog is obese, since the joints have to bear more weight. Treatment is geared to relieving the pain associated with the condition, but if it occurs in a young dog, following a traumatic injury in particular, radical surgery may be necessary.

Neoplasms, or tumors, are also more commonly seen in middle-aged and elderly dogs. These uncontrolled growths are either benign or malignant (cancerous). Benign tumors do not spread or metastasize through the body, but can cause problems according to their site, pressing on part of the respiratory system for example. They usually grow quite slowly compared to malignant tumors and can be removed without fear of recurrence.

Studies reveal that a high proportion of canine tumors affect the skin. Mammary tumors are extremely common in bitches, accounting for nearly half the total cases. The incidence of neoplasia in dogs has been estimated at four cases a year per 1,000 dogs. One-third of these cases are malignant; nearly all bone tumors are in this category. Boxers are extremely susceptible to neoplasms of all kinds, while other breeds which have a high incidence include the Cocker Spaniel and Boston Terrier.

The actual causes of these tumors are not fully understood at present. Parasites can be involved; the worm *Spirocerca lupi* will increase the risk of malignant tumors of the esophagus, especially in hound breeds. Viruses can also be implicated in some instances. Treatment depends very much on the individual case; a total recovery is sometimes possible if the tumor is detected early and affects the body surface.

Surgery is often used to remove the tumor and cryosurgery has been adopted increasingly for dealing with neoplasms in specific sites, such as the anal region. In the case of cryosurgery, liquid nitrogen is applied to the growth using a special probe and the very low temperature that results should kill the tumor cells, leaving healthy surrounding tissue in-

Ageing As in humans, ageing in the dog is an insidious process; the dog will become less active and hearing and sight will deteriorate gradually. Pigmentation is also lost: overall, an older dog will appear paler in color than a puppy, even in the case of pale-colored breeds. A young dog is active and full of energy (right and below).

Towards middle age, there will be a decline in the level of activity. In dark breeds, white hairs may being to show, particularly around the muzzle. There may a tendency to put on weight (right and below).

tact. Over a period of time, the tumor will slough off and, since there has been no direct excision, there is likely to be less risk of cells breaking away from the main mass and being carried round the body in the blood stream to set up new foci of infection elsewhere. Other methods of therapy include radiation treatment and chemotherapy.

EUTHANASIA

There will come a time when an old dog will start to suffer and, although a veterinarian can provide guidance, it is up to the owner to decide on euthanasia. This is invariably traumatic, but, as a general rule, once the dog can no longer walk, or eat without vomiting for example, then it is kinder to put it out of its misery. Keeping a dog which is clearly suffering with no hope of recovery is very distressing for all who come into contact with it.

It is best to take the dog to the veterinarian, bid it farewell and leave it there, rather than staying right to the end, since the dog will detect the emotionally charged atmosphere and become upset as a result. The usual means of euthanasia is to administer an overdose of barbiturate into a vein. The dog gently falls asleep very quickly, as if given a barbiturate anesthetic, but passes away almost immediately, never regaining consciousness.

Owners may prefer to bury their dog in a grave at home if this is permitted, or purchase a plot at a pet cemetery. Graves should be about 3ft (90cm) deep. The veterinarian will deal with the body if asked to; in this case, incineration is most likely to be the procedure that is adopted.

Below The lifespan of dogs can be quite variable. Small breeds, such as the Dachshund, tend to live longer than giant breeds — up to 15 years in some cases. Some giant breeds, such as the Great Dane, may only live for seven or eight years.

In old age, as the synthesis of melanin is reduced, coat and nose color become paler. Particularly in a spayed bitch, obesity will become a major problem unless food intake is reduced — because of the decline in activity. The eyes may become cloudy and vision will diminish (right and below).

Children and dogs *Families with children are twice as likely to have pet dogs as households where there are no children. Caring for a dog helps a child to develop a sense of responsibility. Dogs also make great companions for children of any age* (far right). *While most dogs are patient and tolerant — puppies more so than adult dogs — it is important that children are taught not to handle a dog roughly or provoke it by teasing* (right). *Such treatment may make the dog nervous and more liable to bite.*

DOGS AND HUMAN HEALTH

There are a number of illnesses which can be transmitted from dogs to humans, ranging from relatively minor disorders such as ringworm to the killer disease rabies. These 'zoonoses' have attracted much media attention in recent years, but risks can be minimized by sensible precautions.

Routine worming will help to lessen the likelihood of worm infections; if the dog is trained to defecate on a hard, smooth surface such as concrete the eggs of *Toxocara canis* can be destroyed using a blowtorch. Children are particularly vulnerable: they must be taught not to let dogs lick their faces and to wash their hands after touching a dog, certainly before handling food.

Dog utensils should also be washed and stored totally separately from those used by humans. Recently, the bacterium *Campylobacter* has been shown to be a zoonosis and it can cause severe diarrhea, like *Salmonella*. Dogs should be prevented from scavenging, which is how they acquire such infections, and should be fed exclusively on commercially prepared or cooked foods, rather than raw meat or poultry. The latter is a particular source of salmonellosis if not adequately cooked. The canine form of brucellosis can also be transmitted to humans and results in fever and general weakness and debility. Generally, however, this illness is not as severe as that transmitted by cattle.

Supervising children closely when they are playing with dogs will also help to protect the dog. Children can handle pets roughly and may provoke a bite. Any wounds resulting from a dog bite should be washed thoroughly and an antiseptic applied to the site of injury. The relatively long, pointed canine teeth of dogs mean that puncture wounds are most common, and various types of unpleasant bacteria present in the dog's mouth are likely to be injected deep into the tissue. Tetanus, caused by *Clostridium tetani*, can follow if the person concerned is not protected by vaccination. This disease can have serious consequences.

The most serious zoonosis is rabies. The disease does not occur in some countries, notably Britain, where a strict quarantine is imposed on all imported animals to prevent the disease becoming established. Elsewhere, however, rabies is a threat and pets may be required by law to be vaccinated. Here the danger is more likely to come from strays or abandoned dogs that have become infected by rabid squirrels or foxes, for example. Never approach a strange dog which is behaving oddly and, if you do get bitten, consult a doctor at once.

BREEDING DOGS

It is important for every dog owner to have some understanding of canine reproductive cycles, if only to ensure that accidental pregnancies are avoided. Spaying a bitch is a sensible, acceptable precaution; chemical controls are also available.

Breeding dogs can be a most enjoyable hobby, but it is rarely financially rewarding. In order not to contribute to the vast number of dogs made homeless each year, careful planning is needed to place all members of the litter. Other breeders or pet owners are likely to be interested in good pedigree puppies, but mongrels may prove more difficult.

THE REPRODUCTIVE CYCLE

Male

The onset of maturity, known as puberty, occurs from the age of six months onward in male dogs, although this varies to some extent from breed to breed. As a general rule, males attain puberty at a slightly later age than bitches of the same breed, with certain exceptions such as the Beagle, where the situation is reversed. This delay is usually a matter of weeks, but can extend to months in a few breeds such as the Saluki and Chow Chow.

Dogs should only be allowed to breed after the age of one year, to ensure maximum fertility. They can mate all the year round and will remain sexually competent until well into old age, although their fertility will decline progressively. Stud dogs should not be mated too frequently, as this will cause a temporary decline in fertility.

Female

The bitch has distinct sexual cycles, resulting in periods of estrus. These 'seasons' or 'heats' may be noticed from the age of six months onward, but cer-

tain breeds, such as German Shepherds, are much slower to mature, and may not begin their cycles until the age of 18 months. Estrus occurs every seven or eight months on average, but intervals anywhere between two and 18 months are not unknown. Basenjis, for example, only have one period of estrus annually. Climate may be significant: German Shepherd Dogs come on heat every six months in Britain, but this figure falls to an average of 21 weeks in the United States. The size of the dog has no significant effect on the length of estrus cycles, nor does the time of year appear very significant, although Basenjis generally come into heat during the autumn.

There are four recognized stages of the estrus cycle. The first is pro-estrus, when the vulva swells and a bloody discharge is seen from the vagina. This occurs before ovulation and is in no way equivalent to the menstruation of female humans and primates. Menstruation does not take place in female dogs. During pro-estrus, dogs are likely to be attracted to the bitch, but their advances will not be reciprocated; although a pair may play together, any attempt at mounting by the male will be rebuffed by

TABLE SHOWING SOME OF THE MAJOR INHERITED AND CONGENITAL DISORDERS OF DOGS			
DISORDER	**OBSERVATIONS**	**BREEDS TYPICALLY AFFECTED**	
Clefts of lip and palate	May be hereditary in origin, but other factors, such as a nutritional deficiency in the bitch, may also be responsible.	American Cocker Spaniel American Staffordshire Terrier Beagle Bernese Mountain Dog Boston Terrier	Bulldog Dachshund German Shepherd Dog Shih Tzu
Deafness	Dog often appears unresponsive, even stupid, until this disorder is recognized.	American Foxhound Bull Terrier Collie Dachshund	English Foxhound Great Dane Scottish Terrier
Distichiasis	A double row of eyelashes; most common on upper lids. Causes severe irritation and excessive tear production. Surgery is the only effective treatment in the long-term.	American Cocker Spaniel Bedlington Terrier Boston Terrier Boxer	Griffon Bruxellois Kerry Blue Terrier Lakeland Terrier Yorkshire Terrier
Ectropion	Eyelids directed outward. Causes inflammation of the conjunctiva and cornea, with increased tear production. Needs to be corrected by surgery.	American Cocker Spaniel Bassett Hound Bloodhound	Bulldog Clumber Spaniel St Bernard
Entropion	Eyelids directed inward, more commonly the lower lids. Eyelashes cause severe irritation of the cornea, with increased tear production. Again, requires surgical treatment.	Bloodhound Bulldog Chesapeake Bay Retriever Chow Chow	Irish Setter Labrador Retriever Rottweiler St Bernard
Hip dysplasia	Deformed hip (cox-femoral) joints. Signs extremely variable: lameness in severe cases, yet may pass unnoticed in a mild case. Detected by radiography. Inherited, hence the need to check potential breeding stock for this weakness.	American Cocker Spaniel Black and Tan Coonhound English Setter German Shepherd Dog	Giant Schnauzer Shetland Sheepdog
Intervertebral disc abnormalities	Symptoms influenced by locality of abnormality, as is the prognosis for treatment. Total, confined rest is essential for recovery, irrespective of other therapy. Surgery can be of assistance in some cases.	American Cocker Spaniel Beagle Boxer Dachshund	Dandie Dinmont Terrier Pekingese
Luxating patella	Results in lameness, typically about five months of age. Caused by movement of 'knee bone' or patella. Degree of weakness variable. Surgical correction is the only treatment.	Boston Terrier Bichon Frise Chihuahua	Pomeranian Yorkshire Terrier
Progressive retinal atrophy	The first sign may be that the dog appears to be having difficulty seeing at night. As its name suggests, this disease is progressive, and ultimately blindness will result. The time span may extend for months to years. It appears to be an inherited condition; different forms of PRA are believed to be inherited in different ways, so it can be either a dominant or recessive trait.	Border Collie English Cocker Spaniel English Springer Spaniel Golden Retriever Gordon Setter Labrador Retriever Norwegian Elkhound	Pekingese Pointer Pomeranian Poodle Samoyed Shetland Sheepdog Welsh Corgi
Umbilical hernia	Distinct, noticeable swelling around the umbilicus or 'belly-button', resulting from a partial protrusion of the abdominal contents. Can be corrected by surgery if necessary.	Basenji Bull Terrier Collie	Pekingese Pointer Weimaraner

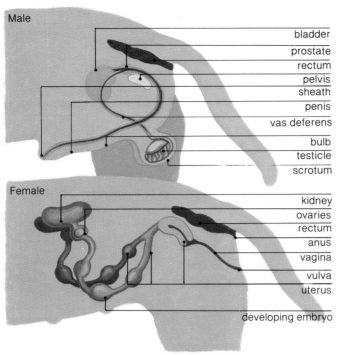

Male

bladder
prostate
rectum
pelvis
sheath
penis
vas deferens
bulb
testicle
scrotum

Female

kidney
ovaries
rectum
anus
vagina
vulva
uterus
developing embryo

the female. Restlessness often accompanies this phase, which lasts an average of nine days, although it can range from two to 27 days.

The next stage is estrus, or sexual receptivity. The bloody discharge will become clear, and the bitch will allow mating to take place. Again, this period of the cycle extends over about nine days, but may be as short as three days or continue for three weeks. The release of ova from the ovaries, or ovulation, usually occurs approximately two days after the start of estrus.

In the following two or three months, the hormone progesterone controls the reproductive tract, whether the bitch is pregnant or not, and this period is known as diestrus. During this phase a pseudo pregnancy may occur.

The longest stage of the cycle is anestrus, when there is no sexual activity apparent, and this lasts until pro-estrus next occurs. Bitches will normally continue to come on heat into old age and will remain fertile, although breeding is not to be recommended after the age of six years old, because of the increased risks. Bitches are not normally mated until their second heat.

Above left *The diagram illustrates the position of the major organs of the reproductive system of the male dog and bitch. Females should not be mated after their sixth year; while males remain active sexually into old age, their fertility will decline.*

Left *Dogs readily detect a bitch in heat and will congregate around her, even is she is not in the receptive phase of the cycle — estrus. During the pro-estrus part of the cycle, the vulva swells and there is a bloody discharge from the vagina. This normally lasts about nine days.*

BREEDING

The choice of a mate for the bitch will be influenced by the purpose for which the puppies are required. Bloodlines are important for those who wish to exhibit but the pet breeder is unlikely to worry about the finer points of a stud dog. Once the stud dog has been chosen, the owner of the dog should be approached well in advance of the anticipated date of mating, to make sure the stud will be available and to ascertain the fee. As an alternative to payment, some owners will accept first choice of a puppy from the litter, especially if the bitch has a good pedigree.

It is a good idea to make an appointment to visit the kennels and see the stud dog in advance. Ideally, it should excel in those points which are relatively poor in the bitch, so that it complements, rather than reinforces, her strengths and weaknesses. Before mating, the bitch should be given a booster vaccination to ensure that a high level of immunity will be passed to the puppies. Once pregnant, the bitch must not receive live vaccines, since these are extremely dangerous to the puppies. Both the bitch and stud dog should be checked for potential defects, such as hip dysplasia.

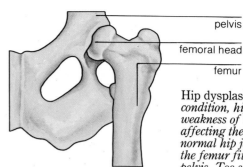

pelvis

femoral head

femur

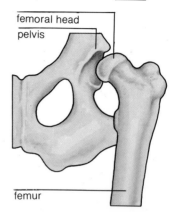

femoral head

pelvis

femur

Hip dysplasia An inherited condition, hip dysplasia is a weakness of the hip joints, affecting the hindlimbs. In normal hip joints, the head of the femur fits into a cup on the pelvis. Too shallow a cup or an abnormal head will affect the stability of the joint. In severe cases, the dog will be very lame. X-rays are used to screen breeding stock for the weakness.

Below At shows, a judge will examine each entry for soundness. It is possible to detect abnormalities such as patellar luxation in this way. Patellar luxation, in which the knee cap moves abnormally, is a congenital weakness most commonly seen in toy breeds.

Left *The dog's penis contains a bone which helps maintain rigidity while the penis is inside the bitch's vagina. During mating, a 'tie' is usually formed in which the muscles of the vagina clamp the penis in place to prevent withdrawal before ejaculation has occurred. Mating lasts about 20 minutes. In addition to spermatazoa, nutritional secretions for the sperm will also be ejaculated.*

Establishing which is the best time for mating during the estrus period can be difficult, especially for the inexperienced breeder. The owner of the stud dog may be prepared to board the bitch for a short period, to ensure the maximum chance of a successful union. The right time is usually about 10 days after the start of pro-estrus, but this again can be variable. No increase in body temperature accompanies ovulation as it does in humans, and the only clinical test of value is examination of vaginal smears under a microscope to detect the characteristic changes in the cells.

Mating will probably take place twice, under controlled conditions, over the four-day period from the tenth day onward. The reaction of the bitch to the dog should be monitored frequently. When ready to mate, she will stand with tail erect, over to one side.

Copulation is a protracted process. The male mounts the female, gripping with the forelimbs and, once penetration has taken place, the tip of the penis swells. The muscles of the vagina contract around the penis, holding it tightly in place, so that withdrawal is not possible. In male dogs there is a bone, known as the os penis, inside the penis, which helps to maintain its rigidity while it is lodged in the vagina. 'Tying' or locking does not occur in every case, notably with Chow Chows, nor is it essential for fertilization.

The dogs remain joined together for about 20 minutes or so, rarely longer than three-quarters of an hour. The semen is ejaculated early during the tie, following the secretions produced by the urethral glands, and the dogs then alter their positions, so they face in opposite directions. Further ejaculation of prostate gland secretions helps to nourish the spermatozoa, and increase the chances of fertilization. A certain amount of struggling by the bitch is normal, but the tie will remain intact. Trying to break a tie can result in injuries to one or both partners. If the liaison is undesired, subsequent treatment to prevent implantation of any fertilized eggs is recommended as an alternative.

It is possible to have a bitch artificially inseminated, using semen from a dog in another part of the country or even further afield, if permission is granted by the governing canine authority. As rabies can be transmitted by semen, its movement from country to country is often controlled strictly by license. Fresh canine semen can be kept viable for nearly a week, or it can be frozen indefinitely, to be thawed when required. Tests will be required to ensure that the bitch is in the estrus phase, and ready to mate. The semen is carefully introduced, using a pipette, and the bitch's hindquarters are kept raised, so that none flows back from the cervical region where it was deposited and out of the vagina. A gloved finger is then inserted for about five minutes into the vagina, to mimic the effect of the tie: this is suppose to improve fertility.

PREGNANCY

There are three major phases of pregnancy. First, the fertilized egg or eggs spend their early life in the uterus, and then implant into the wall. The placenta, which is responsible for nourishing the developing embryo and removing waste products, then develops, and the organs start to form. The major phase of growth takes place in the final part of pregnancy, from day 33 onwards. The gestation period lasts about 63 days in total, but breed variations of a week more or less are not uncommon. Any puppies born more than a week premature are unlikely to survive.

Pregnancy may not be apparent during the first month after mating, although a veterinarian can give an indication about four and a half weeks after mating. Such examinations have to be carried out carefully to prevent any damage to the developing puppies. Obesity, or well-developed abdominal musculature, as present in breeds such as the Greyhound, complicates the task. Some bitches also tense their abdomens, making palpation impossible. The time of examination is quite vital; after five weeks, it is much harder to detect pregnancy by this means, as the fetuses grow and feel like abdominal organs. By six weeks, abdominal distension is likely to be evident, and the mammary glands swell in preparation for producing milk. An earlier change will be evident in bitches which have not given birth before. The teats will become more conspicuous, and will turn pink if the skin is unpigmented, because of the increase in blood flow to the region. A day or so before birth, some clear fluid or milk may be apparent.

A recent innovation in the field of pregnancy detection is the use of ultra-sound machines, which can be divided into two categories, depending on their mode of action. Those of A-mode are quite reliable from about four and a half weeks onward, whereas Doppler machines can be used five weeks after mating. It is also possible to detect the fetuses on radiographs from the seventh week as their developing skeletons will contain sufficient calcium by this stage. Routine radiological examinations are not carried out, however, since unnecessary exposure to radiation must be avoided if at all possible, as it can cause malformations in the fetuses.

BIRTH

Preparation
A suitable box where the bitch can give birth will be necessary and should be placed in a quiet, warm part of the home, such as a spare room. The size of the box will depend on the bitch: it must be large enough to allow her to lie full length without difficulty. Whelping boxes are often made of wood, but a cardboard box will be quite adequate, providing the sides are cut down to an appropriate height. The

Right *During her pregnancy a bitch may act oddly at times, adopting toys or old slippers to mother. Such behavior is also symptomatic of pseudo pregnancy, a condition which can be treated with medication, although the best long-term solution may well be spaying.*

bitch must have easy access, but the sides must not be so low that the puppies could roll or be pushed out. It is also useful to have a bar fitted inside the box around the sides so that the bitch does not accidentally lie on her puppies and kill them. The box should be lined with newspapers, rather than blanketing, as these can be replaced easily and are less likely to hide any puppies. The bitch may tear up the paper to make a nest.

The bitch should be encouraged to sleep in the bed for the last 10 to 14 days of pregnancy. She will not need much extra care for the majority of the gestation period. Exercise in moderation will help to keep a healthy muscle tone, but she should not be encouraged to jump at all, particularly in the latter stages. The diet will need to be adjusted to match the growth of the developing puppies; from the fourth week onward, increased amounts of protein will be required. This extra food is best given in the form of an additional meal, because the expanding uterus will compress the stomach and reduce its capacity.

About four weeks before the birth is expected a veterinarian will provide the necessary tablets for worming the bitch, and advise on the need for dietary supplements. Such products must only be given in accordance with the instructions; overdosing can have serious side-effects. Sterilized bone flour, for example, is a valuable source of calcium and phosphorus, but excessive amounts will lead to skeletal and joint defects. On a balanced diet, little if any supplementation is strictly necessary. In the last few days of pregnancy, pressure from the uterus can result in constipation and if required, up to three teaspoonfuls of medicinal liquid paraffin can be added to the food.

LABOR

The first stage of labor is characterized by restlessness. The bitch may cry out occasionally because of uterine contractions. Bedding will be torn up as a nest is prepared for the puppies. In order to facilitate birth, ligaments along the vertebral column slacken, and the pelvic bones become more obvious. The fibrous connection between them softens to assist the passage of puppies through the birth canal. Loss of appetite is fairly typical about a day before birth takes place, and a fall in body temperature, to about 99.5°F (37.5°C) or lower,

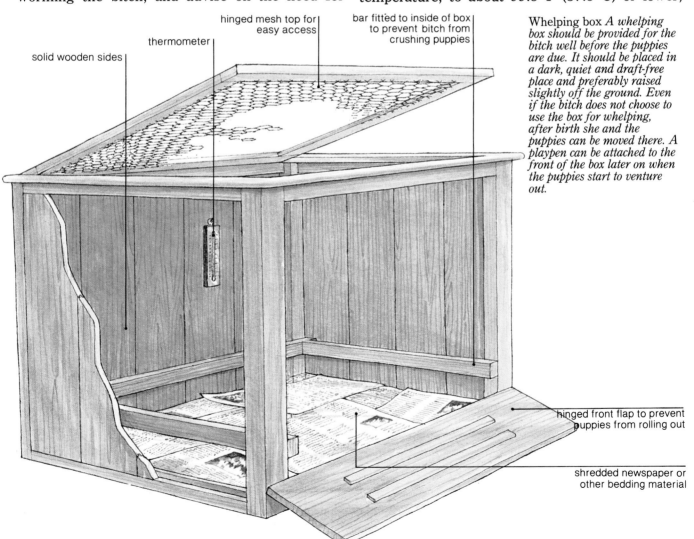

solid wooden sides

thermometer

hinged mesh top for easy access

bar fitted to inside of box to prevent bitch from crushing puppies

hinged front flap to prevent puppies from rolling out

shredded newspaper or other bedding material

Whelping box *A whelping box should be provided for the bitch well before the puppies are due. It should be placed in a dark, quiet and draft-free place and preferably raised slightly off the ground. Even if the bitch does not choose to use the box for whelping, after birth she and the puppies can be moved there. A playpen can be attached to the front of the box later on when the puppies start to venture out.*

Birth *Puppies are normally born head-first* (right). *The bitch will sever the umbilical cord as soon as each puppy is born and the placenta will be passed shortly after. Puppies are born blind and deaf* (below), *usually within half an hour of each other. They should begin suckling soon after birth in order to receive early immunity from their dam's colostrum. The bitch will lick and clean them, stimulating their excretory systems* (far right).

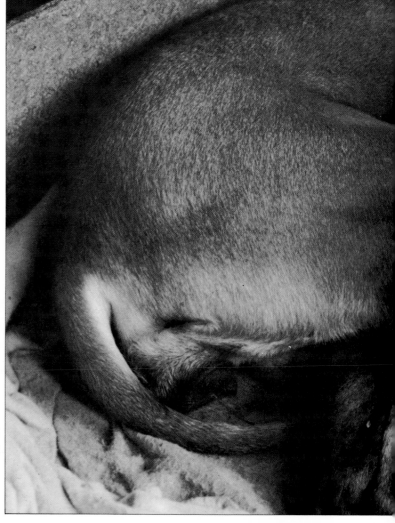

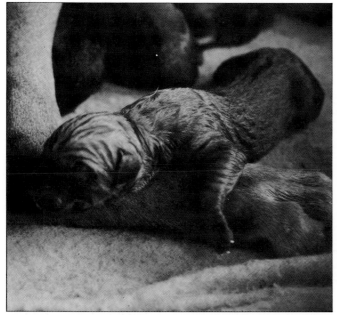

from the normal 101.5°F (38.5°C) is an indication that birth is imminent. A clear discharge will be apparent from the vulva, and the bitch will spend considerable time licking and cleaning this area. This stage lasts for a day, or possibly slightly longer in the case of a bitch giving birth for the first time. It is important that the bitch is kept quiet, with the minimum of disturbance, although food and water should be at hand if she wants them.

The onset of the second stage of labor will be characterized by noticeable abdominal contractions, panting and straining. The vulval discharge will become more noticeable, and the first sign of a puppy is likely to be the appearance of its enveloping water bag, known technically as the chorioallantoic sac, which is full of fluid. This sac can rupture during labor, causing the fluid to pour out, or else it will be broken normally by the bitch once it emerges from the vulva. The umbilical cord connecting the puppy to its placenta will also be bitten through.

The final stage of labor consists of the passing of the placenta or afterbirth, which should follow within a quarter of an hour of the birth of the puppy. The bitch may eat the afterbirth but, if not, it should be removed and flushed down a toilet. One placenta should be voided for each puppy and it is important to keep a check on the number since they are sometimes retained, causing an infection in the uterus later. They are normally green in color, and this is not a sign of infection as a general rule.

Puppies are normally born at intervals of 15 to 30 minutes. In small litters, the gap between puppies may be longer, extending up to an hour or so. The whole litter should be born within about six hours from the onset of the second stage of labor, but in a few instances, a longer period of time may elapse. A few bitches actually pause to rest during labor, which can be distinguished from a physical difficulty in giving birth, by the lack of contractions.

General assistance

The bitch may fail to break the water bag of a puppy, particularly at the end of labor, when she is tired. It will be necessary to carry this out for her, so the puppy can breathe. Make sure the hands are

in place to prevent bleeding. The remaining stump soon shrivels up and ultimately sloughs off naturally. It can be dabbed with iodine to minimize the risk of infection.

PROBLEMS DURING BIRTH

Although in the majority of cases, no problems arise during the birth process, there are certain serious conditions that require urgent veterinary attention. It is a sensible precaution to notify the veterinarian of the expected date for the arrival of the puppies, particularly if difficulties have been encountered with the bitch before. The incidence of dystocia (difficulty in giving birth) is higher in certain breeds, and can be related to their physical characeristics.

One problem is when the bitch goes into labor yet produces no puppies. This is most likely to occur with individuals or small breeds expecting a large litter. Puppies should begin to appear within two hours of the start of obvious uterine contractions; if none do and the contractions weaken, then veterinary advice must be sought. Delays of more than an hour between births are also likely to be a cause for concern. In some cases, a puppy may become stuck, half way out of the birth canal. This is a serious condition, because oxygen starvation may damage its brain irreversibly within five minutes or so. A veterinarian will be able to advise an owner on the best course of action in such an emergency.

Difficulties can also occur if the pelvic canal is relatively small, a common problem of Scottish and Sealyham Terriers. Breeds with large heads, such as the Bulldog, may also encounter difficulties giving birth normally, while deformed puppies are also likely to cause blockages. Difficulties over the positioning of the puppy, or presentation, can be a source of concern. Puppies are normally born head first, but in some cases, reverse or breech presentations do occur.

It may not be possible for a veterinarian to treat these problems by manual means, and a Cesarian section will have to be performed whereby puppies are removed via incisions made in the abdominal wall and uterus. Such surgery is likely to be necessary in the case of bitches which have fractured a pelvis previously, or are overdue by several days, if other methods have not stimulated birth.

Sadly, some puppies may appear malformed at birth, or shortly afterward. The first sign of a cleft palate, for example, is usually milk running back down the nose. Another highly unpleasant congenital defect is hydrocephalus, which is relatively common in Chihuahuas. The skull of affected puppies is abnormally domed, and filled with fluid. Young dogs showing serious malformations usually do not live long, but should be put down by a veterinarian at the earliest opportunity. Some defects are relatively minor, and will not handicap

clean, then break through the membranes with the fingers and lift the puppy out. Hold its head slightly lower than the rest of the body to drain fluid forward, insert a finger in its mouth to stimulate breathing and check its nose is clean. The young dog can be dried gently with a towel which will also encourage it to breathe. Once the puppy is breathing satisfactorily, it should be placed back with the bitch, close to her teats is possible.

If the bitch has not bitten through the umbilical cord, this will have to be done by hand. Breeders sometimes prefer to tear rather than cut it. Excessive force will result in an umbilical hernia, however; cutting the cord will reduce the risk of injury, although blood loss is more likely. Under normal circumstances, the muscle of the umbilical cord contracts after being bitten through, reducing blood loss to a minimum. If the cord is to be cut, a piece of string will need to be tightly tied about 2in (5cm) from the puppy's body. The cord can then be snipped with scissors on the side of the ligature closest to the placenta, leaving the tie

Right *Most bitches do not object to careful handling of their puppies, but disturbances should be kept to a minimum in the first few days.*
Below *The safest way to hold a puppy is to use both hands to support both the forequarters and the rear.*

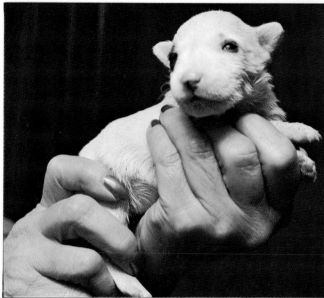

Right *The puppies should be watched when they are suckling to ensure that all appear to be doing well. If their dam resents them suckling from a particular teat, she may be developing a case of mastitis — veterinary advice should be sought without delay.*

the puppy in any way, although it will not be suitable for exhibiting. Double dew claws in the majority of breeds, and even extra toes are included in this category.

POST-NATAL CARE

After giving birth, the bitch will settle down with her puppies, licking them contentedly. They should respond by suckling, normally within 30 minutes of being born. It is vital that the puppies take milk as early as possible, since the first portion, known as colostrum, contains protective antibodies (immunoglobulins) which will help to give immunity against illness until the puppy's own defence system is fully operational. The amount of colostrum ingested directly determines how long this maternal protection will last. The protection declines progressively and will disappear by the time the puppy is 12 weeks old. The actual colostral component of milk is produced for the first two days when the puppies are suckling. During their first week of life, puppies feed about every two hours, sucking the nipple with the forelegs raised, while pushing hard against their dam's body with their hindlimbs. The hind teats are often preferred, but the puppies do not develop a specific pattern of organization, taking whichever teat is available.

The right environment is very important during the early part of the puppies' lives. They are dependent at first on the temperature of their surround-

ings, since they are not yet able to regulate their body temperatures in the same way as adult dogs. The room in which they are housed should therefore be at least 70°F (21°C). If additional heat is needed, an infra-red lamp can be obtained. It is vital that this is positioned in such a way that there is no risk of actually burning the puppies or their dam. Lights of this type are produced exclusively for use with livestock; some emit heat with a minimum light output. They must not be covered, because the heat generated can present a fire risk. An alternative is to use a low wattage heating pad, positioned in the basket under a sheet of newspaper. The running costs of such pads are minimal, even when they are left on constantly. A heating element spreads heat evenly over the surface of the pad when the puppies are in contact with it.

At first puppies normally sleep together in a group, to maintain their body temperature. They will not make any noise, apart from the occasional grunt. Crying is a sign that the puppies are hungry or cold. Their senses are very limited at this stage. Born blind, it will take perhaps a fortnight for their eyes to open, and three weeks before they can hear.

Diet
The bitch will require increasing quantities of food as the puppies grow. Three or four meals may be necessary, with the actual amount of food depending on the breed concerned. As a guide, about one and a half times as much food as usual should be offered in the first week of lactation, twice as much as during the second week. Subsequently, until the fifth week, at least three times the normal food intake will be required. It is vital that a balanced diet is offered throughout this period, to prevent abnormalities such as rickets.

An adequate intake of fluid is also essential for a lactating bitch, and will help to ensure that sufficient milk will be produced for the puppies. Apart from water, one of the milk replacement foods used for rearing orphaned puppies can be given directly to the bitch. These are preferable to cow's milk, which contains relatively low levels of fats and proteins and a high level of sugar.

Weaning
Weaning is a gradual process, which usually starts when the puppies are about three weeks old. In the wild and sometimes in domestic circumstances, bitches begin to wean their litter by vomiting food; as an alternative, a soft food will be required. A little lean meat, or one of the special puppy foods can be given, softened with water beforehand. The bitch will begin to leave her puppies for longer periods from three weeks onward and the litter should be fed when she is not present. Puppies can be slow to feed themselves at first, and to tempt them, the food should be given on a flat saucer, which will make it easily accessible. It may be necessary to place a small amount on their tongues initially, until they acquire a taste for it. There will be a gradual change

Left *During lactation, the bitch should be given more food and fluid than usual to ensure that she can meet the needs of her growing family. A shortage of fluid, in particular, would soon be reflected in a decline in milk production.*

in the puppies' feeding habits, as they take progressively more meat, and their dam will start to discourage them from suckling, as her milk production falls.

By the age of six weeks, the puppies will be virtually independent, and will be acquiring their first, or deciduous, set of teeth. Once weaning is complete, they should be receiving four meals a day. The first and last meals of the day should be milk, perhaps with some soaked biscuit meal. Milk replacement foods mixed with water in the required quantity should be offered. The other two meals should consist of solid foods, given perhaps at midday and six o'clock in the evening. The use of a special canned puppy food, mixed with some fresh cooked items, is recommended. As the puppies get older, their meals can be gradually reduced in number, taking the milky foods out of the routine one at a time. By the age of six months, a young dog

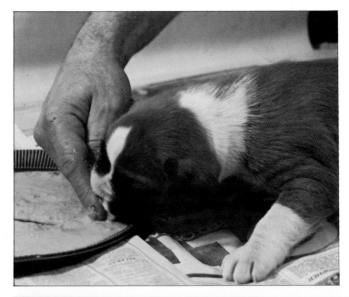

Feeding puppies *A puppy may need to be encouraged to feed on its own by offering it food on a finger* (above right). *Most soon learn to eat from a dish* (above), *although it may be better to feed the puppies individually to ensure they all get an adequate share* (right). *The bitch will gradually tire of her offspring; as soon as they stop suckling, her milk supply will dry up* (far right).

will be receiving two meals a day in increased amounts as it grows.

Rearing problems

Bitches very rarely harm their puppies, but it is safest to keep the sire of the litter away from them, even if he lives on the premises. The bitch will stay very close to the puppies for the first few days, and should not be disturbed unnecessarily. If, however, any teat appears sore and abnormally swollen, there may be a localized infection of the gland, known as mastitis. Veterinary advice must be sought without delay, and the teat should be covered to prevent puppies suckling from it. Antibiotic therapy will probably be required.

A particularly serious problem that occasionally occurs, especially in bitches with large litters, is milk fever, also known as eclampsia. The most obvious signs are that the bitch becomes unsteady on her feet, neglects her puppies and loses her appetite. The condition results form a deficiency of calcium in the blood itself, and if not corrected, coma leading to death is inevitable. An injection of a calcium-containing compound can reverse the condition quickly, if the bitch is seen by a veterinarian as soon as symptoms become evident.

Eclampsia is one of the circumstances in which some or all puppies will have to be fostered or hand-reared, at least until the bitch recovers. If at all possible, they should be transferred to another bitch who has a smaller litter, or even a bitch lactating as a result of a pseudo pregnancy. A veterinarian may be able to suggest a suitable foster parent. Hand-rearing itself is a time-consuming, albeit a rewarding process. The powdered milk replacements for dogs are widely available and are simply mixed as instructed with water. Special bottles and teats are available to facilitate feeding; it is worth obtaining a

Below *Special feeders are available for hand-rearing puppies. Care must be taken not to rush feeding, so as not to choke the puppy.*
Right *Even when puppies are weaned, a milk replacement food can be of value. It is better not to offer food outside; milk rapidly sours and insects may be attracted to the dish.*

stock of such items before a bitch whelps, so that they are on hand for any emergency.

Hygiene is very important when rearing any young creature. Food should never be left standing, but preferably mixed fresh before each feed. Any stored in a refrigerator should be used within a day. Before feeding, milk must be warmed to about 100°F (38°C), with the temperature being checked by means of a thermometer. It is vital not to rush a puppy which is being bottle-fed, as this increases the risk of choking. Any fluid that accidentally passes into the lungs may cause inhalation pneumonia. After feeding, the utensils used should be immersed in a proprietary product used for cleaning babies' bottles and then rinsed.

After each feed, the puppies' faces should be wiped with a cottonwool swab that has been moistened with warm water. The abdominal and anal regions should also be gently rubbed with a clean swab, to mimic the dam's licking which stimulates the puppy to defecate and urinate after feeding.

The temperature of the puppies' environment must be maintained in the absence of their mother, reducing gradually from about 85°F (30°C) in 5°F (2°C) stages from the end of the first week onward. It is quite possible to hand-rear puppies successfully, but any which did not receive colostrum

EARLY SURGERY

There are a number of routine surgical procedures that are normally carried out early in a puppy's life. Some of these help to prevent problems later on, but many are purely cosmetic. There is a growing trend

away from such unnecessary surgery; in Britain, for example, ear cropping is now banned by law.

The removal of a puppy's dew claws is a relatively minor operation if carried out in the first few days after birth. These claws, corresponding to the human thumbs and big toes, are vestigial in the dog, and serve no useful purpose. In certain cases a puppy may not even possess a full set. Only breeds like the Briard must retain the dew claws on their hindlegs if they are to be exhibited.

If the dew claws are not removed, they often get caught up and torn quite seriously later in life. The hind dew claws are the source of most problems, and will need regular trimming. Since these claws

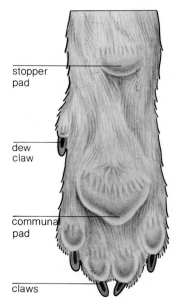

stopper pad

dew claw

communal pad

claws

Left *The nails on the dog's feet do not need cuttting normally — they are worn down gradually. The dew claws, however, may need to be clipped since they are not in contact with any surface. Dew claws can be surgically removed when the dog is young to prevent them being caught and torn later in life.*

do not touch the ground they are not worn down naturally, but continue growing and can twist right round and back into the flesh itself. The claws in the pads rarely need trimming if the dog walks on hard surfaces such as pavements, but if in doubt, then a veterinarian will advise accordingly. A claw will bleed profusely if it is cut incorrectly, especially when inadequate tools are used for the task, and this will make the dog nervous of such treatment at a later date. Dew claws can also be removed on older dogs, but this is a more serious operation, which may have to be carried out if one is torn accidentally.

Tail docking was originally performed for practical reasons, to prevent hunting dogs being caught by their tails in thick undergrowth. Subsequently, it has become fashionable just for show purposes. Approximately 45 breeds are required to be mutilated in this way. Breed standards specify the amount of tails which should remain. The Airedale Terrier, for example, must only lose the tip of its tail, while the Boxer will have just a stump left after docking. In certain breeds, such as the Cavalier King Charles Spaniel, it is left up to the owner to decide as to whether their dog should be docked for the show ring. If such surgery is carried out, then a veterinarian will perform the task, using an anesthetic.

There are a number of other operations of a cosmetic nature which it is unethical for a veterinarian to perform on pedigree dogs, if these would disguise a fault which would be penalized under the show standards concerned. Obvious cases include alteration of ear and tail carriage.

REPRODUCTIVE DISORDERS

Diseases
Certain diseases are sexually transmitted in the dog. These include a venereal tumor, which causes swellings close to, or actually on the genitalia.

Infections acquired at the time of mating can lead to problems during pregnancy. A form of brucellosis, caused by *Brucella canis* was first identified in the United States in 1966, but is virtually unknown in Britain at present. The signs of infection are infertility in both sexes, or puppies being born dead or dying shortly after birth. In some cases of apparent infertility, the bitch may have actually conceived but the developing embryos died and were reabsorbed at an early stage. Abortion during the final third of pregnancy is also common, with a vaginal discharge being present for a long period afterward. This discharge will be infectious, and the organism is likely to persist in the body for at least 18 months. Abortion is likely to occur again, if the bitch is mated again during this period.

The bacterium responsible for this disease can be present in aborted pups, as well as their dam. Like other forms of brucellosis, the canine type can be transmitted to humans, so that protective clothing, including gloves, should be worn when dealing with dogs that might be infected. The signs of illness in humans are weakness, enlarged lymph nodes throughout the body and an accompanying fever, although generally this disease is less severe than brucellosis infections acquired from cattle.

Brucella canis is not the only cause of early death in puppies, and a variety of infectious causes can be implicated in the so-called 'fading puppy syndrome'. A dirty, cold environment is likely to lead to puppies dying early in life. Toxins produced by bacteria responsible for mastitis can be passed to puppies via contaminated milk and may prove lethal. Viruses can be implicated in some case, with canine herpes virus being considered especially significant, partly because infection causes no apparent disease in older dogs, yet is invariably fatal to puppies under three weeks of age. Veterinary help must be sought urgently when a number of puppies are born dead, or die shortly afterward. In breeding kennels, every effort should be made to keep the bitch and any surviving offspring isolated, especially from other pregnant dogs.

Contraceptives should not be confused with the various deodorant preparations which are marketed to disguise the bitch's output of pheromones, scents that attract male dogs. These deodorants have no actual contraceptive value. It must also be remembered that once a bitch has mated with a dog, this will not prevent her conceiving again if she mates with another dog shortly afterward and both sets of puppies will be born in the same litter. This phenomenon is known as superfecundation.

When an unplanned mating is known to have taken place, it is possible to give an hormonal injection to ensure that conception does not occur. A veterinarian should be contacted at once to arrange this, since a delay can make such treatment worthless. There is no truth whatsoever in stories that a bitch which has mated with a dog of another breed or a mongrel will not be able to conceive normally in the future. Reseach has been carried out into the possibility of reversible sterility by chemical means for a set period of time in male dogs, but at present no such treatments are available.

Neutering
The neutering operation known as castration is normally performed to decrease the problems associated with male dogs, such as wandering and urinating around the home to leave their scent. The degree of success of this operation varies, but approximately 90 percent of male dogs show a decreased tendency to wander following castration. Mating behavior may persist if dogs have previously mated with bitches.

The risk of surgery is very slight but the operation is not reversible. The testes are removed via a single incision in the scrotum and the wound is then closed with a few external stitches. The best time for the operation is before the dog is sexually competent, yet sufficiently mature for surgery.

Both testes should have descended into the scrotum from the abdomen where they developed early in life, certainly by the time the puppy is six months old. In some breeds, such as the Yorkshire Terrier, there is an increased incidence of failure of one or both testes to descend normally. This condition is known as cryptorchidism and is potentially serious because a retained testis is very likely to become cancerous later in life, forming a sertoli cell tumor. Such dogs should always be castrated, with the testis being removed from the abdomen. They should not be used for breeding purposes, since this condition is likely to be inherited.

In the case of the female, neutering is referred to as spaying or, technically, as ovariohysterectomy, and entails the removal of both uterus and ovaries. Changes in behavior will be obvious. Periods of heat will not occur and neither will pseudo pregnancies, but there is also an increased risk of incontinence. Surgery is not normally carried out during a period of heat, or when a bitch is lactating. Ideally, the operation should be performed during anestrus, although a case of pyometra will require immediate attention.

A bitch can be spayed either via the flank, or through the midline of the ventral surface of the abdomen. The abdominal cavity has to be opened, but the wound will heal quickly and external stitches should be removed about 10 days after the operation. If the stitches break open before healing has begun, and if any of the abdominal contents, such as a loop of intestine, become evident through the incision, the veterinarian must be contacted without delay. The bitch should be kept quiet for several days after surgery, exercised on a lead and prevented from jumping if at all possible.

Once a dog of either sex has been neutered, it is very likely to start putting on weight, and its food intake must be reduced accordingly. Such dogs sometimes want less exercise as well, although they remain just as alert. The hair of neutered dogs can also become coarser, and it will take several months for hair to regrow fully over the site of the operation.

Pseudo pregnancy
This state is due to an ovarian disorder associated with the bitch's reproductive cycle. Under normal circumstances, the corpora lutea, which form at the sites where eggs were released, only produce the hormone progesterone for a limited period of time. This hormone acts to ensure that the embryo implants successfully in the uterus, and also stimulates milk production. In cases of pseudo pregnancy, the corpora lutea persist, causing the typical signs of pregnancy six to eight weeks after estrus. The effects can be variable in intensity. There can even be abdominal swelling as well as milk production. Behavioral changes are also likely. The bitch will attempt to make a nest, and adopt items such as slippers as part of the phantom litter. She is likely to be aggressive if such items are taken away.

Pseudo pregnancies often recur and the situation will not necessarily be resolved by allowing the bitch to breed. Medication prescribed by a veterinarian will help to alleviate the symptoms if they become severe, but spaying is undoubtedly the best long-term solution.

Repeated pseudo pregananacies are also thought to make a bitch more prone to uterine infection, known as pyometra, later in life. Pyometra is first indicated by loss of appetite, and increased thirst and urination. Vomiting may also occur after the bitch drinks. If the condition is left untreated, the bitch will become increasingly weak and her abdomen will swell in size. A discharge from the vulva is likely to become evident. Pyometra is most common in bitches from the age of five years onward, and follows a period of heat.

A veterinarian will be able to confirm a case of pyometra by radiography. Spaying will be necessary, although fluids may have to be given before surgery can be undertaken. Since kidney failure can be a common adjunct to pyometra, a period of convalescence under observation at the surgery is likely to be required.

CONTROL OF THE BREEDING CYCLE
Chemical
When a bitch is in heat, to prevent her from breeding she must be kept isolated from other dogs and confined to the house, which can prove an intolerable burden. Contraception by chemical treatment is possible, and is particularly useful if the bitch is being taken on holiday, for example, at a time when a heat could be due. Control by this means also ensures that the bitch will be able to breed satisfactorily at a later date if required.

The drugs used for contraception fall into two main categories, either those related to progesterone, known as progestagens, or androgens, commonly known as male sex hormones. Neither group is free from side-effects. Progestagens are, however, less likely than progesterone itself to stimulate the development of mammary tumors but still cause fluid retention, and are likely to lead to weight gain, unless the diet is closely watched. The androgen group may interfere with future reproductive cycles and cause physical problems such as a vaginal discharge and clitoral enlargement. A veterinarian will be able to advise and administer the safest preparation of this type. Drugs are administered by injection or tablets.

Right Breeding dogs is often very rewarding, repaying in enjoyment the time and expense involved. Finding good homes for all the puppies is a major responsibility. Pedigree puppies, especially those with champion parents, are likely to attract interest from other breeders.

GLOSSARY

AKC American Kennel Club

Almond eyes Eyes that resemble almonds in shape

Angulation Term describing the conformation of a particular joint such as the hock; may be expressed in degrees

Apple-headed A domed or irregularly rounded skull

Apron Longer hair on the chest, at the base of the neck, creating a frill in some cases

Back Defined in various ways, depending on the breed concerned, but generally taken to be the region extending from the withers to the base of the tail, along the vertebrae

Bad-doer A dog which fails to thrive; usually applied to a young individual

Bad mouth Faulty dentition — teeth may be absent for example, or fail to meet correctly

Balanced All parts of the body are considered to be in proportion to each other

Bandy legs Term for legs that bow abnormally outwards

Barrel The rounded body shape created by the ribs in some breeds

Barrel hocks Hock joints that are directed outwards, causing the feet to point inwards as a result. Sometimes termed 'spread hocks'

Bat ears A characteristic feature of the French Bulldog. The ears are erect, wide at the base and rounded at the tip, with the ear canals directed forwards

Bay The howling call of a hound in pursuit

Beard Long, thick hair on the lower jaw

Benched Show dogs are placed on benches, and secured by special chains

BIS The 'Best in Show' award, conferred on the best winner of all the breed winners in a competition

Bird dog A dog trained for hunting birds

Bitch Female dog

Bite The position of the lower and upper teeth relative to each other when the jaws are together. If they meet, this constitutes a level bite

Blanket The color of the saddle area in hounds

Blaze A white stripe running down the face, usually between the eyes

Bloom The glossy appearance of a healthy coat

Blue belton Blue flecking on a white background, typically associated with English Setters

Blue merle Marbling effect created by the presence of blue and grey hair in a black coat, typically associated with Cardigan Corgis, Collies and Shetland Sheepdogs

Bobtail A dog without a tail; alternative name for the Old English Sheepdog

BOB 'Best of Breed' award

Bone Strong, muscular legs

Bossy Excessive development of shoulder muscles

Brace Two individuals of the same kind

Bracelets Rings of hair remaining on the legs of Lowchens and Poodles in show clip

Brindle Black hairs intermingled with brown or another lighter color

Brisket The area of the body under the chest, between the forelimbs

Broken-coated Wire-haired or rough-coated

Brood bitch A breeding female

Brush Bushy tail, resembling that of a fox

Burr Inner surface of the ear

Butterfly nose Partial loss of pigmentation from the nose

Button ears Ears are semi-erect, with the tips falling forward

Canid (Canine) Member of the genus *Canis*, e.g. wolves

Canines Long, pointed teeth next to the incisors, present on both jaws

Castration Neutering of male dog by surgical removal of testicles

CC Challenge certificate awarded at KC Championship Show for best entries of both sexes of a specific breed

CD Companion Dog — a suffix given by the AKC for a dog that has achieved the minimum points score in Novice Classes at a specific number of shows

Ch Champion — a prefix used to indicate a winner of three Challenge certificates, under separate judges in Britain, or the accumulation of a specific number of points in other countries

Cheeky Rounded, thickish and protruding cheeks

Chest The part of the body encompassed by the ribs

China eye A clear blue eye

Chiseled Term describing a head with a clear-cut appearance, especially below the eyes

Choke chain A collar around the dog's neck which, when correctly applied, should loosen or tighten, depending on the handler's grip

Chops Jowls, particularly significant in the Bulldog

Clip Trimming of the coat, particularly significant in Poodles

Clipping Front legs are hit by the hind when the dog moves

Cloddy Low, thickset and relatively heavy

Coarse Unrefined; a dog of poor quality

Cobby Compact, short-bodied

Collar White markings around the neck; also a means of restraining a dog

Condition General state of health, from its overall appearance

Corky Keen, lively

Couple Two hounds

Coupling The loins (area between the ribs and pelvis)

Coursing Pursuit of hares by greyhounds; hunting by sight

Covering ground Stride, involving fore and hindlimbs

Cow-hocked Hocks turned in towards each other

Crabbing Sideways movement

Crank tail A tail carried low

Crest Uppermost arched part of the neck; also the hair present on the head of a Chinese Crested Dog

Cropping Cutting of the ear leathers to make the ears remain erect

Crossbred Offspring from the mating of two different breeds

Croup The part of the back nearest the tail

Crown The top of the skull

Cryptorchid An adult dog with one (unilateral) or two (bilateral) of its testicles retained in its body, and thus absent from the scrotum

Culotte Relatively long hair at the back of the thighs in certain breeds

Cur A mongrel

Cushion Thickness or fullness of the upper lips, typically associated with Pekingese, Boxers and Bulldogs

Dam Female parent

Dapple Genuinely mottled appearance, with no color predominating in the coat

Dew claw A claw occurring on the inside of the legs, often removed

Dewlap Pendulous skin under the throat

Dock Amputate all or part of the tail

Dog Specifically, a male dog

Double coat A weather-resistant outer coat, with a softer insulating layer beneath

Down in pasterns Weakness of the metacarpus, causing the feet to be at an angle from the forelimbs, rather than in a relatively straight line

Drag A scent trail laid by dragging a strong-smelling lure, later to be followed by hounds in lieu of a fox

Drop ear Pendulous, long ears lying close to the head

Dry neck Taut skin

Dual Champion or **Bench and Field Champion** Both a working and show winner

Dudley nose Light brown nose

Ectropion Eyelids directed outwards

Elbow Joint below the shoulder

Entropion Eyelids directed inwards towards the eye

Even bite Both rows of incisor teeth meet directly

Ewe-necked Concave arch of the neck

Expression Combined features of the head

Eye teeth Upper canines

Fall Hair which overhangs the face

Feathering Fringes of hair on the body, ears, legs or tail

Fiddle Front feet turned in, while the elbows are turned out

Flag Long tail or hair thereon

Flanks Sides of the body extending from the last ribs to the hips

Flews Pendulous upper lips

Floating rib Final (thirteenth) rib on each side which is not joined to the others

Flush Driving birds or animals from cover

Forearm Extends from the elbow to the pastern

Foreface Muzzle or front of the head

Foul color Untypical marking or color

Front The part of the body that is visible when the dog is viewed from the front

Furnishings Long hair on the foreface

Furrow Line running from the center of the skull to the stop

Gait Leg movement. Categorized into types, including the walk, trot and gallop

Gay tail Trail inclined vertically upwards

Gazehound A hound that hunts by sight

Grizzled Bluish-grey color

Guard hairs Longish hairs which conceal the undercoat

Gun-barrel front Straight forelimbs

Gun-shy A dog which is nervous of the sound or sight of guns

Hackles Hair on the neck and back erected when the dog feels threatened

Hackney action Lifting of the forelegs abnormally high

Handler Person responsible for the dog in the show ring or at a field trial

Hard-mouthed A dog which marks retrieved game with its teeth

Hare foot Elongated foot

Harlequin Black or blue patches set against white; associated with Great Danes

Harsh coat Stiff and wiry

Haunch Region above the hips

Heat A term applied to a bitch which is reproductively active, i.e. in season

Height Shoulder height, measured from the ground to the withers in a vertical line

Hindquarters Rear part of the dog's body

Hock Hindleg ('heel') joints between stifles and pasterns

Hocks well let down Hocks in close proximity to the ground

Hound marked Hound coloration of tan, black and white

Inbreeding Mating of dogs which are closely related, such as dam to son

Incisors Teeth at the front of the mouth, between the canines

Jowls Fleshy part of the lips and jaws

Knuckling over Weak carpus, causing the joint to protrude forwards

Lay back The position of the scapula relative to a vertical plane

Leathers Ear flaps

Line-breeding Breeding of related stock together

Lippy Excessive development or overhanging of the lips

Litter A term for the puppies resulting from one whelping

Liver Reddish-brown color

Loaded shoulders Overdevelopment of the shoulder muscles, creating a heavy appearance

Loins Extend from the last ribs to the hindquarters

Lumber Excess musculature

Lurcher Crossbred hound

Mane Long hair on and around the neck, resembling that of a lion

Merle Combination of blue, grey and black

Milk teeth Deciduous teeth

Miscellaneous Class A class for breeds that cannot yet be shown competitively in other AKC classes

Molar Teeth with relatively large surface areas, at the back of the mouth

Molera Faulty ossification of the skull

Mongrel Offspring resulting from the mating of crossbred dogs

Muzzle Region of the face in front of eyes

Nick A beneficial mating

Nose Ability to track by following a scent

Occiput Highest back part of the skull

Ottertail A tail which is thick at its base, round and showing no feathering, with hair divided on the underside

Out at elbow Elbow points away from the body

Out at shoulder Shoulder blades are weak, tend to deviate from the body

Outcross Mating of a dog and bitch which are unrelated but of the same breed

Overshot Upper incisors protrude past those of the lower jaw

Pace Legs on one side of the body move before those on the other

Pack A number of hounds kept specifically for hunting

Pad Tough yet vascular covering of the base of the foot; 'soles'

Paper foot Thin-soled, flat foot

Parent club National breed club

Particolor Variegated patching

Pasterns Part of the foreleg extending from the carpus to the digits

Patella Knee cap

Pedigree The ancestry of a particular individual

Penciling The black line present on tan-colored toes

Pig eye Abnormally small eye

Pigeon-toed Toes point inwards towards the midline

Pile Thick undercoat

Plume Fringe of hair on the tails of breeds such as setters

Point The rigid posture adopted by a hunting dog to reveal the location of prey

Points Color of the hair on the legs, face, ears and tail

Poke Carriage of the neck at an abnormally low angle

Pompon Circular tuft of hair at the end of the tail, associated with Poodles

Prefix The name of the kennel where the dog was bred, which appears in front of the dog's individual name

Premolars Teeth located between the canines and molars

Pricked ears Ears carried erect, but with pointed tips

Puppy A dog under 12 months old

Quality A reflection of the dog's conformation and character

Rangy Tall, long body

Rat tail A tail with hair absent from the tip

Ribbed up Long, well-angled ribs

Ring Area where dogs are judged

Ring tail Tail carried high, almost forming a circle

Roached back Curved back

Roan Intermingling of colored and white hairs, typically associated with Cocker Spaniels

Roman nose Nose with a high ridge whose point turns down

Rose ear A smallish ear which folds down and back, thus revealing the burr

Ruff Long and relatively thick hair around the neck

Sabre tail Tail in the shape of a semi-circle

Sable Black hair intermixed with lighter colored hair

Saddle Black marking over the back resembling a saddle

Saddle back Excessively long back

Scissor bite Upper incisors overlap their lower counterparts when the jaw is closed

Screw tail A tail which is short and twisted

Season The reproductively active stage of the bitch's estrus cycle

Second thigh Lower thigh

Self-colored Of one color only

Semi-prick ears Ears carried erect, with tips pointing forward

Service Mating of the bitch by a dog

Set-on Point where the tail joins the body

Set-up Dog displayed in the show ring

Shelly Lack of bone and substance

Slab-sided Ribs directed too vertically, creating a thin appearance

Sloping shoulders Shoulders positioned well back

Snipy Weak, thin muzzle

Spay To prevent bitches from breeding, by surgery

Spectacles Dark markings or shadings around the eyes, extending to the ears in some breeds, such as Keeshonds

Splashed Patches of white contrasting with a solid color

Splay foot Toes spread wide apart

Squirrel tail Tail carried upright, falling quite flat over the back

Standard The breed description specified by the governing canine authority

Staring coat A coat in poor condition

Stern Tail of a hound or other sporting dog

Sternum Breastbone

Stifle Joint located between thigh and second thigh

Stilted Gait associated with a straight-hocked dog

Stop The point between the eyes where the nasal bone and skull meet

Straight-hocked Insufficient angulation at the hocks

Substance Good development

Symmetry All parts of the dog are in proportion

Team More than two working dogs

Terrier front Straight profile at the front

Texture Describes the type of coat

Throaty Excessive skin below the throat

Thumb marks Black spots close to the pasterns, typically associated with Manchester Terriers

Tickled Isolated areas of darker coloration, in a predominantly whitish coat

Timber Bone, especially of the limbs

Tongue Call of hounds when they are on a trail

Top knot Tuft of hair on the top of the skull

Topline Profile extending from the withers to the tail

Trace Dark stripe along the back, characteristic of Pugs

Trail Follow by means of a scent

Tri color Three colors — white, black and tan

Trim Grooming which involves clipping or plucking

Tuck up Curve under the stomach

Type Qualities specified for the breed in its official standard

Undercoat Softer, insulating hair under the top coat

Undershot Lower incisors extend beyond the upper when the jaws are closed

Upper arm Humerus; foreleg

Wall eye Eye has a whitish iris; can be bluish

Weaving Front legs interfere with each other as the dog moves

Well let down Short hocks

Wet neck Excessive or loose skin over the neck

Wheaten Yellowish-fawn

Whelping Giving birth

Whelps Puppies still dependent on their dam

Whip-tail A straight and pointed tail

Whiskers Hairs on the sides of the muzzle and lower chin

Wire-haired Rough, textured coat

Withers Uppermost point of the shoulders

Wrinkle Loose skin forming folds on the face

Wry mouth Twisting of the jaws (especially the lower) so that they are not parallel

ACKNOWLEDGMENTS

The pictures on the following pages have been reproduced by kind courtesy of the following: 6 Michael Freeman; 8 (1) Ronald Sheridan's Photo-Library, (al, a, t) The Mansell Collection; 9 The Mansell Collection; 10, 12 (a), 14 (ar) Quarto Publishing Ltd; 18-9 Pete Weaver; 20 (b), 23 (tl) 34 Quarto Publishing Limited; 42 (c) Australian News and Information Services; 61 (a) Quarto Publishing Ltd; 64 Mr Goodchild; 70 (l), 91 (b), 125, 133 (ar), 134-5, 142, 146, 150 (l), 151, 152, 160 Quarto Publishing Ltd; 164, 167, 171 (a) Royal Veterinary College; 173 Quarto Publishing Ltd; 175, 177 Royal Veterinary College; 178-9, 187, 188 Quarto Publishing Ltd.

All other photographers courtesy Spectrum Colour Library.

KEY: (a) above; (b) below; (l) left; (r) right; (t) top